MW00624195

Despite their tiny numbers, the nobility are central to our understanding of early modern European society. Well into the nineteenth century, they controlled a large share of Europe's wealth and dominated its politics. As a result they had a disproportionate effect on the entire society's economic and cultural life. In fact, the nobles of Europe offer an excellent vantage point for understanding the interplay of tradition and innovation in early modern society. This book provides a comprehensive history of the European nobility between the Renaissance and the French Revolution. Designed to introduce students and non-specialists to the subject, it explains the principal themes and problems in an authoritative and accessible manner. Professor Dewald surveys the changing numbers, self-perceptions, wealth, and political power of the European nobles, and explores their changing modes of life. Arguing against conventional views, he maintains that the nobles adapted effectively to the profound changes that marked society and culture at this time. He also argues that this group evolved in essentially the same ways throughout Europe; although different countries had different numbers of nobles and accorded them different privileges, nobles everywhere faced similar problems and responded to them in similar ways.

The European Nobility, 1400–1800

NEW APPROACHES TO EUROPEAN HISTORY

Series editors
WILLIAM BEIK *Emory University*
T. C. W. BLANNING *Sidney Sussex College, Cambridge*
R. W. SCRIBNER *Clare College, Cambridge*

New Approaches to European History is an important new text book initiative, intended to provide concise but authoritative surveys of major themes and problems in European history since the Renaissance. Written at a level and length accessible to advanced school students and undergraduates, each book in the series will address topics or themes that students of European history encounter daily: the series will embrace both some of the more "traditional" subjects of study, and those cultural and social issues to which increasing numbers of school and college courses are devoted. A particular effort will be made to consider the wider international implications of the subject under scrutiny.

To aid the student reader scholarly apparatus and annotations will be light, but each work will have full supplementary bibliographies and notes for further reading: where appropriate chronologies, maps, diagrams and other illustrative material will also be provided.

The first titles in the series are

1 MERRY E. WIESNER Women and Gender in Early Modern Europe
2 JONATHAN SPERBER The European Revolutions, 1848–1851
3 CHARLES INGRAO The Habsburg Monarchy 1618–1815
4 ROBERT JÜTTE Poverty and Deviance in Early Modern Europe
5 JAMES B. COLLINS The State in Early Modern France
6 CHARLES G. NAUERT, JR Humanism and the Culture of Renaissance Europe
7 DORINDA OUTRAM The Enlightenment
8 MACK P. HOLT The French Wars of Religion, 1562–1629
9 JONATHAN DEWALD The European Nobility, 1400–1800

The European Nobility, 1400–1800

JONATHAN DEWALD
SUNY at Buffalo

CAMBRIDGE
UNIVERSITY PRESS

Published by the Press Syndicate of the University of Cambridge
The Pitt Building, Trumpington Street, Cambridge CB2 1RP
40 West 20th Street, New York, NY 10011–4211, USA
10 Stamford Road, Oakleigh, Melbourne 3166, Australia

© Cambridge University Press 1996

First published 1996

Printed in Great Britain at the University Press, Cambridge

A catalogue record of this book is available from the British Library

Library of Congress cataloguing in publication data
Dewald, Jonathan
  The European nobility, 1400–1800 / Jonathan Dewald.
  p. cm. – (New approaches to European history)
Includes bibliographical references.
ISBN 0 521 41512 8 (hc). – ISBN 0 521 42528 X (hc)
  1. Nobility – Europe – History. 2. Europe – Social conditions.
I. Title. II. Series.
HT653.E9D48 1996
305.5′223′ 094–dc20 95–32843 CIP

ISBN 0521 41512 8 hardback
ISBN 0521 42528 X paperback

For Emma, Nicolas, and Elise

Contents

Illustrations

Preface

The book that follows examines a complex group, during a long and tumultuous period in its history. As in all historical writing, making sense of this complexity and tumult has required choices; the book addresses some tasks and neglects others. One task that I have not undertaken here is that of comprehensive survey of the early modern nobilities.[1] The book does not summarize the large body of legislation that early modern states devoted to the nobles, nor does it systematically narrate the principal events in which they participated; indeed, given their prominence in early modern life, such a narration would amount mainly to retelling the political history of the period. Much that seems picturesque about the nobles, that makes them "other" to our sensibilities, has also been left out of this account. There is almost nothing here about armor, tournaments, coats of arms, pageantry, chivalric gallantry; duelling and jousts appear only briefly.

Rather than survey, narrative, or picturesque detail, I offer here an interpretive essay, directed to understanding the most important ways in which this mass of people evolved during the centuries between the late Middle Ages and the French Revolution. Readers will encounter important events and striking facts, many of which I hope will seem picturesque – but events and facts are offered mainly to illustrate interpretation, rather than as ends in themselves. Those who need more systematic overviews of events, legislation, and chivalric practice may turn to several excellent studies.[2]

[1] A note on terminology. In English usage, the distinction between "nobility" and "aristocracy" is delicate and often ignored. Thus the *Oxford English Dictionary* describes nobles as "belonging to that class in the community which has a titular pre-eminence over the others" – and aristocracy as "a ruling body of nobles, an oligarchy," or "the collective body of those who form a privileged class with regard to the government of the country; the nobles." In what follows I have usually followed the sense of this distinction, using the term nobles to refer to the entire order, aristocracy to refer to its most powerful members. But like the *OED* I view the terms as covering overlapping realities.

[2] These include recent works by M. L. Bush, *Noble Privilege* (New York, 1983) and *Rich Noble, Poor Noble* (Manchester, 1988); and the forthcoming book by Samuel Clark.

Interpretation of the sort presented here poses obvious risks, for no historian could command the historical literature that concerns the nobles across western and central Europe. Certainly I do not claim to, and I have not even attempted to extend the analysis eastward, to Poland, Russia, and the Balkans. Risks have seemed worth taking, however, because historians' understanding of the European nobles has changed significantly in recent years. Longstanding verities have collapsed, creating a need for new assessments of what the nobles were and how they changed.

The problem of change itself holds the central place in this process of reinterpretation. Until fairly recently, historians organized their under-standing of the nobility's early modern history around ideas of crisis and transition. Conservative historians saw the period as marking the decline of a once-cohesive "aristocratic world," a world ordered by bonds between respected leaders and rustic followers, a world little touched by marketplace calculations.[3] Marxist historical writing took a surprisingly similar line. Economic change (it was argued) necessarily rearranged society's ruling groups: in the early modern period, this meant the rise of merchants, industrialists, and commercially minded landowners, who could respond adequately to the market economy's increasing range. Yet a third group, historians writing in the tradition of Weberian sociology, likewise emphasized transition, albeit of a somewhat different order: these historians spoke of change from the "ferocity, childishness, and lack of self-control" (the terms used by the greatest exponent of this view) that had prevailed from Homeric times until about 1600, to the relative self-control required in modern life.[4] This "civilizing process"[5] resulted partly from the needs of a new economy, partly from the development of the modern state, partly from new forms of religion and culture. All required that individuals repress their anarchic impulses, if they hoped to retain positions of power and responsibility. For conservatives, Marxists and Weberians alike, the ruling classes had in some sense to grow up, had to be modernized so as to cope with modernity's complex apparatus of production and rule.

A new approach to the nobles' history must start from the fact that "crisis" and "transition" now seem inadequate terms for describing the nobles' experiences in these years. Specialists have discovered that in many regions of Europe they were a startlingly resilient group, which

[3] See the summary of this view in Rudolf Endres, ed., *Adel in der Frühneuzeit: Ein regionaler Vergleich* (Cologne, 1991), ix–xi.
[4] Lawrence Stone, *The Crisis of the Aristocracy, 1558–1641* (Oxford, 1965), 223.
[5] The term is that of Norbert Elias: *The Civilizing Process*, trans. Edmund Jephcott, 2 vols. (New York, 1978).

maintained wealth and power through apparently cataclysmic social changes. This book underlines other important continuities in their lives. The movement of commoners into the nobility was frequent in the late Middle Ages, and so was contemporary awareness of it. The group's economic practices early acquired a highly rational quality, in some ways indistinguishable from those of capitalist entrepreneurs. Even criticism of the nobility had a long history: there may never have been a time when nobility represented an unchallenged ideal in European society.

Continuity in such matters does not mean that nothing in the nobles' situation changed during the early modern period. On the contrary, the nobles' continued hold on power and wealth required constant adaptation, often of surprising kinds. Hence this book's main task is to sort out what changed in the nobles' situation and what remained constant. In many domains, I argue here, this sorting-out reveals surprises. The book seeks to show the unexpected ways in which change and continuity might combine in the life of a ruling group.

If the problem of continuity forms the book's organizing focus, three additional arguments recur throughout and require clear statement at the beginning. First, I argue here for a fundamental similarity in the nobles' experiences across Europe, at least to the regions of eastern Germany and Bohemia. Similarity had its limits. Different societies had differing numbers of nobles and accorded them different privileges. Yet across Europe the nobles confronted similar economic, political, and cultural problems, and they responded to them in basically similar ways. In a study of this scope, such resemblances can only be suggested (rather than proven) through the presentation of parallel examples, drawn from diverse regions of western and central Europe. Readers may find that a disproportionate number of these examples come from France. To some extent this imbalance reflects my own scholarly interest in France, but it also reflects important realities of early modern history. Especially where the nobility were concerned, France was not simply one society among many. It was by far the largest European state, and it provided a series of models that other countries emulated, in matters ranging from politics to culture. Comparisons of the sort presented here, I believe, suggest the power of this process of emulation in some domains; in others, comparison suggests the degree to which all of Europe experienced common economic and cultural currents.

A second argument concerns the starting-point for the changes that the book explores, the society of the late Middle Ages. I believe that historians have misread some of the changes of the early modern period because they have tended to view late medieval Europe as a traditional society, dominated by a combination of Homeric ferocity and reverence for the past. The problems of change in the early modern period acquire a different appearance if we note other aspects of the period. Late medieval society was never so stable as to allow its members to view past practice as an adequate guide to the present; nor were the nobles so coherent a group that they could view themselves as an unchallenged ruling elite. At the same time, late medieval nobles were expected to command a complicated culture and to reason carefully about their political choices. We cannot view the early modern period as a "modernization" of the nobilities, because in many ways they were already "modern" in 1400.

Hence the book's third theme, that of drawing together in a unified description the most fundamental changes that the nobles underwent in the early modern period. The nobles survived the changes of the early modern period (I argue here) by progressively shedding their order's weakest members. In the late Middle Ages, poor nobles were numerous. Society offered them an honorable place, usually as dependants of the rich, with whom they shared the experiences and culture of warfare. Over the early modern period, this assemblage of rich and poor nobles fell apart. Money became increasingly necessary to lead a life that contemporaries would recognize as suitable to noble status. By their very existence poor nobles had come to symbolize contradictions within the social order. They were now a subject for uneasy laughter, and, unable to keep up their status, they tended to drop out of the order altogether. As a result, over the early modern period nobles became less numerous and on average richer – because poverty increasingly precluded access to the attainments and entertainments that life within the nobility now required.

One way of describing this process is to say that the nobles became a coherent social class during the early modern period. Such a formulation does not accord with Marxist readings of social class, for nobles' relations to the means of production became more varied rather than more similar as the period advanced. Late medieval nobles relied for most of their income on landownership; their seventeenth- and eighteenth-century successors held a wide array of investments, and some had given up landowning entirely. According to a less exact understanding of what class means, however, we can usefully speak of a process of class formation. In a basic sense, the European nobles became more like one another as the early modern period advanced. The diversity of their incomes and modes of life diminished. They came to share a larger number of experiences and expectations.

A final preliminary remark. Any effort at sympathetic analysis of a ruling group risks misreading as rehabilitation or endorsement. The risk is especially great for studies of the European nobilities, whose influence on our own culture remains so powerful, and for studies (such as this one) that emphasize the complexity of the group's culture and choices. It should be evident in what follows that I also view the nobles as a violent and exploitative ruling group, whose prosperity depended heavily on the coercion of others. Early modern aristocratic society did not offer rule by the best, at least in terms that most of us can find appropriate.[6] Yet for a book such as this, denunciation of the group's failings seems especially inappropriate. It limits our capacity to understand the inner logic of the group's thoughts and actions. Worse, it encourages smugness about the virtues of our own world. We have our virtues, but they are perhaps weakest in the matters of social inequality and power that this study explores.

William Beik first proposed that I write this book, and he has since supplied both encouragement and careful criticism. I am also indebted to his fellow series editors for their suggestions and corrections. Charles Stinger read the entire manuscript with characteristic care, insight, and graciousness. The project has been greatly helped by the material support I have received from the Dean of Social Sciences at SUNY Buffalo and from the Institute for Advanced Study, Princeton; a year's residence in that idyllic setting allowed me to rethink and deepen many of the book's arguments.

Most of all I am indebted to Liana Vardi, for the encouragement, criticism, and knowledge that she has brought to this project. She introduced me to many of the questions and materials discussed here, suggested alternative interpretations, and corrected errors. Despite our disagreements on some specific issues, this has been a collaborative project from the beginning – and as a result it has been a pleasure as well.

6   In Greek, "aristocracy" means literally "the government of a state by its best citizens" (in the words of the *OED*).

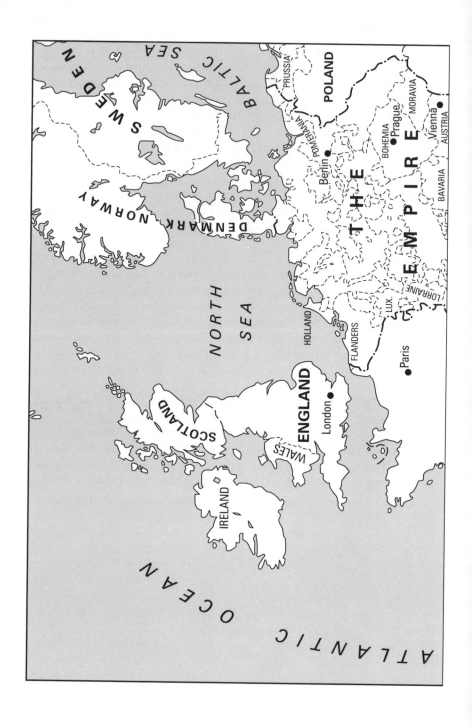

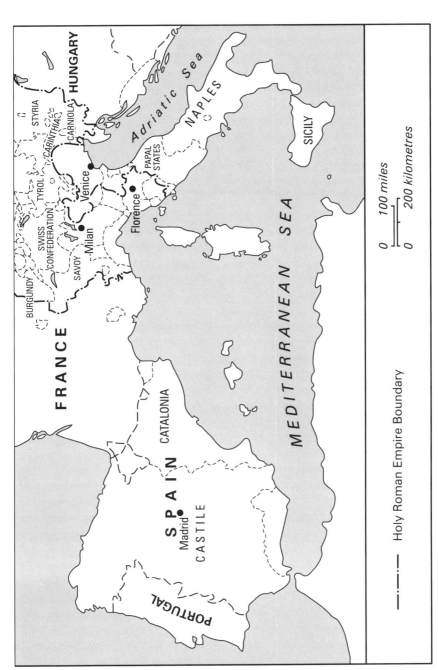

Europe in 1500

Holy Roman Empire Boundary

FRANCE

HUNGARY

STYRIA

CARINTHIA

CARNIOLA

TYROL

SWISS
CONFEDERATION

Venice

Milan

Florence

Adriatic Sea

NAPLES

PAPAL
STATES

SICILY

SAVOY

BURGUNDY

MEDITERRANEAN SEA

SPAIN

CATALONIA

CASTILE

Madrid

PORTUGAL

0   100 miles

0   200 kilometres

Introduction
The European nobilities as an
historical problem

From the early Middle Ages until the threshold of our own era, a small group of people dominated European society. These were the nobilities, constituting in most countries 1 or 2 percent of population but holding much larger shares of their societies' wealth, political authority, and esteem. Such claims to privilege had many sources, but ultimately they rested on ideas about personality and identity. Nobles saw themselves as different from other people. By their birth, so they argued, they had inherited distinctive qualities, qualities that their educations had refined and strengthened. This combination of genetic and cultural inheritance, so they claimed, separated them from others and gave them special aptitudes for protecting and commanding. In turn these social roles justified wealth and honor: because they commanded others, the nobles needed esteem and deference, and they needed to be free of the material cares that dominated ordinary lives. Privilege, they argued, was both a precondition of effective rule and a suitable reward for its troubles. In most parts of Europe, these privileges acquired the force of law. An extensive body of law defined who was noble and what advantages they enjoyed. Thus nobles usually enjoyed special standing in the lawcourts, and special provisions governed their property transactions.

The book that follows sketches the history of these ruling groups during the years in which their hold on European societies was tightest: between the end of the Middle Ages, around 1400, and the beginnings of the industrial age, around 1800. The book explores the nobles' numbers and backgrounds, their wealth, something of their daily lives. It considers their place in Europe's political development. It tries to understand their contributions to European culture, and more broadly their impact on the rest of society. A final chapter explores the impact on them of political and social changes after the French Revolution of 1789.

These were tumultuous years in European history. During the four centuries that this book examines, Europeans first encountered the New

World, then organized an increasingly profitable domination of it. In the long term, the encounter led to radical changes in Europeans' outlooks and values, changes that were especially powerful because they coincided with other cultural encounters: with Greek and Roman knowledge in the fifteenth century, with new religions during the Reformation of the sixteenth century, with a new science in the seventeenth and eighteenth centuries. And there were radical political and social changes. Most European states became more powerful, better organized, and more centralized in these years; most economies became more active, more productive, more reliant on monetary exchanges. By the end of the period, the beginnings of industrial revolution were visible in some parts of Europe, and a few great cities had attained a modern scale; London already had a million inhabitants, and Paris would soon reach that mark. The task of a book like this, then, is to set the history of Europe's traditional ruling group – a ruling group that justified its position by reference to the past – within a series of revolutionary changes in the world around it.

No single book, of course, could adequately summarize Europe's diverse experiences of aristocratic society in these years. Even in the simplest matters, profound differences divided the nobilities of different nations. Nobles were common in eastern Europe and in Spain, much less numerous in most of the west; they represented at least 8 percent of Polish population, about 1 percent of French. Definitions of who belonged to the order might vary widely. In England, only a few hundred families enjoyed official titles as nobles, while thousands of others formed a loosely defined gentry, whose existence rested only on ancestral wealth and assertions about good birth. Elsewhere, for the most part, all nobles enjoyed official titles, and few legal barriers separated the greatest dukes from the least significant village squires; in these countries, the nobility formed a single order, and its members – rich and poor alike – claimed a common superiority to all those who lacked noble birth. Attitudes to urban life might likewise differ from one country to another. Near the Mediterranean nobles had long lived in cities, whereas to the north they tended to live in the countryside and only hesitantly moved to the cities in the seventeenth and eighteenth centuries. Aristocratic political powers might be equally varied. During much of the early modern period, nobles in central and eastern Europe had local powers undreamed of in the west; within their estates, they ruled with little outside interference. In contrast, by the eighteenth century British nobles held unequalled control over centralized state power, but had few formal powers as landowners. Variations of this kind make generalization about European patterns a risky matter, especially since much necessary primary research remains to be done.

Yet differences do not constitute the whole story. If national differences mattered greatly, so also did patterns of resemblance. Throughout
Europe, nobles held to common ideologies. Everywhere they justified
their privileges by a common set of images about the nature of their group
and the services that they performed for the rest of society. There were
also common experiences. In fact the nobilities formed one of a relatively
few groups that had a genuinely European history during the early
modern period. Like artists and intellectuals but in much greater
numbers, they moved about Europe, in search of education, pleasure, and
employment. Royal marriages typically sent large numbers of nobles to
distant lands, as courtiers and advisers to newly married princesses.
Warfare had the same effect, placing nobles for prolonged periods in
foreign settings and (because of the leisurely pace of much early modern
campaigning) allowing them significant interchange with local residents.
This movement of people (mostly of men, but involving many women as
well) produced in turn shared sensibilities. Ideals of dress and deport-
ment tended to be shared by aristocratic circles throughout Europe, but
so also did more fundamental ideas about human life. "The polite of
every country seem to have but one character," as a mid-eighteenth-
century Englishman put it. "A gentleman of Sweden differs but little,
except in trifles, from one of every other country."[1] The story of the
nobilities is partly one of national differences, but it is also one of shared
Europe-wide patterns. A central argument of this book, in fact, is for the
importance of these common patterns. Across Europe, the nobilities
changed in essentially similar ways, under the impact of essentially
similar forces.

What is at stake in a history of these men and women? In one sense very
little. Their tiny numbers made them wildly atypical of the societies in
which they lived. Nor can a study of the group be justified by its
spectacular achievements. Throughout Europe, to be sure, there were
individual nobles who displayed remarkable abilities and made impressive use of them. Because in most parts of Europe they monopolized high
political and military offices, the nobles supplied most of the early
modern period's great generals and statesmen. Many nobles participated
actively in Europe's cultural life as well. Many even involved themselves
in the most dynamic and innovative efforts of European capitalism,
financing overseas exploration, new corporations, and technological
advances. Yet such efforts remained the work of a minority among the
nobles. The majority (so it seems necessary to conclude) led vacant and
parasitic lives, without the justification even of service to their countries.

[1] Quoted J. C. D. Clark, *English Society 1688–1832* (Cambridge, 1985), 99.

"Five hundred . . . ordinary men, chosen accidentally from among the unemployed" – so a hostile observer in 1909 described the British peerage of his day, probably the most energetic and best educated, certainly the richest, nobles in European history.[2] However lacking in sympathy or imagination, the judgment in one sense was fair enough. The European nobles made uneven use of enormous advantages. There is little to suggest that they were an especially distinguished or even public-spirited ruling group. Probably they took more from the societies around them than they gave back.

Yet even the historian who believes that most early modern nobles were of mediocre ability and self-indulgent character finds that they demand close study, and study that does not focus only on the minority of achievers among them. That is because the nobles' situation has become central to how historians understand processes of social change in the early modern period, and even beyond. Their centrality has resulted from one of the great discoveries of historical research in the generations since World War II. In one national history after another, historians have come to realize that the nobilities were an astoundingly resilient ruling group, repeatedly able to withstand apparently overwhelming historical forces.

The English Revolution of the mid-seventeenth century has provided an especially clear example. Historians once interpreted this series of events as the result of a weakening of aristocratic power, which allowed commoners to dominate national politics and eventually to abolish the high nobility altogether. Historians no longer think in these terms. Instead, they have come to see the House of Lords dominating English politics throughout the period leading up to the Revolution, and they have seen the English nobles as maintaining their economic preeminence with the same effectiveness. If anything, so historians have come to believe, the high nobles dominated and directed English politics in its age of greatest turmoil. Even more important, they emerged successfully from the ordeal, still the richest group in society and quite ready to direct politics over the two centuries to come. For the same awareness of aristocratic resilience has characterized thought about the eighteenth and early nineteenth centuries. The industrial revolution did little to shake aristocratic rule. The richest people in mid-nineteenth-century England, after a century of industrialization, remained aristocratic landowners. Political arrangements directly translated this economic power. The British cabinets of the late nineteenth century were among the most aristocratic in the nation's history.

England represents an extreme instance of the continuity of aristocratic

---

[2] David Cannadine, *The Decline and Fall of the British Aristocracy* (New Haven, 1991), 49, quoting the British prime minister David Lloyd George.

power in European history, but there were parallels throughout Europe. In France, historians have shown that the nobles managed to capture for themselves many of the profits of absolutist government in the seventeenth century – a government that once was believed to be hostile to their interests. More startlingly, similar conclusions have emerged concerning the great French Revolution of 1789. The revolutionaries killed many individual nobles, damaged many more nobles' fortunes, and developed a ferociously anti-aristocratic rhetoric; their efforts permanently changed the rules of political practice in France. Yet for all this, they left most aristocratic families and their properties in place, ready to take up anew their leading position in nineteenth-century society; and the rules of nineteenth-century life continued to favor the well-born. In France as in England, historians have pushed the date for ending the Old Regime – the social order based on distinctions of birth and assumptions of social privilege – steadily later, to the political cataclysms of the early twentieth century and the complicated economic changes that accompanied them.

Such emphasis on the "persistence of the Old Regime"[3] in western Europe, the enduring vitality there of aristocratic social forms, has in turn reshaped historians' approach to the problems of central Europe. For historians of Germany and the rest of central Europe have long recognized that there aristocratic society remained vital and dominant up to World War I. Precisely this continuity, in fact, was once offered as an explanation for the peculiarities of German history – for bellicosity in 1914 and totalitarianism a generation later. Germany (so interpretation used to run) failed to challenge aristocratic rule and to establish in its place the dominance of the bourgeoisie. In their eagerness to protect the economic interests and military institutions on which their order rested, German nobles were ready to encourage destabilizing adventures both abroad and at home, and they were determined to destroy forces that might have produced a stable, democratic polity. But discovery of aristocratic continuities in England and France has made the German case seem less unusual. Aristocratic social and political structures survived everywhere in nineteenth-century Europe; their survival cannot be made an explanation for Germany's peculiar history.[4]

Historians' growing realization of the continuing vitality of aristocratic social forms everywhere in early modern Europe thus sets some of the agenda for a study like this one, and makes clear the significance of the

---

[3] For the phrase and strong arguments justifying its use, Arno Mayer, *The Persistence of the Old Regime: Europe to the Great War* (New York, 1981).

[4] See the discussion in David Blackbourn and Geoff Eley, *The Peculiarites of German History: Bourgeois Society and Politics in Nineteenth-Century Germany* (Oxford, 1984), 39–61, 144–55, *passim*.

subject. The nobles matter to us as we try to understand early modern societies because they dominated them with such persistence, and because their domination survived into the modern age, indeed into the twentieth century. We need to ask how the nobles did it, how they managed to adapt to so many historical changes. This means in particular examining the nobles' confrontations with two of the dominant forces of the early modern period, the bureaucratic state and market capitalism. Both forces developed rapidly in Europe from the sixteenth century on. Both modernized European society by changing the rules of social action: that is, changing the methods for accumulating and keeping wealth and power. Together, economic and political developments over the early modern period repeatedly challenged the methods by which nobles in earlier generations had established their rule. Yet the nobles were as firmly in command of their societies at the end of these years as at the beginning, in fact probably more firmly. How had this astounding fact come about? This is part of what a history of the nobilities can tell us. It is one reason that such a history leads directly into fundamental facts about European society before 1900.

But there is another side to the history of aristocratic adaptation, the history of its failures. As a group the nobles by and large succeeded in keeping and even increasing their powers. But they did not succeed equally in all domains, and not all groups of nobles shared equally in the success. The bare fact of success, so forcefully established in recent scholarship, thus conceals as much as it reveals. The process of adaptation favored some groups within the nobility over others; it required certain forms of dealing with the surrounding societies, and penalized others; it encouraged certain tendencies in the social environment and stifled others. The continuity of aristocratic power and wealth, in other words, accompanied important changes in society and in the aristocracy itself. Alongside the theme of adaptation and success, then, this book will treat the themes of failure and change. It will try to identify the qualitative changes that nobles' successes may mask from view.

Such questions demand a history that is in some degree social, that is, a history that attempts to understand daily realities of substantial groups of people. Ideas and ideologies are an important part of this history, but its core remains the effort to establish typical patterns of behavior, against which the unusual, whether successful or failed, can be charted. The claim to social history may ring strangely in a history devoted to ruling groups. And in fact much thought in the development of social history since World War II stressed the need to turn attention away from such groups as the nobles, who, it was argued, had enjoyed historians' attention long enough. It was time, so these historians argued, that more attention be given to peasants and workers, and less to social elites like nobles. Yet the methods of social history can as profitably be employed on the privileged as on the weak. An important achievement of social historians has been to show the power that working people could exercise in the aristocratic societies of early modern Europe (as indeed in other societies). They have given less attention to understanding the forces that limited what the rich could do, to seeing the rich like the poor as caught in the societies of which they are a part and as impelled by social forces that they could not control.

The "persistence of the Old Regime" has been a surprising fact for historians, and it is worth asking why this should be so. One reason, clearly, lies in the fact that much European historiography since the French Revolution has focussed on the rise of the middle classes and the consequent decline of the nobilities. Nobles themselves contributed to this interest, because from very early times they repeatedly bewailed their loss of power and wealth, and complained that these had passed to other groups. Around the nobilities, in other words, there gathered images of crisis and decay, usually allied to nostalgia for times when the nobles' situation was more solid and less subject to questioning and complaint. In fact, the great French social theorist and observer (and nobleman) Alexis de Tocqueville in the mid-nineteenth century offered the nobility's decline as the central thread of European history. "If, beginning at the eleventh century, one takes stock of what was happening in France at fifty-year intervals, one finds each time that a double revolution has taken place in the state of society. The noble has gone down in the social scale, and the commoner has gone up; as the one falls, the other rises. Each half century brings them closer, and soon they will touch. And that is not something peculiar to France. Wherever one looks one finds the same revolution taking place throughout the Christian world."[5] What Tocqueville saw as a broad and inexorable process of social change, other writers claimed to observe in the details of the world around them. "If I had time," lamented William Cobbett as he wandered the southern English countryside in 1823, "I would make an actual survey of one whole county, and find out *how many of the old gentry have lost their estates*, and have been supplanted by the Jews, since PITT began his reign. I am sure I should prove that, in number, they are one-half extinguished . . . The little ones are, indeed, gone."[6]

Complaints like these, coming from observers as acute as Tocqueville

[5] Alexis de Tocqueville, *Democracy in America*, ed. J. P. Mayer (New York, 1969), 11.
[6] William Cobbett, *Rural Rides*, ed. George Woodstock (London, 1967), 119 (emphases in original).

and Cobbett, pose problems that are partly logical and partly empirical. Even if there were evidence for the nobles' decline relative to the middle classes, for instance, we have trouble understanding how Tocqueville could have imagined a social class in steady decline during eight consecutive centuries. Surely, we think, there must have been some bright moments to interrupt this centuries-long decline; and in any case after such steady decay, what could have remained of the class in his own time? In fact, though one would not know it from reading Tocqueville, nobles remained rich, powerful, and socially visible in nineteenth-century France, where the Tocqueville family itself enjoyed a distinguished position; they were even richer elsewhere in Europe. Tocqueville's own experience ought to have made him skeptical about the historical picture that he drew.

Another fact ought to have made him even more skeptical. Complaints such as his enjoyed a long history, which can be traced back through the sixteenth century and into the Middle Ages. At even the most glorious moments in their history, the nobilities complained of poverty and neglect, often in the hope of obtaining government assistance. "Such as were gentlemen's houses . . . are since dwindled into cottages & such as were then cottages are now advanced to gentlemen's houses, some of whom (though they are not many) would pass for palaces in former days; and yet neither they nor their owners were known to the parish . . . sixty years ago," as another English observer worried in the 1720s.[7] "The princes of the blood and the other great nobles are so poor and so lacking in authority . . . because all the lands and wealth of importance of the greater families of the kingdom have fallen at various times into the hands of the crown . . . They have little authority." Thus an Italian visitor in 1561, commenting on the state of the French nobility.[8] The same observer saw problems for the lesser nobles, who faced a difficult choice between ruinous expense if they came to court and political impotence if they stayed home. "The nobles, who are usually not very rich, are ruined when they come to court, where everything is dear . . . On the contrary, when they stay in their chateaux and lead a private and simple life, they have all they need without livery, sumptuous garments, expensive horses, banquets, and other things necessary to a courtier."[9] A century and a half later, La Bruyère used almost the same language, though his point was different: "A nobleman, if he lives at home in his province, lives free but

---

[7] Quoted E. P. Thompson, *Whigs and Hunters: The Origin of the Black Act* (London, 1975), 112.
[8] James Bruce Ross and Mary Martin McLaughlin, eds., *The Portable Renaissance Reader*, rev. edn (Middlesex–New York, 1968), 316.
[9] Ibid., 310.

without substance; if he lives at court, he is taken care of, but enslaved."[10]
Soon after, the duc de Saint-Simon complained that French government
was in the hands of the "vile bourgeoisie," leaving the nobility powerless
and neglected.[11]

Just as these complaints had been repeated, generation after generation, for centuries before Tocqueville wrote, so also they have ritually
been repeated since. Late in the nineteenth century, at the moment of the
British aristocracy's greatest wealth and power, administrators had so
taken these ideas to heart that they greeted with surprise surveys proving
aristocratic prosperity.[12] Even today the rhetoric of aristocratic decline
retains its force. "The picture, says [photographer Richard] Avedon, is a
Proustian look at the death of aristocratic Europe, taken at the last great
ball on the Continent." Thus the caption in *Newsweek* magazine of a
photograph taken in 1991 – a photograph of wealthy and handsome
people, lavishly bedecked, and apparently enjoying themselves in an
exclusive, elegant setting.[13]

The language of complaint is often the work of acute and careful
observers, and (we shall see) it often described significant realities. Yet,
repeated so regularly generation after generation, this language cannot
only reflect factual observation. After all, while complaints of aristocratic
decay recurred from one generation to the next, aristocrats themselves
continued their social dominance and their wealth. The disjuncture
between reality and anxious contemporary comment suggests that the
language of decline formed something more than observation of reality. It
was also, perhaps primarily, a set of expectations *through which* reality
was understood, or even given shape. Around the nobility, it appears,
there has clung a permanent rhetoric of nostalgia; what was once solid and
assured, so observer after observer tells us, has reached the verge of
collapse.

If this rhetoric of nostalgia cannot be explained as a direct reflection of
reality, why did it emerge, and why did it retain such power in the
European imagination? To some extent, as a simple misreading of
realities. At any time, as we shall see in detail, individual nobles and their
families might be in difficulties. The spectacle was often moving, as
indeed financial collapse remains today: cherished homes and possessions
having to be sold, daughters unable to find suitable marriage partners,
unpolished newcomers taking positions in high society. Such scenes were

[10] Quoted Franklin Ford, *Robe and Sword* (repr. New York, 1965), vii.
[11] Quoted René Pommeau and Jean Ehrard, *Littérature française, 5: de Fénelon à Voltaire* (Paris, 1984), 252.
[12] Cannadine, *The Decline and Fall*, 22, 54–55.
[13] *Newsweek*, 13 September 1993, 51.

real, and not surprisingly they attracted the attention of social observers in all periods. Yet individual misfortunes did not mean the decline of the social group as a whole. Observers have too easily leapt from individual cases to assertions about the condition of the group. The leap has been especially easy when personal interests have been involved: for nobles who found themselves in difficulties and needed to interpret these in larger than personal terms; or for conservatives of all kinds, frightened by signs of imminent social change.

Yet nostalgia has also deeper sources, in the qualities that western culture has tended to assign to aristocracies and in the ways it has used those qualities to think indirectly about other issues. Nobility has represented, first, biological stability. European nobles have always defined themselves in terms of descent from admired ancestors. Usually they have tried to preserve the purity of that descent by marrying with others whose blood is pure; even today, according to opinion polls, most French nobles say that they would be most comfortable marrying another noble. Through his/her presumed racial purity, the noble seemed to embody connectedness to a distant historical past. "It is a reverend thing to see an ancient castle or building not in decay, or to see a fair timber-tree sound and perfect: how much more to behold an ancient noble family which hath stood against the waves and weathers of time." Thus the English jurist and scientific propagandist Francis Bacon, early in the seventeenth century.[14] A still more powerful belief that noble descent could somehow preserve contact with ancient virtues flourished in the mid-nineteenth century. Thus the heroine of Benjamin Disraeli's novel *Sybil*, who offers pure Anglo-Saxon nobility somehow surviving uncontaminated in a mid-nineteenth-century present, displays the purity of faith, constancy, and courage of her ancestors – ancestors of whom she knows nothing, and whose influence on her is purely genetic. Disraeli's novel expressed the conviction that noble birth preserved specific qualities, qualities that others possessed to a much lesser degree: generosity, courage, indifference to calculation. Those who disliked the calculations and moral cowardice of capitalist society could view the nobles as living monuments to a better, morally heroic past.

The significance thus attached to biological contact with the past helps to account for the anxieties nobles expressed about presumed threats to the purity of their blood. It is not accidental that William Cobbett, in his worries at the replacement of the old English gentry by new men, described the threat as coming from "Jews." He meant to speak of the threatening new wealth that government finance had generated – but his

[14] Francis Bacon, *The Essays*, ed. John Pitcher (London, 1985), 99.

language referred equally to the racial identities that clustered around the nobles. Survival of the nobles was linked in this language to an image of racial purity, a racial purity somehow linked to national history.

European thought attached nobles to nature in another sense, by emphasizing the nobleman's special position as a landowner, committed to preserving his property for his descendants. In the mid-nineteenth century, Tocqueville analyzed this attachment in detail and with powerful emotions. "In nations where the law of inheritance is based on primogeniture, landed estates generally pass undivided from one generation to another. Hence family feeling finds a sort of physical expression in the land. The family represents the land and the land the family, perpetuating its name, origin, glory, power, and virtue. It is an imperishable witness to the past and a precious earnest of the future . . . as soon as landowners are deprived of their strong sentimental attachment to the land, based on memories and pride, it is certain that sooner or later they will sell it . . . Where family feeling is at an end, personal selfishness turns again to its real inclinations. As the family is felt to be a vague, indeterminate, uncertain conception, each man concentrates on his immediate conveniences; he thinks about getting the next generation established in life, but nothing further."[15]

Tocqueville here discussed explicitly what many others took for granted. Long possession of landed estates in itself, he argued, created among nobles a familial psychology and a set of economic values. By their possessions, Tocqueville believed, nobles were in some sense shielded from the egotism of the market economy. They would sacrifice immediate personal advantage – which would lead them to sell their estates and invest in something more profitable – for the sake of preserving a trust for their descendants. It is important to note the range of qualities that Tocqueville here invoked. There is permanence: the nobleman is rooted to a place, in contrast to the fluidity of modern societies. There is family feeling, a sense of continuity with both the dead and the unborn. There are forms of self-sacrifice, of current pleasures forgone, and there is the corresponding absence of economic calculation.

Tocqueville and many others saw yet a further element contributing to this solidity of aristocratic identity, assurance of knowledge, taste, world view. "An aristocratic people interested in literature," he wrote, will "soon prescribe rules that cannot be broken" for all the arts. "Their code will be both strict and traditional," so that they will have no uncertainties about artistic taste and no profound debates about the subject matter under discussion. They will have, in fact, assurance about what they

[15] Tocqueville, *Democracy in America*, 52–53.

believe and say, freedom from the doubt that seems to characterize so much of modern life.[16] The American critic Edmund Wilson offered a comparable view in 1931, demonstrating the persistent power of the images that surrounded the aristocrat: "It was easy" for the English poet of the sixteenth and seventeenth centuries "to express himself both directly and elegantly, because he was a courtier or, in any case, a member of a comparatively small educated class, whose speech combined the candour and naturalness of conversation among equals with the grace of a courtly society." Assurance of this kind, resting on absolute stability of identity, Wilson finds impossible for the poet of his own day.[17]

Nostalgia for aristocratic society and fear for its future, it seems, related to deeper conceptions of the person and her/his place in society, and to longings about what these ought to be. The images quoted present the nobleman as rooted, literally grounded. His background and his possessions gave him cultural assurance, freed him from doubts and uncertainties. His identity derived from elemental realities, from feelings about family, land, and the caste to which he belonged. Aristocratic identity thus visualized was autonomous, independent from the societal pressures that mark so many aspects of modern life. It rested on an immediately usable possession, land, rather than on the uncomfortable interchanges of commerce and other forms of economic life. The nobleman in fact scarcely needed a surrounding society, because his estates could supply most of his needs. This was an identity free from change, because it rested on possessions immune from challenge or control by others. Thus solid within itself, aristocratic identity of this kind could bring assurance of knowledge, taste, and language. In all of these ways, the image of the nobleman represents a solid antithesis to the world we know, the world of change, doubt, unstable identities and knowledge.

We can understand the appeal of such an image of the person, and also the anxieties that would surround it. For if the image of nobility was one of pristine selfhood, free from the mess of so much social interchange, threats would seem to be everywhere – in anything that appeared to mar the image of autonomy thus constructed. At the same time, so pristine a vision made it seem unlikely that the nobles could in a fundamental way cope with the rise of market capitalism and of modern society. They represented in this ideological vision something removed from the demands of market exchange; these were men and women governed by a different economic and social calculus.

---

[16] Ibid., 472.

[17] Edmund Wilson, *Axel's Castle: A Study of the Imaginative Literature of 1870–1930* (repr. London, 1961; first published New York, 1931), 39.

A central theme of this book is that these nostalgic visions of the noble are fundamentally misleading. The early modern nobles, throughout Europe, survived the shocks that the period handed out by a continuous process of adaptation. At the simplest level, this meant changes in the persons who made up the nobility. There was a continuous flow of newcomers to the nobility over the period, partly as replacements for families that died out, partly because the period brought new definitions of nobility. As a result, in most places only a small minority of the nobility could accurately claim medieval roots for their family trees. When Cobbett and others observed with such horror new families buying up landed property, they were seeing only the continuation of a longstanding process. The biological pretensions of early modern aristocratic ideology were simply false. Nor do the psychological qualities that nostalgia attributed to the nobles hold up well to careful historical analysis. Nobles did not demonstrate quite the cultural assurance – or the cultural limitations, for that matter – that Tocqueville and others ascribed to them. In the seventeenth and eighteenth centuries, indeed, the culture produced by and for them displayed especially powerful qualities of doubt and passionate conflict. Family relations too were more complex than we might expect, for the pressures to preserve lineage might produce explosive conflicts between parents and children, or between siblings.

In other ways too, so this book argues, the images of stable identity that have surrounded the European nobility mislead us. From very early in European history, nobles found themselves unable to evade the complications of the exchange economy. In 1400 there were already large areas of Europe where estates could not be imagined as autonomous, free from buying and selling on a large scale. By 1600, autarky of this sort had largely disappeared from England and France, and was soon to disappear from Germany. An especially significant marker of the disappearance, we shall see, was the flourishing land market that characterized much of fifteenth- and sixteenth-century Europe, a market that nobles joined as both sellers and buyers. By 1400 too the state played a large role in many nobles' lives, as a source of money, employment, and regulations. Nobles' identities were intimately bound up with state service, a relationship that only tightened in the following years. Had there ever been a time when the nobility led an existence free from these dependencies and exchanges with the world beyond the estate? Perhaps, but by 1400 such an existence had ended.

Alexis de Tocqueville believed that the history of the European nobilities was one of steady decline, from the eleventh century to his own day in the mid-nineteenth. In fact the nobles' history exhibited long periods in which their wealth and power expanded. Despite periods of decay and crisis that periodically intervened in these years, they were arguably richer and more powerful in 1914 than in 1414. As significant, perhaps, the nobles remained in 1914 at the center of the European imagination. They, their country mansions, and their supposed values played central roles in the high and the low culture of the early twentieth century, in ways that continue to touch us. We continue to read about them in the novels of Turgenev, Henry James, Marcel Proust, and Giuseppe di Lampedusa, in the plays of Anton Chekhov, in country house detective stories. Survival in this measure is a remarkable fact. It suggests the need for a close look at the nobility, but it also suggests that the nobles themselves were more complicated, more various, more chameleon-like – and also more interesting – than traditional images suggest.

1   Nature and numbers

"From the beginning, mankind has been divided into three parts, among men of prayer, farmers, and men of war." With these words, an early eleventh-century French bishop laid out the foundations of medieval social thought. He and his imitators divided society between clergy like himself, the workers who fed and supplied the rest, and the nobility, who contributed to the common good by protecting their fellows. Writers repeated the formulation throughout the early modern period, to the eve of the French Revolution itself, because it offered potent advantages. It presented society as symmetrical, each group having its tasks and its responsibilities for serving the others, and it glossed over the vast numerical disproportion among the three classes; in this vision of society, the 1 percent who were nobles counted for as much as the 99 percent who were not, because each group served equally. Perhaps this vision corresponded to the relative simplicity of medieval society – but it certainly corresponded to men's hopes for a simple and stable social order. For here was a vision that answered in simple terms the questions, who was a nobleman and what social role did he play. The nobleman fought to protect others, and protected them as well through the advice and aid that he gave to the king.[1]

Writers and politicians continued into the eighteenth century to repeat these ideas from early feudal society. By the early sixteenth century, however, everyone knew that such questions could not be so simply answered. By this time, the recently invented printing presses were turning out a growing number of tracts debating questions about nobility, asking who was noble, how one arrived at that status, and what use it had. Dividing society into the three orders of medieval theory no longer sufficed, for there were too many people who fitted awkwardly into its categories and too many situations that it did not capture. Some nobles worked, blurring one of the primary divisions among the three orders. More important, a growing number of nobles did not fight. Instead, they were to be found living as country gentlemen, managing

[1] Quoted in Georges Duby, *The Three Orders: Feudal Society Imagined*, trans. Arthur Goldhammer (Chicago, 1980), 13.

their estates, or at court, entertaining and advising their kings, or in the cities, working as royal officials and judges. This growing diversity of social roles was only one cause of debate over the nobility. Changing ideas – many of them allied with Renaissance humanism – had the same effect. Whatever the causes, such public discussion is the first significant fact about the early modern nobilities. Contemporaries held divergent views about definitions and their implications; they could differ about who was noble and about how they had become so; they could disagree as to what nobility was worth. Nobility had ceased to be a stable or simple idea.

Race and status: the biology of social mobility

Debates over nobility tended to be organized around fundamental alternatives, exemplifying that reasoning by oppositions that was one of early modern Europe's preferred modes of thought. Nobility could rest on birth, on genetic inheritance from the past; or it could be newly acquired, as a public reward for exceptional qualities and accomplishments. It could rest on antithetical modes of life: on military activity, in keeping with Europe's violent medieval past, or on peaceful service to the state, service that typically demanded education and the exercise of learning. Finally, nobility could rest on explicit grant from the state, on a formal process of ennoblement; or it could reflect the unspoken consensus of the community, the longstanding belief that families had always behaved in ways that justified special standing.

Only a few daring writers could envision a simple resolution of these antitheses and argue that there could be only one form of genuine nobility. One who took this step was the French duc de Boulainvilliers, writing early in the eighteenth century. Boulainvilliers proposed viewing the French nobility as a conquering race, a race that by his day had maintained its purity for over a thousand years. The nobles around him, he claimed, descended from the Franks, the Germanic race that had conquered France in the sixth and seventh centuries and had supplied France with its kings thereafter. Conquest gave the nobles the right to their properties and social preeminence. Racial purity in the centuries since the conquest meant that the conqerors' traits survived in the nobles Boulainvilliers saw around him. They were bold, courageous, and unwilling to accept tyranny from the monarchical state. In contrast to the slavish tendencies of the Romans and their descendants, they demanded liberty. They even looked different from other Frenchmen.[2]

[2] For recent review of Boulainvilliers' ideas, Harold A. Ellis, *Boulainvilliers and the French Monarchy: Aristocratic Politics in Early Eighteenth-Century France* (Ithaca, 1988).

Boulainvilliers was expressing views that had circulated widely in the previous two centuries. These views had an obvious appeal to many nobles. But they ran into problems in the daily life of early modern Europe, problems which meant that no one could take them altogether seriously. Far from being a compact conquering race, noble families were continually dying out and being replaced by new ones. There was a steady process of movement into the nobility – and contemporaries knew it. They could see it happening all around them.

Historians of several countries have established the dimensions of this dying out and replacement process, and it could be astoundingly rapid. Among the lesser nobility of fifteenth-century France, about one-fifth of the family names disappeared with each generation; in the course of a century, most of the group had been replaced by new families. More or less the same happened in Germany. In lower Saxony, just over half of the noble families disappeared between 1430 and 1550; in two regions of the Rhineland, fewer than one-fifth of the fifteenth-century noble families survived in 1550. In Spain, only six of the noble families prominent in 1300 survived to count among the fifty-five titled nobles of 1520. And the same process had been seen in England. Of 136 peerage families in 1300, fewer than half survived in the male line by 1400, and only sixteen survived in 1500. These were the richest of the English landowning classes, those who had the least difficulty sustaining their rank. Lower in the English social hierarchy, the story was the same. Between 1603 and 1642, 102 of 859 gentry families in the northern county of Yorkshire failed to produce male heirs.[3]

Disappearances at this rate reflected both basic facts of early modern life and pressures specific to the nobility. Everyone faced the likelihood that children would die in infancy and childhood, and wealth offered scant protection against early modern diseases. In the seventeenth and eighteenth centuries, when living conditions had improved substantially, child mortality remained high among even the richest European nobles. One-third of the children of the English peerage died before the age of twenty, and a slightly higher percentage of the German nobles' children did so.[4] Nobles faced the added possibility of their sons dying in combat:

---

[3] Edouard Perroy, "Social Mobility among the French Noblesse in the Later Middle Ages," *Past and Present*, 21 (1962), 25–38; Hellmuth Rössler, ed., *Deutscher Adel, 1450–1555* (Darmstadt, 1965), 179, 129–30; J. N. Hilgarth, *The Spanish Kingdoms, 1250–1516*, 2 vols. (Oxford, 1978), II, 54; K. B. McFarlane, *The Nobility of Later Medieval England* (Oxford, 1973), 173–4; Joan Thirsk, ed., *The Agrarian History of England and Wales, IV: 1500–1640* (Oxford, 1967), 298. For yet another example, H. F. K. Van Nierop, *The Nobility of Holland: From Knights to Regents, 1500–1650*, trans. Maarten Ultee (Cambridge, 1993), 51.
[4] Gregory Pedlow, *The Survival of the Hessian Nobility, 1770–1870* (Princeton, 1988), 53.

nearly half the men in the fifteenth-century English peerage died violent deaths. Perhaps most important, economic pressures affected noble families' organization, and thus their chances of reproducing themselves. Most families wanted to concentrate their resources, leaving the next generation as solidly established as possible so as to carry on the family's name and political role. Very often this meant leaving younger sons or daughters in poverty, without the resources to marry properly and establish other branches of the family; in turn this meant that families died out when their principal heirs failed to produce offspring. In any case, impoverished families could not hope to sustain their place within the nobility. As their landholdings shrank and their debts mounted, they had less hope of finding marriage partners, and it became increasingly likely that they would sink into the peasantry. And it was commonly believed that nobles *would* become impoverished, "it being of necessity that many of the nobility fall in time to be weak in fortune," in the Englishman Francis Bacon's phrase; to be born noble, he thought, "commonly abateth industry," by the easy advantages the nobleman found himself enjoying.[5] In Bacon's view, aristocratic psychology added to the likelihood of downward social mobility, by weakening aristocrats' ability to sustain their economic position.

Awareness of such social mobility – of the extinction of old families and their replacement by new ones – appeared everywhere in Europe, just like the facts of disappearance and replacement themselves. At Paderborn, in northwest Germany, a fifteenth-century inscription listed the eighty families of the region who had died out in the previous century, and concluded: "God help us in the coming century, or else all honor will disappear." A knight in eastern England at about the same time established a similar monument to families that had disappeared: a stained-glass window in the local church that gave the names and coats of arms of some eighty-seven "lords, barons, bannerets and knights who had died without issue male in Norfolk and Suffolk since the coronation of Edward III," a century earlier. Early in the sixteenth century, the French high official and nobleman Claude de Seyssel included in his analysis of French society a chapter entitled "How Men Go from the Third Estate to the Second and from the Second to the First." In France, Seyssel believed, such mobility "is so easy that every day we see men of the popular estate ascend by degrees, some to nobility and innumerable to the middling estate."[6] Across Europe, late medieval observers knew

[5] Francis Bacon, *Essays*, ed. John Pitcher (London, 1985), 99, 100.
[6] Rössler, ed., *Deutscher Adel*, 165; McFarlane, *The Nobility*, 145–46; Claude de Seyssel, *The Monarchy of France*, trans. J. H. Hexter, ed. Donald R. Kelley (New Haven and London, 1981), 62–63.

about social mobility, whether they approved of it like Seyssel or dreaded it like the anonymous German and English donors. With old families disappearing and new ones appearing, only the rigidly self-deluded could cling to an idea of the nobility as a pure-bred caste. Even defenders of the idea knew of alternative interpretations and knew that the caste model was in some degree a myth – that is, an occasionally useful way of thinking about the world, but in no sense an absolute truth.

Processes of mobility

Biology alone, then, meant that the nobility had never been a closed caste of the sort that Boulainvilliers imagined. Without a steady flow of new recruits to the nobility, the order would simply have disappeared – and late medieval men and women knew that this was the case. Where then did new nobles come from, and how did they establish themselves within the nobility? Late medieval conditions offered propitious circumstances for the socially ambitious, for political turmoil and warfare favored rapid advancement. England, France, Spain, and Germany all endured years of civil war during these centuries. Some nobles lost their lives in battle, and many others fell victim to kings' fear of disloyalty. In Castile, king Peter "the Cruel" earned his nickname by executing sixty of the country's leading nobles during the twenty years of his reign; and kings in France and England might be almost as brutal. In these circumstances, there were places open at the top of aristocratic society – and princes were eager to fill them by advancing those who served loyally.

As a result, the fourteenth and fifteenth centuries witnessed spectacular examples of rapid advancement. In the early fourteenth century, the Mendoza family were minor backcountry nobles in northwest Spain. But involvement in royal military ventures and shrewd political choices raised them to the top of the social hierarchy by 1370; thanks to royal generosity, they were the richest nobles in fifteenth-century Castile. Enguerran de Marigny likewise began as a poor provincial noble in western France; an introduction to the queen allowed him entry to royal service, and he too rose to great wealth. A few years later, Robert de Lorris began as a small-time Parisian bourgeois; after successful royal service, he acquired a series of lands and titles, and his sons married daughters of two great aristocratic houses. England offers the example of the Boleyn family. Ann Boleyn's great-grandfather was a merchant in mid-fifteenth-century London; his son married the daughter of an earl, one of the loftiest ranks in the British peerage, and established himself as a landed gentleman; *his* son, Ann's father, married the daughter of a still more important earl, secured knighthood and high government positions from the crown, and (having watched complaisantly as Henry VIII seduced his daughter) himself advanced to the peerage – and to his place in history as the king's father-in-law.[7] This was a story of advancement from the mercantile middle class to the heights of aristocratic society within three generations. It was unusual but hardly unique in the fifteenth and early sixteenth centuries.[8] Families who reached the top of the social hierarchy often did so rapidly.

Far more frequent, of course, was the movement of commoners – both rich peasants and urban businessmen – into the lower levels of the nobility. For such lesser figures as well, the military and political circumstances of the late Middle Ages favored social mobility. Both princes and great nobles needed loyal followers, and they readily handed out titles of nobility as rewards. In 1387 John I, king of Castile, promised noble status to any horsemen who joined his army for two months. His successors made similar offers throughout the fifteenth century, in sufficient numbers that urban authorities complained: their cities were being emptied, as the ambitious rushed off to war.[9] In fifteenth-century France, well-to-do peasant families eased themselves into the nobility simply by acquiring fiefs and entering the service of more powerful local landowners. There were no formal ceremonies of ennoblement: the new families simply took to calling themselves noble.[10] Rapid and informal mobility characterized fifteenth-century England as well. Between 1450 and 1500, about one-third of the more successful London merchants' sons became landed gentlemen. In England such movement went both ways, suggesting the porousness of social boundaries. Country gentlemen were as eager to apprentice their sons to merchants as merchants were to establish their sons in the countryside.[11] Similar exchanges between nobles, burghers, and peasants occurred in northwest Germany. Intermarriage was frequent, and non-nobles, many of them peasants, held about half of all fiefs in the region.[12]

---

[7] Helen Nader, *The Mendoza Family in the Spanish Renaissance, 1350 to 1550* (New Brunswick, 1979), 37–40; Marie-Thérèse Caron, *Noblesse et pouvoir royal en France, XIIIe–XVIe siècle* (Paris, 1994), 60, 110; Neville Williams, *Henry VIII and His Court* (London, 1971), 100–05. For other examples of mobility, Caron, *Noblesse et pouvoir royal*, 118–19; Angus MacKay, *Spain in the Middle Ages: From Frontier to Empire, 1000–1500* (New York, 1977), 174.

[8] McFarlane, *The Nobility of Later Medieval England*, 164–67.

[9] Marie-Claude Gerbet, *La Noblesse dans le royaume de Castille: étude sur ses structures sociales en Estrémadure de 1454 à 1516* (Paris, 1979), 108–09.

[10] Perroy, "Social Mobility among the French Noblesse."

[11] Sylvia Thrupp, *The Merchant Class of Medieval London, 1300–1500* (Ann Arbor, 1948; repr. 1962), 205–22.

[12] Rössler, ed., *Deutscher Adel*, 159ff.; see also 192–93, for similar patterns in the region of Saxony; for France, Jonathan Dewald, *Pont-St-Pierre, 1398–1789: Lordship, Community, and Capitalism in Early Modern France* (Berkeley, 1987), 93–94, 97–98.

Social boundaries were easily crossed in the fourteenth and fifteenth centuries, even by relatively humble men. After about 1500, however, the nature of social advancement began to change. For one thing, this was a more settled age, which offered fewer openings for freewheeling adventurers like the Mendozas. For another, governments increasingly intervened to channel and restrict social mobility. In Spain and France, governments had a direct interest in the matter, because in those countries nobles paid no taxes. Hence, early in the sixteenth century the new Spanish king Charles V revoked previous grants of nobility and forbade the granting of future ones. In fact no early modern government could consistently live up to these good intentions, but they did produce a sharp drop in ennoblements in sixteenth-century Spain.[13] Charles also introduced more elaborate rankings within the nobility, and in 1520 he established the grandees as a distinct category for the greatest Spanish families – a form of categorizing that was essentially new in the early sixteenth century. Pressures of a similar kind emerged in France, with efforts in several domains to close off institutions and privileges to the non-nobles. In 1600 Henry IV in fact explicitly closed off ennoblement by military service – testimony both to the new attitudes to social advancement that were developing in these years and to the fluidity of movement that had previously characterized French society. In the 1660s, the French crown undertook still more dramatic efforts to limit advancement: it sent officials into the provinces to hunt out false nobles; those who failed to prove noble status were subjected to fines and public humiliation. From now on, monarchs meant to control social mobility themselves.[14]

Governmental efforts, however, do not fully account for the restrictions on social mobility that emerged after 1500. For in these years nobles themselves also came to attach growing importance to matters of lineage; they became less tolerant of newcomers. Nobles became more interested in their genealogies, and they made distinguished ancestry a precondition for important positions. In the mid-sixteenth century, German cathedral chapters began requiring evidence of noble ancestry for those who sought positions in them.[15] Such restrictions became still more widespread in the

---

[13] Gerbet, *La Noblesse dans le royaume de Castille*, 109.

[14] François Isambert, *Recueil général des anciennes lois françaises* (Paris, n.d.), XV, 226–38: "Edit portant règlement général sur les tailles, sur les usurpations du titre de noblesse . . ." March, 1600; for a clear overview of the closing of the French nobility, Jean Meyer, "Noblesse des bocages: essai de typologie d'une noblesse provinciale," in Béla Köpeczi and Eva H. Balys, eds., *Noblesse française, noblesse hongroise, XVIe–XIXe siècles* (Budapest-Paris, 1981), 54–55 (this essay briefly summarizes themes developed in detail in Meyer's great work, *La Noblesse bretonne au XVIIIe siècle*, 2 vols. (Paris, 1966).

[15] J. H. Elliott, *Imperial Spain, 1469–1716* (New York, 1967), 111; Rössler, ed., *Deutscher Adel*, 168–69.

seventeenth and eighteenth centuries. Under pressure from its nobles, the French monarchy in 1751 established a military academy open only to nobles, and in 1780 it restricted commissions in the army to those with four noble ancestors. Even this seemed insufficient to many nobles: in 1789 one group of French nobles demanded that new schools be established in each province for the nobles' exclusive benefit. In mid-eighteenth-century Prussia as well, nearly all important governmental and military positions came to be reserved for the nobility; commoners who nonetheless found their way to high office were denied authority to command subordinates who happened to be noble.[16] In significant ways, the nobilities became more caste-conscious as the early modern period advanced.

Numbers

Efforts to regulate flows into the nobility had implications for the order's numbers. Table 1 brings together some of the data that historians have gathered on the nobility's numbers. It displays two important patterns, one spatial, the other temporal. First, it shows that early modern Europe divided between regions where nobles were numerous and regions where they were scarce. The latter regions constituted the core of Europe – France, Germany, Bohemia, and Italy – and here nobles might be scarce indeed. There were only 25,000 noble families in pre-revolutionary France, 0.52 percent of the population; in 1835 there were only 435 adult nobles in the small western German state of Hesse-Kassel, 0.3 percent of total population, about the same percentage as in Bavaria and the ecclesiastical state of Munster. In eighteenth-century Luxembourg, a possession of the Austrian empire lying between France and western Germany, nobles constituted 0.7 percent of the population in the mid-eighteenth century – a mere 1,500 individuals within a total population of 215,000. In Bohemia, Germany, lower Austria, and Italy the numbers were similar. In all of these regions, there were few enough nobles that, at least among the order's richer members, there was little room for anonymity.

But the situation was very different on the frontiers of Europe, western and eastern alike. In these settings, ongoing warfare against ethnic outsiders – Slavs and Moslems in eastern Europe, Moslems (until 1492)

---

[16] R. R. Palmer, *The Age of the Democratic Revolution, 1760–1800*, 2 vols. (Princeton, 1959–64), I, 73–74; Dewald, *Pont-St-Pierre*, 278; Hans Rosenberg, *Bureaucracy, Aristocracy, and Autocracy: The Prussian Experience, 1660–1815* (Cambridge, MA, 1958), 163; David Bien, "The Army in the French Enlightenment: Reform, Reaction, and Revolution," *Past and Present*, 85 (November, 1979), 68–98.

Table 1   *Evidence on numbers*

1   Bohemia: 1557 – 1,834
           1656 – 1,880
           ca. 1600 – about 1 percent of population
2   Moravia: 1619 – 279
3   Catalonia: 1518 – 488 in total population of about 400,000
             1626 – 780
4   Spain: Castile, mid-fifteenth-century – about 10 percent of population
           Castile, 1541 – 108,358 families = about 10 percent of population
           Castile, ca. 1600 – 650,000 = about 10 percent of population
           Spain as a whole, 1787 – 480,589 = 4.6 percent of population
           Spain as a whole, 1797 – 402,059 = 3.8 percent of population
5   Luxembourg: 1766 – about 1,500 individuals, in total population of 215,000 (= 0.7
    percent of population)
6   Savoy: 1702 – 795 families, 3,400 individuals, in population of 320,000 (= 1.06 percent)
           1787 – 500 families
7   German states
    (a) Hesse Kassel: 1835 – 0.3 percent of population
    (b) Bavaria: 1815 – 0.3 percent of population
    (c) Munster: ca. 1450 – about 100 families
        eighteenth century – 63 families, 0.4 percent of population
    (d) Prussia: eighteenth century – 1 percent of population
    (e) Saxony: ca. 1700 – 0.55 percent of population
8   France
    (a) Brittany: 1668 – 30,000 = 1.7 percent of population
        1750 – 14,000 = 0.6 percent of population
    (b) *élection* of Bayeux:
        1463 – 211 families
        1523 – 273 families
        1540 – 309 families
        1598 – 559 families
        1624 – 520 families
        1666 – 592 families = 3.5 percent of households
    (c) province of Franche Comté:
        1789 – 2,000 individuals = 0.3 percent of population
    (d) France as a whole:
        ca. 1450 – 1 percent of population
        ca. 1789 – 0.52 percent of population
9   England, gentry and peers
    ca. 1300 – 3,200 families
    ca. 1700 – 15,000 families
    ca. 1800 – 20,000 families
10 Italy
    (a) Venice: 1509 – 2,570, 2.2 percent of population
        1550 – 2,520, 1.6 percent
        1594 – 1,970, 1.4 percent
        1620 – 2,000, 1.4 percent
        1631 – 1,660, 1.6 percent
        1797 – 1,090, 0.8 percent

Table 1   (cont.)

(b) the Kingdom of Naples: seventeenth century – about 1 percent of population
(c) Siena: 1631 – 757 families
        1701 – 380
        1723 – 302
        1743 – 250
        1764 – 170
11   Holland: ca. 1500 – 0.4 percent of population
        ca. 1550 – 0.3 percent

Sources: Thomas Winkelbauer, "Krise der Aristokratie? Zum Strukturwandel des Adels in den böhmischen und niederösterreichischen Ländern im 16. und 17. Jahrhundert," 331–32; J. H. Elliott, "A Provincial Aristocracy: The Catalan Ruling Class in the Sixteenth and Seventeenth Centuries," repr. in *Spain and Its World: Selected Essays* (New Haven, 1989), 71–91; Angus MacKay, "The Lesser Nobility in the Kingdom of Castile," in Michael Jones, ed., *Gentry and Lesser Nobility in Late Medieval Europe* (Gloucester – New York, 1986); Antonio Dominquez Ortiz, *Las clases privilegiadas en la España del Antiguo Régimen* (Madrid, 1973), 26; Lynch, *The Hispanic World*, 181; Richard Herr, *The Eighteenth-Century Revolution in Spain* (Princeton, 1958), 86, 95; Richard Herr, *Rural Change and Royal Finances in Spain at the End of the Old Regime* (Berkeley, 1989), 75; Calixte Hudemann-Simon, *La Noblesse luxembourgeoise au XVIIIe siècle* (Paris, 1985), 23–24; Jean Nicolas, *La Savoie au XVIIIe siècle: noblesse et bourgeoisie*, 2 vols. (Paris, 1978), I, 11–12, II, 767–77; Gregory Pedlow, *The Survival of the Hessian Nobility, 1770–1870* (Princeton, 1988), 17; Gerhard Theuerkauf, "Der Adel in Westfalen," in Hellmuth Rössler, ed., *Deutscher Adel, 1430–1555* (Darmstadt, 1965), 153–76, 164; Rudolf Endres, ed., *Adel in der Frühneuzeit: Ein regionaler Vergleich* (Cologne, 1991), 127; Roland Mousnier, *Les Institutions de la France sous la monarchie absolue*, 2 vols. (Paris, 1974), I, 121; Alain Croix, *La Bretagne aux XVIe et XVIIe siècles: la vie, la mort, la foi*, 2 vols. (Paris, 1981), I, 150–53; James Wood, *The Nobility of the Election of Bayeux, 1463–1666: Continuity through Change* (Princeton, 1980), 45; Jacques Dupâquier, *Statistiques démographiques du bassin parisien, 1636–1720* (Paris, 1977), 160–62; Claude Brelot, *La Noblesse en Franche Comté de 1789 à 1808* (Paris, 1972), 17–18; Guy Chaussinand-Nogaret, *The French Nobility in the Eighteenth Century: From Feudalism to Enlightenment*, trans. William Doyle (Cambridge, 1985), 30; Chris Given-Wilson, *The English Nobility in the Later Middle Ages* (London, 1987), 13–15; G. E. Mingay, *English Landed Society in the Eighteenth Century* (London, 1963), 6; James C. Davis, *The Decline of the Venetian Nobility as a Ruling Class* (Baltimore, 1962), 58; Tomasso Astarita, *The Continuity of Feudal Power: The Caracciolo di Brienza in Spanish Naples* (Cambridge, 1992), 17, n. 30; George F. R. Baker, "Nobilità in declino: il caso di Siena sotto i Medici e gli Asburgo-Lorena," *Revista storica italiana*, 84, 3 (September, 1972), 584–616; H. F. K. Van Nierop, *The Nobility of Holland: From Knights to Regents, 1500–1650*, trans. Maarten Ultee (Cambridge, 1993), 50.

in Spain – gave large numbers of new men access to higher status; and the booty of conquest provided the material bases for their advancement. Even when conquest slowed, in these regions warriors played an especially important role in national identity, and sovereigns remained ready to reward loyalty with titles. As a result, in fifteenth-century

Castile, nobles constituted at least 10 percent of the population, possibly
more. In Poland nobles were about as numerous: 8–10 percent of the
population, perhaps even more. In Hungary, yet another frontier region,
nobles made up 5 percent of the population in the late eighteenth century,
and probably more in the previous centuries; in some regions of the
country, they counted for as much as 16 percent of the population.[17]

England, despite its less clear-cut definitions of what constituted
"gentility," fitted somewhere in the middle of this range, with its gentry
more numerous than in Germany or France, but less so than in Spain. In
the fourteenth century, there were about 200 great nobles, the barons
who would come to form the House of Lords, and about 3,000 knights
and esquires, the lesser figures who would come to be viewed as the
gentry. With their wives and children, these 3,200 men constituted
perhaps 2 percent of total population. Three centuries later, Gregory
King attempted to anatomize English society, and arrived at a total of
about 16,500 gentry and lords – closer to 5 percent of total population.[18]
Here the nobles' presence reflected not the society's warlike nature, but
its wealth. England was rich enough to support a large leisured class, and
its wealth increased – mainly to the gentry's benefit – all through the
period.

Just as important, Table 1 suggests a chronology in the nobles'
numerical development. In some regions, their numbers expanded
during the sixteenth century, for reasons that will be considered below.
But almost everywhere nobles became dramatically scarcer after 1600. In
the eighteenth century, at least, contemporaries had no doubt that
numbers were declining. "There used to be many more nobles than there
are now, up to twice as many," reported a provincial French observer in
the later eighteenth century.[19] In some regions, numerical decline came
still faster: the number of Bohemian nobles fell by one-half between 1557
and 1656, and continued to fall thereafter.[20] Decline had complicated
causes. It reflected the legal changes and snobbishness that made it more
difficult for newcomers to enter the nobility. It also reflected changing
attitudes toward marriage and familial life. Nobles (like many other
groups in European society) began in the seventeenth century to limit the

[17] Angus MacKay, *Spain in the Middle Ages: From Frontier to Empire, 1000–1500* (New
York, 1977), 2–3; Winkelbauer, "Krise?," 330; Peter Schimert, "Between the Double-
Headed Eagle and the Crescent Moon," forthcoming, 8–10.
[18] Chris Given-Wilson, *The English Nobility in the Later Middle Ages* (London, 1987),
13–15; Peter Laslett, *The World We Have Lost: England before the Industrial Age* (New
York, 1965), 26, 32.
[19] Quoted Claude Brelot, *La Noblesse en Franche Comté de 1789 à 1808* (Paris, 1972), 17.
[20] Winkelbauer, "Krise?," 331–32.

numbers of their children; by the eigtheenth century, noble families might be very small indeed. In the same years, there seems to have taken place a fundamental change in aristocratic conceptions of marriage itself. Men and women alike wanted more personal fulfillment from marriage and more personal autonomy; they were less willing to marry solely to sustain their families' prosperity, or to accept arranged marriages. As a result, significant numbers failed to marry at all, and there was a growing number of marital disputes among those who did.[21]

But one group remained immune to this process of contraction. While the nobilities as a whole contracted in early modern Europe, the loftiest groups in aristocratic society, those with the most imposing titles, became everywhere more numerous. We have seen that the Spanish king Charles V first introduced such titles to Iberia in 1520, creating the specific group of nobles known as grandees of Spain. Elsewhere such titles had long existed, but their numbers expanded dramatically. For early modern rulers had discovered the political advantages of creating lofty new noble titles. These could be sold for cash, as a way of balancing budgets, or they could be given to men who were already powerful, to secure their gratitude and political allegiance.

As a result, the beneficiaries formed a mixed group, one that included both wealthy businessmen and long-established nobles, who could acquire lustrous new titles for themselves and their relatives. For this reason, the sale of titles often upset social conservatives, who disliked seeing new men receiving public honors. Certainly this was the case in England, where royal greed produced a 56 percent increase in the size of the high nobility between 1615 and 1628, and even more dramatic changes among the highest level of gentry: in the first two years of his reign, king James tripled the English knighthood. In about the same years, the Spanish king Philip III created three new dukes, thirty marquises, and thirty-three counts. In France the story was similar, and it provoked public complaint. "The titled have become a multitude that is less honored and esteemed than in the past," as a royal edict stated in 1566. "The order of the past has been perverted." Italy and eastern Europe witnessed the same phenomenon. The Kingdom of Naples had ninety-nine high nobles in the early sixteenth century; by the mid-seventeenth century, the number had reached 438. In Hungary, the

---

[21] Lawrence Stone, *The Family, Sex, and Marriage in England, 1500–1800* (New York, 1977), 375–404; Jean Nicolas, *La Savoie au XVIIIe siècle: noblesse et bourgeoisie*, 2 vols. (Paris, 1978), II, 768 ff. For other examples of declining numbers, Roland Mousnier, *Les Institutions de la France sous la monarchie absolue*, 2 vols. (Paris, 1974–80), I, 120–22; Dewald, *Pont-St-Pierre*, 113–14; Theurerkauf, "Der Adel in Westfalen," 164.

Table 2   *The high nobilities: inflations of honors*

1	England, the peers
	1487: 57 1615: 81
	1559: 62 1628: 126
	1603: 55 1760: 204
2	France, the "ducs et pairs de France" (excluding ecclesiastics and royal princes)
	1589: 11 1661: 38
	1610: 17 1715: 48
	1643: 28 1723: 52
3	The Kingdom of Naples, titled nobles
	1444: 56 1620: 296
	1528: 99 1672: 446
	1599: 165 1750: 649
	1613: 239
4	Spain, titled nobles (*grandes de España* and *titulos*)
	1520: 55 1665: 236
	1598: 99 1700: 528
	1621: 144 1787: 654
5	Lower Austria, titled nobles (the *Herrenstand*)
	1612–1720, 212 new members

Sources: Lawrence Stone, *The Crisis of the Aristocracy, 1558–1641* (Oxford, 1965), 758; R. R. Palmer, *The Age of the Democratic Revolution*, I (Princeton, 1959), 45; Jean-Pierre Labatut, *Les Ducs et pairs de France au XVII siècle* (Paris, 1972), 80; Tommaso Astarita, *The Continuity of Feudal Power: The Caracciolo di Brienza in Spanish Naples* (Cambridge, 1992), 220; John Lynch, *The Hispanic World in Crisis and Change, 1598–1700* (Oxford, 1992), 183; Richard Herr, *The Eighteenth-Century Revolution in Spain* (Princeton, 1958), 96; R. J. W. Evans, *The Making of the Habsburg Monarchy, 1500–1700* (Oxford, 1979), 170.

Habsburgs created over 100 new titles of nobility between 1606 and 1657, effectively tripling the country's high nobility. The "inflation of honors" was a European phenomenon in the later sixteenth and early seventeenth centuries.[22]

Together, the numerical changes described in Tables 1 and 2 meant a reconfiguration in the nobility's most basic structure. There were many fewer nobles overall, but many more nobles at the highest levels. The titled nobility – in England the peers and baronets, in France the dukes, peers, and marquis, in Spain the grandees and *titulos* – formed a much larger share of the order in the eighteenth century than ever before.

[22] Quoted Robert Harding, *The Anatomy of a Power Elite: The Provincial Governors of Early Modern France* (New Haven, 1978), 80–84; Schimert, "Between the Double-Headed Eagle and the Crescent Moon," 12–13.

Privileges

Just as uncertainties surrounded the genetic bases of nobility, so also might there be confusion about its privileges. Privilege, of course, might vary widely from one country to another, a variation that usually was to be explained by local political circumstances. Where states were strong, by and large, nobles enjoyed fewer marks of special standing, for governments saw these as infringements of their own power. With significant exceptions, then, privilege tended to diminish over the early modern period, under the steady pressure of centralizing governments. Yet privilege was fundamental to the nobles' existence. It rendered visible the gap between them and the rest of society, and by implication it demonstrated the importance of their contribution to society. For this was the essence of ideas of privilege, that it rewarded the nobles' own services and those of their ancestors.

Some privileges were basic and nearly universal. There was the right to bear arms, and in particular to wear a sword; this testified to the nobles' traditional function, that of defending the rest of society. There was the right to certain forms of dress; periodically governments sought to restrict expensive clothing and other elegancies to those of high status. But these were complex and fragile privileges. Governments were more concerned to affirm their own officials' right to wear elaborate clothing, whatever their social status, than to defend the rights of nobles; and in any case violations were frequent. By the mid-eighteenth century the Bavarian government had to use troops to enforce its sumptuary laws, so common had violations become, while the English government simply gave up the attempt after 1604.[23] More solid were privileges concerning careers. Nobles might have exclusive right to certain political and military offices, and this monopoly tended to become more absolute as time went on. By the eighteenth century in most of Europe, it had become difficult for commoners to enter the officer corps and some bureaucracies. There were other positions as well, notably in the church, over which nobles enjoyed an increasingly complete monopoly. Cathedral chapters, the collections of clerics who resided in Europe's bishoprics and enjoyed a large share of church wealth, increasingly were reserved for nobles, especially in Germany.

Other privileges might vary more widely from one country to another. There was the question, for instance, of special legal position for the nobles. Did they have special rules for the inheritance of property? In

---

[23] Neidhard Bulst, "Kleidung als sozialer Konflikstoff: Probleme kleidergesetzlicher Normierung im sozialen Gefüge," *Saeculum*, 64, 1 (1993), 32–46.

most regions, yes, in keeping with the concern of feudal law that properties pass intact to one heir, so as to allow him to fulfill the functions for which his fief had been granted. Could nobles demand trial before specific law courts? Again, usually they could, and usually they could claim forms of punishment specific to the order; nobles were to be beheaded, commoners hanged or executed in still more degrading ways.[24] Again, these discriminations rendered social status visible in the daily round of practical life, hence their importance.

Political privileges were equally varied. In most parts of Europe, nobles had the right to sit in representative assemblies, known as estates, and typically this gave them a significant voice in political matters. In many regions, *all* nobles, no matter how poor, could join in this exercise of political power. Like so much else, the power of these representative assemblies varied widely across Europe. In some regions, their approval was required before governments could levy taxes; elsewhere, they functioned only to rubber-stamp the governments' decisions. Yet where they existed, they gave significant opportunities for profit to those who could control them. The estates of the French province of Languedoc under Louis XIV provide an especially clear example. The French monarchy had largely destroyed the estates' real political autonomy, yet it usually sought consensus with their representatives about such matters as taxation, and it did so by offering solid material advantages to individual members. Thus the crown involved the nobles in its political projects by allowing them to participate in advantageous financial operations, for instance as tax farmers. These were advantages that not all nobles received, but for some within the order they could be very important. In the same way, the crown went out of its way to entertain and flatter members of the estates of Brittany, so as to secure their support for its fiscal aims.[25]

For most nobles, the most important privileges concerned taxation: nobles claimed freedom from the state's heaviest demands. Here too, national differences might be important. Noble tax exemption did not exist in England; in fact the English gentry and nobles probably paid higher percentages of taxation than other Englishmen. Elsewhere, as in parts of Germany and in southern France, property rather than people enjoyed privileges: properties that were classified as noble (in most cases, because they were believed to have been granted as rewards for military

[24] Pedlow, *The Survival*, 26ff.
[25] William Beik, *Absolutism in Languedoc: State Power and Provincial Aristocracy in Seventeenth-Century Languedoc* (Cambridge, 1985); James Collins, *Classes, Estates, and Order in Early Modern Brittany* (Cambridge, 1994). These issues are discussed more fully below, Chapter 3.

1 Elegance in the provinces: two nobles of Lorraine, ca. 1620 (Jacques Callot, *The Nobility of Lorraine*)

service) were not taxed at the usual rates, whoever owned them, while even nobles had to pay taxes on properties they acquired from non-nobles. But in sixteenth-century Spain, northern France, Sweden, and much of Germany, to be noble was to avoid the most onerous fiscal burdens.

Yet even tax exemptions failed to distinguish the nobles clearly from all other social groups, for fiscal privilege was not their exclusive preserve. In France, a wide range of people enjoyed the same exemption from basic income taxes. These included royal officials and most residents of the larger cities, precisely the groups closest to the nobles in status. More important, after about 1650 tax exemptions tended to weaken, producing a profound change in nobles' relations to other social groups. In Spain, from the mid-seventeenth century the government turned increasingly to indirect taxes imposed evenly on all classes, making nobles' exemption from income taxes steadily less meaningful; the Spanish government during the same years reduced fiscal privileges in its domains in northern Italy.[26] In France the critical change came in 1695, when Louis XIV subjected his nobles to a form of income tax. The tax, variously modified over the next century, never weighed as heavily as the taxes most villagers paid, but it nonetheless became steadily more burdensome.[27] In Prussia, a mild form of taxation was imposed on the nobles in the early eighteenth century, and in the duchy of Savoy, nobles were subjected to the same taxes as other residents starting in 1731. The heart-rending protests that the change provoked suggested its symbolic as well as economic significance: "Henceforth what will be sacred and solid," complained one nobleman, "now that rights consolidated by centuries of possession . . . are now destroyed by a new system?"[28] In the Habsburg territory of Luxembourg, nobles lost all fiscal privileges in 1771.[29] By this point, nobles' fiscal privileges seemed to most administrators an outmoded abuse rather than a normal right.

---

[26] Ignacio Atienza Hernández, *Aristocracia, poder y riqueza en la España moderna: La Casa de Osuna, siglos XV–XIX* (Madrid, 1987), 44; Domenico Sella, *Crisis and Continuity: The Economy of Spanish Lombardy in the Seventeenth Century* (Cambridge, MA, 1979), 140–43.

[27] For a summary of the principal taxes on the nobles, Marcel Marion, *Dictionnaire des institutions de la France aux XVIIe et XVIIIe siècles* (Paris, 1923; repr. New York, 1968), 69–71, 556–59; for an example of their real weight, James Lowth Goldsmith, *Les Salers et les d'Escorailles: seigneurs de Haute Auvergne, 1500–1789* (Clermont Ferrand, 1984), 207–08.

[28] Peter Baumgart, "Der Adel Brandenburg-Preussens im Urteil der Hohenzollern der 18. Jahrhunderts," in Rudolf Endres, ed., *Adel in der Frühneuzeit: ein regionaler Vergleich* (Cologne, 1991), 150–51; quoted Nicolas, *La Savoie au XVIIIe siècle*, II, 632–36.

[29] Calixte Hudemann-Simon, *La Noblesse luxembourgeoise au XVIIIe siècle* (Paris-Luxembourg, 1985), 239–46.

An ideology under attack: criticism of the nobility

Early modern nobles thus occupied a contradictory position. They enjoyed significant privileges, yet their privileges overlapped disconcertingly with those enjoyed by numerous commoners – and in any case privileges tended to erode as the period advanced. Nobles claimed descent from medieval heroes, yet their contemporaries knew the claim to be often hollow. These contradictions became more painful in the early modern period because of the directions taken by public discussion of the idea of nobility. Nothing, so numerous handbooks proclaimed, was more glorious than noble status. Yet from 1500 on, commentators proved ready to make fun of nobles' pretensions and proclaim the falsity of the myths with which nobles surrounded themselves. Let us listen to Erasmus, the Dutch humanist, the recipient of honors from the English and French kings and from the Holy Roman Emperor, and probably the most influential intellectual of the early sixteenth century. Erasmus imagined the dialogue between a wise old advisor and a handsome youth eager to get on in the world, hoping to become a nobleman, something that would make him "honorable in the eyes of the vulgar" – already an indication that nobility is in some degree a sham quality. The pair explore but reject some established paths to title: buying noble status from the king (dismissed because purchased titles are not taken seriously); performing virtuous actions (too difficult and too slow). They finally settle on an alternative method: the young man is to move away from home, put on noble manners, and simply pretend to be a nobleman. Proper clothing, so the advisor tells the young man, will do as a beginning, but he then needs to act the part. "Unless you are an expert gamester at cards and dice, a rank whoremaster, a stout drinker, a daring extravagant, and understand the art of borrowing and bubbling, and have got the French pox [syphilis] to boot, scarce anyone will believe you to be a knight." Then there is the problem of money. The young man will need to borrow beyond his means, "for nobody is more in debt than great princes," and he need not hesitate to steal when he encounters merchants on the open road: "for what can be more dishonorable than for a pitiful tradesman to have money enough, and a knight at the same time wants it to spend upon his whores, and at dice?"[30] The point was straightforward. Nobles, Erasmus argued, were whoring, irresponsible, inglorious frauds.

Awareness of social mobility and thoroughgoing critique of noble status mingle in Erasmus's satire. He presents his young man as sharing a

[30] Colloquy "The False Knight," in W. T. H. Jackson, ed., *Essential Works of Erasmus* (New York, 1965), 131–39; quotations 135, 136.

commonplace ambition, to raise his social standing by rising into the nobility; geographical mobility, so his advisor counsels, will be a necessary part of the project, for among people he does not know he can easily counterfeit high rank. In fact Erasmus did not reject the idea of nobility wholesale. The dialogue mentions those who attain it through virtuous actions or by birth. Yet his essential point is that most nobles have no real claim to social superiority.

Readers throughout Europe bought Erasmus's books and followed his ideas. He represented a wide current of sixteenth-century opinion, and in fact numerous other writers echoed his views. In Germany, Sebastian Franck concluded a discussion of the nobility's faults with the reflection that "the nobility in our time is almost entirely heathenish"; a few years later, the poet Nikodemus Frischlin likewise described the nobles as impious blasphemers, and complained that "the most ignorant and crudest little nobles, . . . puffed up with an incomprehensible madness about their ancestry," wanted to be given precedence over the learned and competent.[31] In England, Erasmus's friend Thomas More included them in the first part of *Utopia* (1516), presenting Europe's supposedly glorious warrior class as mere ruffians who were otherwise unemployable. In Italy at about the same time, Niccolò Machiavelli urged his prince to watch his nobles carefully but not to take them too seriously, because they were inherently greedy and oppressive. "These two dispositions are to be found in every city; . . . the people are everywhere anxious not to be dominated or oppressed by the nobles, and the nobles are out to dominate and oppress the people." There was no question which group the prince had to support. Nobles who made trouble should be killed and new ones created to take their places. "A prince must always live with the same people," ran the conclusion, "but he can well do without the nobles, since he can make and unmake them every day, increasing and lowering their standing at will." In spite of his criticisms, Machiavelli thought that a ruler needed a nobility, to give grandeur and order to his state, and he thought that "the nobles have more foresight and are more astute, they always act in time to safeguard their interests." But he entirely dismissed the idea that ancient families might bring special qualities to the role. Anyone whom the prince selected would do. If nobles were more astute than others, this merely reflected wealth and high position. Like Erasmus but in darker tones, Machiavelli assumed that social mobility characterized his society. Movement in and out of the nobility was a fact of life.[32]

[31] Cited and analyzed by H. C. Erik Midelfort, "Adeliges Landesleben und die Legitimationskrise des deutschen Adels im 16. Jahrhundert," in Georg Schmidt, ed., *Stände und Gesellschaft im alten Reich* (Stuttgart, 1989), 245–64; 250–52.
[32] *The Prince*, ed. George Bull (London, 1961), 67–68.

Part of this broad challenge to conventional ideas about social status was a critique of the very function of the warrior nobility. Machiavelli, of course, had no such objections, but Erasmus and Thomas More vigorously criticized the whole enterprise. More described the impact of war in *Utopia*: the subjects of one of his fictional warlike kings found "their money was being taken out of the country, they were shedding their blood for the little glory of someone else, peace was no more secure than before, their morals at home were being corrupted by war, the lust for robbery was becoming second nature, criminal recklessness was emboldened by killings in war, and the laws were held in contempt." Later in the book More compared the warrior with the butcher, reducing what the Middle Ages had deemed a glorious function to a form of manual labor.[33] Such mockery remained vibrant in the seventeenth and eighteenth centuries; it was no longer obvious to educated Europeans that a military career was the most glorious that a man might follow. In 1600 an English writer complained that "gentlemen who were wont to addict themselves to wars are now grown good husbands [estate managers], and well know how to improve their lands." There were similar observations from Italy and France; and numerous commentators, even from the nobility itself, underlined the squalor of military life and the ugly disfigurement of many ex-soldiers.[34]

These were extremist views. But even those most committed to ideals of military glory accepted that there were other valid forms of high status. Baldesar Castiglione, the early sixteenth-century Italian whose *The Courtier* became an international best-seller and revered guide to elegant behavior, noted as a form of backwardness that "the French recognize only the nobility of arms and reckon all the rest as naught; and thus not only do they not esteem, but they abhor letters, and consider all men of letters to be very base." Even in France, another of Castiglione's characters noted, attitudes were changing.[35] Many nobles still regarded fighting as the only life-work suited to them, but the ideology that placed the warrior at the top of society had lost its cogency.

Comparable uncertainties surrounded the question of noble birth. A voice of moderation in this as in much else concerning the nobility, Castiglione took the view that the status could be acquired through

---

[33] Thomas More, *Utopia*, ed. Edward Surtz (New Haven, 1964), 42–43.

[34] Quoted John Hale, *War and Society in Renaissance Europe, 1450–1620* (Baltimore, 1985), 91; Hale also describes the larger evolution of values. See also Theodore K. Rabb, "Artists and Warfare: A Study of Changing Values in Seventeenth-Century Europe," *Transactions of the American Philosophical Society*, 75 (1985), 79–106, which likewise documents growing disenchantment with military values.

[35] Baldesar Castiglione, *The Book of the Courtier*, trans. Charles Singleton (Garden City, New York, 1959), 67, 68.

personal virtue as well as through birth, and that both forms were admirable. Others offered more extreme statements of this view, claiming that personal worth formed the *only* grounding for nobility. Not the actions of distant ancestors but one's own were to be the basis for social standing. As one mid-sixteenth-century Frenchman proclaimed, "there is no true nobility, but that which proceeds from virtue and good conduct."[36]

Already by the mid-sixteenth century, then, ideas about nobility had lost much of their coherence. Radically incompatible ideas circulated even among those who praised nobility. Others ridiculed the whole idea. This intellectual disarray is important as we try to understand how nobles actually lived in the early modern period. We might imagine a stable ideology of noble excellence slowly eroding over the early modern period, under pressure from modernizing social and political changes – a "world we have lost," slowly breaking up in the face of new forces. Clearly that is how Alexis de Tocqueville in the mid-nineteenth century saw the matter. But in fact anti-aristocratic ideas were among the early and best-selling products of Europe's sixteenth-century publishing industry. If at times their readers accepted ideas about a great chain of being, along which each man's rank was clearly fixed and which held together by deference and mutual service, mockery of these images found also a vigorous market. This was a European market, perhaps with different emphases but with a common enjoyment of anti-noble humor. The theme could be found in the picaresque novels of Spain, and in *Don Quixote* itself; in Germany, France, England; and in the international Latin humanist culture within which Erasmus and More starred.

The rise of the administrative nobilities

But social conditions in the centuries after 1450 opened up new fissures in the ideology of nobility, because they significantly changed the order's membership. New groups joined it, and the values attaching to old practices changed. Most important was the creation of a fundamentally new social class in these years, a class of university-trained administrators. The growing, increasingly sophisticated governments of the period demanded more and more such men. Governments wanted their servants to be better trained, typically with law degrees. When medieval governments had needed such men, typically they had turned to the church. But a series of noisy conflicts between church and state in the late Middle Ages made churchmen less attractive as governmental administrators,

---

[36] Quoted Ellery Schalk, *From Valor to Pedigree: Ideas of Nobility in France in the Sixteenth and Seventeenth Centuries* (Princeton, 1986), 57.

and the new breed were mostly laymen. Governments rewarded these men well; in fact state service more than commerce offered the leading avenue to riches in the early modern period. And increasingly it offered them a special status as well. Enjoying the honor of education and positions of command within their societies, these men came to see themselves as a kind of nobility, a nobility that did not fight but instead based itself on state service.

Their development was most visible in France, where in the course of the sixteenth century this group officially established its claim to nobility, coming to be known as the nobility of the robe – in reference to the long robes usually worn by early modern judges and officials. In the mid-fourteenth century this group had scarcely existed. There had been a handful of great lay administrators around the king, and there were the eighty-odd judges, only thirty-four of them laymen, of the Paris Parlement, established in 1345 as the kingdom's chief appeals court – a task until then handled by a floating assembly of the king's greatest vassals.[37] In the course of the next two centuries, this small group expanded many times over. New appeals courts like the one at Paris were established in eight leading provincial cities, and about the same number of courts were established to deal with administrative disputes, mainly concerning taxation. Hundreds of lesser jurisdictions were set up throughout France and required thousands of judges to staff them, and large numbers of new financial offices were created. In 1515 France counted one royal official for every 4,700 inhabitants; by 1665, there was an official for every 380 inhabitants. A new and highly visible ruling group had established itself.[38]

From the beginning these men and their families enjoyed a special standing within French society. Their power of judgment over the lives and properties of those around them compelled recognition that these were not mere bourgeois. But in the years after 1500 this consensus received increasingly explicit formulation. By the early eighteenth century, it had been established that the 1,100 highest positions in the French judiciary officially conferred noble status, and hundreds of others might confer nobility on the office-holder's descendants.[39]

Similar processes occurred throughout Europe, with similar chronology: in most of Europe, the sixteenth century was the crucial period of change, during which civil services expanded several times over and

[37] Françoise Autrand, *Naissance d'un grand corps d'Etat: les gens du Parlement de Paris, 1345–1454* (Paris, 1981), 21.
[38] Roland Mousnier et al., *Le Conseil du Roi de Louis XII à la Révolution* (Paris, 1970), 17–20.
[39] Mousnier, *Les Institutions de la France*, II, 318; I, 122–24.

during which their members established themselves as comparable in status to the traditional military elites. Governments were growing everywhere, and they needed more civil servants; increasingly these men were university-educated, and increasingly they had a sharp sense of their importance in the world. Though usually not so explicitly as in France, they came in most places to enjoy a status comparable to that of the nobility. In Spain up to the late fifteenth century, for instance, there had been only a relative handful of positions for the university-educated, known as *letrados*, and the group itself was looked down upon. Under Ferdinand and Isabella and their immediate successors, however, the group underwent a rapid expansion in numbers, wealth, and esteem. A series of new councils and courts were established and staffed with university-trained men. At the highest level, the number of such positions tripled over the sixteenth century, then remained essentially unchanged over the seventeenth – roughly following the chronology seen in France; at lower levels, the numerical increase seems to have been still more rapid. And whereas fifteenth-century officials had been dismissed as second-rate figures, "mere clerks," sixteenth-century officials became rich, in some cities the richest inhabitants. "If before, grandees were greater than *letrados*," wrote one of them in 1641, "now *letrados* have become the grandees." Along with money came status – the Spanish crown regularly rewarded its civil servants with titles of high nobility.[40]

England is sometimes seen as an exception to this development of bureaucratic elites in the sixteenth century, but in fact it had a similar history of bureaucratic development in the sixteenth century. If somewhat more haltingly than on the continent, sixteenth-century England also saw a dramatic expansion in the ranks of the civil service. The Reformation and the expansion of litigation made the king's business far more complex than it had earlier been. Universities and law schools bulged with men eager to get the training that would allow them to profit from this situation; and even more dramatically than elsewhere, the crown rewarded its leading servants with grants of land and other forms of wealth – dramatically, because the crown's confiscation of monastic lands gave it such ample resources to use in rewarding its servants. Acquiring landed estates and often titles from grateful rulers, these officials quickly and effectively merged into the high gentry.[41]

[40] Richard Kagan, *Students and Society in Early Modern Spain* (Baltimore, 1974), 84–87; quotation from Charles Jago, "The 'Crisis of the Aristocracy' in Seventeenth-Century Castile," *Past and Present*, 84 (1979), 68.

[41] Lawrence Stone and Jeanne Fawtier Stone, *An Open Elite? England 1540–1880* (Oxford, 1987), 197–201. Other studies of expanding bureaucracies include R. Burr Litchfield, *Emergence of a Bureaucracy: The Florentine Patricians, 1530–1790* (Princeton, 1986) and Rosenberg, *Bureaucracy, Aristocracy, and Autocracy*.

2 The administrative nobleman: a French royal official,
ca. 1540 (Jean Clouet, *Guillaume Budé*)

Families like these posed a number of challenges to conventional ideologies of nobility. Glaringly, they were nobles who did not fight; where did they fit within a vision that divided society between warriors, priests, and farmers? More troubling still, their existence suggested a separation of real political power from military might. These men did not fight, but seemed nonetheless to hold effective control over their societies, including control over men who did fight. The civil servants seemed to embody the anti-military ideas that Erasmus and More had developed early in the sixteenth century. They could easily see themselves as just the sort of alternative elite that the humanists had called for: one oriented to government rather than to violence, one shaped by rigorous education. The civil servants were a receptive audience for humanists propounding this new vision of how society ought to be organized; many humanists' books were dedicated to them and some were written by them.

The administrative nobilities that arose in the sixteenth and seventeenth centuries posed another challenge to conventional ideas about social status. Many came from families that already enjoyed nobility, but many others did not; a few came from the bottom of the social hierarchy, from families of artisans and even peasants. They exemplified the possibility of social movement, the more clearly because of the education needed to reach such positions.

Rich and poor nobles

To the question, what is a nobleman, the sixteenth century thus brought confusing new answers. It could no longer be assumed that a nobleman was a warrior or lived on a country estate; it was more clear than ever that the nobleman did not necessarily descend from an old family, and that there was a constant movement of new families into the order; it was not even clear that warfare – the nobleman's traditional contribution to his society's welfare – was a good thing.

Another division increasingly complicated early modern ideas about what was noble, the division between ranks within the nobility. Even among nobles who claimed equally ancient lineage and equally devoted themselves to military activity, sharp differences separated rich and poor nobles.[42] These differences had a long history. In the early Middle Ages, so it appears, there had been no poor nobles, for contemporary definitions limited titles of nobility to a small group of great families. In the eleventh and twelfth centuries, however, this understanding of nobility changed. Lesser figures who surrounded the great nobles and fought with them increasingly acquired the trappings of high status. The knight, whose title had originally implied subservience and social inferiority, came to share in the glory of his master; great men, including kings, came to have themselves knighted; and the ceremony became increasingly elaborate. The former military servants had become part of the ruling group, and the ceremonies of knighthood affirmed this common bond among men of

---

[42] Chapter 2 will examine nobles' wealth.

diverse situations. But ceremony was not the essential point. In the thirteenth and fourteenth centuries (we have seen) many men fought without bothering with the ceremonies of knighthood. Noble status settled on a diffuse collection of families recognized as genteel – the gentry, the esquires.

Throughout the early modern period, thus, a common status covered men of diverse economic conditions and political authority. The economic distances might be enormous. In terms of income, the difference between the typical lesser nobles and those at the top of the noble hierarchy might easily be on the order of one to 100; still greater differences separated the richest nobles from the poorest. Rather than a single social class, then, the European nobilities included a hierarchy of wealth. There were a small number of the great, a substantial middle class, and a mass of the poor – some of whom might be very poor indeed, in fact poorer than some of the farmers around them. Almost invariably, other differences accompanied these differences in income. In most regions, the wealthy nobleman had other marks of status, specific titles and significant legal privileges. Inequality within the nobility, as a result, involved more than money. Clear differences in status marked and accentuated economic differences.

Noble poverty was an apparently permanent part of the nobles' history in these centuries. It did not signal an order in decay or disarray – quite the contrary, there had always been poor nobles, at least since the twelfth century, when the order broadened out to include the mere knights, the military followers of greater men. If not a sign of social change, however, the poor nobles did constitute yet a further challenge to any simple reading of the social order. Whatever claims to social superiority, nobles were not necessarily the richest people in their communities.

Given such disparities within the order, what forces held it together and how strong were they? How close could rich and poor nobles feel themselves? Until well into the seventeenth century, rich and poor were united by the bonds of patronage, centering on the households of the rich. In medieval Europe rich and poor had been united by a system of vassalage and feudalism: formal mechanisms by which one man placed himself in dependence on another, and received in return a formal gift of property. By 1400 or so these rites and agreements had lost much of their vigor, but more informal relations remained lively. Rich men continued to offer financial support for lesser gentlemen, and they continued to receive in return services, both immediate and long-term. This was the patron–client relation, and it remained central to much European social life from 1400 into the seventeenth century.

For the lesser man, the client, the benefits of the relationship were obvious. He received material support, very often a place at the table and in the household of his richer patron, and he could expect advancement in his career. He could call on the patron for protection in conflicts with others. For the patron, there was a combination of practical, social, and psychological benefits. Few in early modern society wanted solitude, and few had much experience of it. To be surrounded by many companions, at table and even in the bedchamber, was normal and proper. At the same time, followers served immediate needs for protection in violent times, and they might be enrolled in military adventures either at home or abroad; local patronage networks remained at the center of royal armies in England and France. But more important, much of a great nobleman's standing lay in the fact that as he moved about he was accompanied by large numbers of followers, and at home too he was expected to be surrounded by large numbers of people.[43] In fifteenth-century England, the duke of Clarence had 299 followers wearing his livery, the badges identifying them as loyal followers. Though the practice declined in popularity thereafter, in 1571 the earl of Pembroke still had 210 liveried retainers. Many of these were gentlemen; there was nothing demeaning for a man who himself claimed high status to serve as a dependant to such great nobles as these. The same practices were to be found in France; in the seventeenth century the Cardinal de Richelieu showed the continuity of these ideals, going out always attended by a mass of armed dependants. His great Spanish rival the count duke of Olivares had almost 200 servants, and other Spanish grandees in the early seventeenth century had still more: the duke of Osuna 300, the duke of Medinaceli 700. In Bohemia in the 1620s, the great duke Albrecht von Wallenstein maintained a court of nearly 900 individuals; when the duke visited the baths of Karlsbad in hopes of soothing his gout, his officials rented out the entire town – for three months.[44] Liveried followers of this sort had above all to be big and tough; their job was to make an impression, and perhaps to fight. But the patronage networks of the great took in other sorts as well. Great noblemen needed legal counsellors, and they needed friendly faces in the lawcourts which decided their lawsuits. Hence lawyers and judges too figured among the followers.[45]

[43] On early moderns' distaste for solitude, Philippe Ariès, *Centuries of Childhood: A Social History of Family Life*, trans. Robert Baldick (New York, 1962), 375–98; on patronage more generally, Sharon Kettering, *Patrons, Brokers, and Clients in Seventeenth-Century France* (Oxford, 1986).

[44] Lawrence Stone, *The Crisis of the Aristocracy, 1558–1641* (Oxford, 1965), 212; J. H. Elliott, *Imperial Spain, 1469–1716* (New York, 1963), 311; Golo Mann, *Wallenstein*, trans. Charles Kessler (New York, 1976), 222–26.

[45] On military nobles' need for clients among the jurists, Caron, *Noblesse et pouvoir*, 153; Jonathan Dewald, *The Formation of a Provincial Nobility: The Magistrates of the Parlement of Rouen, 1499–1610* (Princeton, 1980), 87–94.

Contemporary writers might present these bonds of patronage in highly emotional terms, as a complete and mutual commitment of loyalty, even as a submersion of the follower's identity in that of his leader. Examples of such commitment abounded. In 1346, the aged and blind king of Bohemia insisted on participating in battle against the English. To accommodate him, "because they cherished his honour and their own prowess," several of his followers roped their horses to his and led him into the thick of the battle; "they were found the next day lying around their leader, with their horses still fastened together." This was how loyalty was supposed to function, and well into the seventeenth century nobles continued to proclaim fidelity of this kind. Thus a German nobleman, describing his devotion to the French king Henry IV, recalled telling the future king "that he had so charmed me that I would go no further in seeking a master; if he wanted my service, I would devote myself to him until death." Childhood experiences often strengthened the rhetoric of fidelity, for many nobles had spent parts of their childhoods in the homes of the great men they eventually followed.[46]

More often, however, relations between patron and client had a hard-edged, calculating quality. They were marked by shifts of attachment and frequent accusations of disloyalty. Lesser nobles were especially prone to note "the indifference that a prince can direct to a gentleman in his service," in the words of one French noble, but in fact the calculations were mutual; clients were quite ready to desert their patrons when they could find better conditions elsewhere. One result, as in fifteenth-century England, was carefully drawn-up contracts, spelling out the obligations and benefits that each side expected in the relationship.[47]

Clearly men entered patronage relations with hard calculations of their potential profits. Yet these relations remained fundamental to nobles' lives in these years, for they united the potentially divided nobility into a single order, overcoming differences of income, education, and social standing. But at some point after 1550 – earlier in England, later in France – these relations began to snap. Rich and poor nobles became steadily less able to view themselves as part of a single order, united by

[46] Jean Froissart, *Chronicles*, selected, ed., and trans. Geoffrey Brereton (London, 1968), 89, 90; quoted Mousnier, *Les Institutions de la France*, I, 185. In a variety of other works, Mousnier has vigorously argued for the depth and strength of these relationships.

[47] Quoted Jonathan Dewald, *Aristocratic Experience and the Origins of Modern Culture: France, 1570–1715* (Berkeley, 1993), 32; K. B. McFarlane, "'Bastard Feudalism,'" *Bulletin of the Institute for Historical Research*, 20, 61 (May–November, 1945), 161–80; for overviews of recent research, P. R. Coss, "Bastard Feudalism Revised," *Past and Present*, 125 (November, 1989), 26–64, and David Crouch, D. A. Carpenter, and P. R. Coss, "Debate: Bastard Feudalism Revised," *Past and Present*, 131 (May, 1991), 164–203.

bonds of service and assistance, and they became steadily more aware of what divided them. As they did so, they brought to an end habits that had a very long history in European societies. In this sense, without regard to the formalities of law and landholding, the sixteenth and seventeenth centuries marked the end of feudalism in Europe.

In some degree, this momentous breakdown of patronage relations reflected economic changes. Adam Smith, the eighteenth-century Englishman who founded liberal economic theory, believed that patronage relations of this kind reflected medieval Europe's economic underdevelopment. Landowners had few opportunities to spend money or even to get money in exchange for the goods that their lands produced. They had thus little choice but to use their properties to support hospitality for their followers. The widening array of consumer goods that the sixteenth and seventeenth centuries made available, and the increasing possibilities they brought for marketing the estate's produce, Smith argued, dramatically changed the situation. Landowners could now devote the entire product of their estates to their own enjoyment, and they suddenly found maintaining open house for large numbers of retainers less attractive. In the same way, wealthy nobles could buy services from paid professionals, rather than rely on household dependants to perform them. Urban lawyers, estate managers, even specialized cooks and gardeners could fill the roles that in-house servants had once performed. There was not only the positive stimulus of new items to purchase, but also the negative stimulus of economic pressure and even debt. For many nobles, we shall see, early modern economic changes made it harder to be generous; nobles had to watch their expenses more carefully and had to be more ruthless in drawing revenues from their estates. There was less room for the follower.

But there was also less desire to have him around. Hesitantly from the sixteenth century on, and enthusiastically from the mid-seventeenth, Europeans of all classes became more interested in privacy. They began to design houses with smaller rooms, suited to intimate exchanges, and they added hallways, which allowed them to dispense with the medieval practice of passing through one another's bedrooms. As a result, numbers of servants began to diminish; even those who could afford the expense no longer desired to have large numbers of men in their homes.[48]

If masters became less willing to have followers, gentlemen at the same time were becoming less willing to serve. The mid-sixteenth-century Spanish novel *Lazarillo de Tormes*, an anonymous work possibly written by a great nobleman, offered one example of the tensions that already surrounded the figure of the poor nobleman in service to a greater. "I'm often asked," says an impoverished gentleman whom the hero encoun-

---

[48] See below, Chapter 4.

ters, "to be the right-hand man of a minor nobleman, but it's very hard working with them because you're no longer a man, just a thing they use. If you don't do what they want then it's 'Good-bye to you.' When they feel conscience-stricken and want to reward you for all the work you have put in on their behalf, you are paid in the old clothes' room with a sweaty doublet or a worn-out jacket or cloak. And even if you get a job with a titled lord you still go through the mill . . . Rich men . . . don't want honest men in their houses; in fact they hate and despise them and call them stupid and say they're not men of the world and that a gentleman can't relax when he's in their company."[49] Patronage was breaking down, such examples suggested, partly because lesser nobles no longer wanted the kinds of subjection that the relation implied. *Lazarillo*'s nobleman preferred starvation to service, because service had come to seem servitude.

A final cause of change was closely related: cultural differences between great nobles and lesser increased from the sixteenth century on, leaving them less interested in common pursuits, less able to speak to each other. For the great nobles – partly because of the economic changes to which Adam Smith pointed – were acquiring new centers of activity, away from the landed estates that had been the foundation for much patronage activity. One such center was the royal court, the grouping of high nobles, officials, servants, and entertainers who lived around the king. As we shall see in detail below, courts grew both in size and in importance during the early modern period. Those who could afford to (and the cost could be high) spent an increasing share of their time there, and spent less time in their country houses. This meant physical separation from the country nobles left behind, but more importantly it also meant psychological separation. For the court became a cultural center as well as a center of power. At court there were new styles, new objects, new pleasures, and new beliefs. By contrast, country gentlemen increasingly seemed backward, out of touch, dull. The great nobles almost always had a place at court; indeed, they could not refuse such a place, without arousing suspicious irritation from the monarch. Some lesser nobles might be welcomed as well, but ultimately the rise of the courts meant yet another fracture within the nobility, as high and low came to occupy different cultural worlds. By about 1700, variations on this theme had been replayed throughout Europe: even in distant Hungary court and country nobles found themselves alienated from one another, as most of the country's great nobles found themselves drawn to the Habsburgs' court in Vienna.[50]

[49] Michael Alpert, trans., *Two Spanish Picaresque Novels* (London, 1969), 63.
[50] Schimert, "Between the Double-Headed Eagle and the Crescent Moon," 52ff. More generally, Perez Zagorin, *Rebels and Rulers, 1500–1660*, 2 vols. (Cambridge, 1982), II, 138–46.

Great nobles sought privacy from their one-time dependents, and lesser nobles increasingly found the constraints of dependency humiliating rather than gratifying. To these private reasons for the breakdown of patronage ties, the early modern state added public reasons. For the state viewed patronage as a danger to public order and a source of rebellion. In fact princes had always looked suspiciously at great nobles' power over their followers. They were especially displeased when patronage extended, as it very often did, to the state's own officials. Until well into the sixteenth century, few states in Europe could do much to end patronage, for the practice served political needs that could not otherwise be met. This was how the state recruited soldiers, and it was an important means of assuring obedience in distant regions. Governments relied on lesser nobles obeying their patrons, and in this way preserved relative peace in the countryside. In effect, they subcontracted the local maintenance of law and order to the great nobles.

But such means of governing always involved confiding the state's powers to the nobles themselves, and they led quickly to political crisis when leading patrons disagreed with state policy. As sixteenth- and seventeenth-century states grew, their bureaucracies allowed them to perform the same functions with fewer risks. Increasingly, the state could by-pass the patronage networks that centered on the great nobles, and instead govern directly. Thus the state began to exert its influence against patronage relations. English kings sought to outlaw liveries, the badges by which followers signalled their allegiance to a great noble. Monarchs everywhere forbade civil servants from serving great nobles. They increasingly sought to assign great nobles to governmental offices far from their territorial bases, so as to reduce the influence of patronage bonds on their political behavior. Underlying these efforts was a belief that noble patronage easily shaded into mere brigandage, that the state had to exert its control for the sake of public order. A Catalan town in the early seventeenth century complained that "there are . . . many unemployed vagabonds, and as they have no occupation to earn them a living, they take service with the gentry . . . and go out to rob and kill."[51] Here was a real-life parallel to Thomas More's imagined scene from early sixteenth- century England, linking nobility with brigandage and bringing into question the ethical value of the semi-feudal patronage bond.

One consequence of this breakdown of patronage bonds was a change in what it meant to be a poor noble. In the fifteenth century as in the seventeenth and eighteenth, poor nobles had been numerous, constituting the large majority of the order's members. But in the fifteenth century the poor noble lived as an honorable dependant of a rich one, with

[51] Quoted J. H. Elliott, *The Revolt of the Catalans: A Study in the Decline of Spain, 1598–1640* (Cambridge, 1963), 64.

chances to share in his master's material well-being and political power. The great noble house was partly his. After 1600, such sharing became harder for all concerned, and after 1700 it almost ceased to exist. The poor noble was on his own. He could compensate for the poverty of his own dwelling only by occasional visits to those of greater neighbors. These circumstances made the impoverished noble an altogether more serious problem, because s/he represented a blatant inconsistency within the social order – poverty allied to high status. Sixteenth- and seventeenth-century definitions of nobility required fine dress, elaborate manners, and elegant speech. Lack of education or ignorance about wine and food exposed the nobleman to mockery, but this was precisely the contradiction that poor nobles increasingly represented: many simply could not afford the external trappings needed to sustain gentility, yet they noisily insisted on their noble birth. Contemporaries understood the problem, and some sought to rectify it. The period after 1650 saw a flowering of institutions designed to alleviate noble poverty, by aiding poor nobles. Madame de Maintenon, Louis XIV's unofficial queen, established a prototypical version, a school designed to educate young women from the impoverished nobility and to prepare them for solid marriages. Military schools in the eighteenth century sought to do something similar for impoverished young noblemen, training them for a military career and giving them the polish and skills that their status demanded.

Such institutions might help individual poor nobles, but they did not erase the ideological contradiction that they posed. Disconnected from the great aristocratic household and its patronage bonds, poor nobles incarnated a disjuncture between claims of status and economic position. Undeniably noble, they nonetheless lacked attributes that now seemed essential to high status. Fiction displayed the problem with particular vehemence. *Lazarillo*'s nobleman, so poor that he lives off the bread that his servant begs, nonetheless has comically lofty ideas about the honor of nobility. "'A gentleman owes nothing to anybody except God and the King,'" he explains, "'and it's not right for a gentleman to sacrifice any of his proper pride'" – this despite the fact that he cannot even supply himself with the barest necessities of life.[52] The humor was meant to illustrate a serious point. Without support from the rich, nobles like this could scarcely survive; they certainly could not establish families and sustain a lineage. In the long run the poor nobles would thus disappear, but while they existed they posed an ideological problem: despite contemporary theory, nobility could not rest on lineage alone. It required substantial wealth.

---

[52] Alpert, trans., *Two Spanish Picaresque Novels*, 62.

The urbanization of the nobility

Both the weakening of ties between patrons and clients and the prolifer-
ation of administrators reinforced a third change: nobles' increasing
tendency to reside in cities. The change first became visible in southern
Europe, in Spain and Italy. Complaints that Spanish nobles were
deserting the countryside for the cities began in the mid-sixteenth
century. By the early seventeenth century, almost one-fourth of the
Catalan nobility lived in the capital city of Barcelona, and many of the
others spent considerable amounts of time there. In most regions of Italy,
nobles had always spent much of their time in the cities, but the sixteenth
century witnessed a significant jump in the frequency of urban residence.[53]
   Elsewhere, the habit of city life came more slowly. Into the mid-
sixteenth century, the French and English nobles saw the countryside as
their real home and the city as an alien place. An Italian traveller noted,
"the English think it ignominious for noblemen to stay in cities."[54] But
the following century brought a revolutionary change, as northern nobles
who could afford to moved to the cities. Between 1550 and 1650, real
estate speculators in Paris, London, and a variety of provincial cities
created new aristocratic neighborhoods, with elegant houses that would
appeal to the greatest nobles. In Paris the Place Royale (now the Place des
Vosges) provided a model of such urban architecture: constructed along
the regular lines that the newly classicizing mentalities called for, an
elegant enclosure that allowed its residents to feel free of the dirt and
bustle of the rest of the city. The Place Royale became so much a center of
aristocratic life as to be a site of duels. In Paris the vogue for aristocratic
mansions grew steadily from these beginnings, with different neighborhoods finding favor as the years progressed. The process culminated in
the full development of the faubourg St-Germain in the eighteenth
century and the building of still greater palaces in the faubourg St-
Honoré later in the century.[55]
   By that point, the mode of urban living had completely taken over
among the French nobles who could afford it. The Englishman Arthur
Young travelled through France in the 1780s to inspect the countryside,
but found no nobles there. He had been told before leaving England "that
nobody but farmers and labourers in France lived in the country"; and
his travels confirmed his expectations. "What a miracle, that all this

[53] John Lynch, *The Hispanic World in Crisis and Change* (Oxford, 1992), 2; Elliott, *The
Revolt of the Catalans*, 69; Astarita, *The Continuity of Feudal Power*, 119ff.; Richard
Goldthwaite, *Wealth and the Demand for Art in Italy, 1300–1600* (Baltimore, 1993), 43.
[54] Quoted Stone and Stone, *An Open Elite?*, 16; on late medieval France, Bernard
Chevalier, *Les Bonnes Villes de la France du XIVe au XVIe siècle* (Paris, 1982), 63–64.
[55] Emmanuel Le Roy Ladurie, ed., *Histoire de la France urbaine, 3: la ville classique* (Paris,
1981), 130–44, 391–408, 464–69.

splendour and wealth of the cities in France should be so unconnected with the country!" he wrote. "The country [is] deserted, or if a gentleman in it, you find him in some wretched hole, to save that money which is lavished with profusion in the luxuries of a capital."[56] The countryside had become a secondary residence for nobles, even for those who owned extensive properties there. Similar situations could be found further east. In one region of the German state of Prussia, by the late eighteenth century one-third of all nobles owned no land whatsoever and depended entirely on urban professions.[57]

Young's scandalized response to the French situation, of course, implied that things were different in England, and in some measure they were. English gentry remained more attached to rural living, and whole genres of English art and literature celebrated the fact. There were poems in honor of the gentry's country homes, and paintings of gentry families among their rural possessions – horses, dogs, houses. Yet the English gentry too had effectively been urbanized, though in a somewhat different manner from the French. In London as in Paris aristocratic neighborhoods developed, and there developed the fashion of the London season in the years around 1600, a fashion that survived vigorously in the years thereafter. The image of rural purity that so many English families sought to project was in fact an illusion, which concealed their regular familiarity with the city.

What drew the nobles there? In part, political changes. As administrators and judges themselves increasingly acquired noble status, an important group of nobles came to be urbanites almost by definition. For other nobles, the state's development made regular visits to the cities imperative. They had to go if they hoped for employment in the growing civil services or at court; and they had to spend time there in order to supervise the extensive business all landowners had before the king's judicial system. Among the high nobility, there was also a growing awareness of cities' political importance. Figures like the duc de Guise in late sixteenth-century France took pains to cultivate the loyalty of urban artisans and merchants; and their efforts paid off, for Guise and his family could mobilize thousands of supporters in Paris and other cities, closing them off even against the king himself. Similar efforts characterized the political upheavals of the seventeenth century; and even phases of the French Revolution of 1789 showed the high nobles' continuing influence within urban politics. Whatever their wealth and political ambitions, by

---

[56] Arthur Young, *Travels in France during the Years 1787, 1788, and 1789*, ed. Constantia Maxwell (Cambridge, 1950), 5, 115–16; for statistical verification of Young's impressions, Le Roy Ladurie et al., *Histoire de la France urbaine*, 391ff.

[57] Deborah Hertz, *Jewish High Society in Old Regime Berlin* (New Haven and London, 1988), 31–32.

1600 few indeed nobles could escape regular contact with urban life.

As important, nobles increasingly found themselves wanting to spend time in the city, for it had become the site of pleasures that could not be found elsewhere. The development of the theater throughout western Europe was one instance of this larger process. Professional actors and dramatists emerged first in the mid-sixteenth century, with striking parallelism in such different societies as England, Spain, and France; Barcelona acquired Spain's first covered theater in 1598. Other such urban institutions followed – the first coffee houses after 1650, opera first in Italy around 1600, then spreading north.[58] Increasingly it was evident that the pleasures of high society were to be found in the city, and that those condemned to country life only were pitiful bumpkins. "Nobility is gained and exercised in cities, among people, and less easily among wild beasts in solitude or in dealings with farmers" – so argued a fifteenth-century Italian humanist.[59] By the eighteenth century, these views were shared throughout Europe. James Boswell, son of a Scottish jurist and lord, captured his contemporaries' feelings as he described his return to London in 1762: "I was all in a flutter at having at last got back to the place which I was so madly fond of, and . . . had formed so many wild schemes to get back to."[60]

For the richest nobles across Europe, the shift from country to city was an easy and untroubled process. The urban mansion, despite the different styles that it assumed in Paris, London, Berlin, Barcelona, Madrid, and Vienna, performed a comparable function to the great country house. It formed a solid center of aristocratic sociability, a dazzling manifestation of the family's standing and wealth. In these conditions, feudal standing could survive very well in the city.

For lesser nobles, however, moving to the city meant encounter with the same challenges that urban living presented to their plebeian neighbors. For them as for everyone else, city living might be anonymous, uncomfortable, and expensive. Only the great could afford houses of their own. The rest lived instead in apartments, rented either for the season or for a longer term. They might be unknown and neglected, and they found themselves in a highly competitive situation. As important, the city could be a scene on which outsiders, non-nobles, could adopt the manners of high standing and claim the status. The city blurred the theoretically clear lines of social difference. In the eighteenth-century city, middle class and nobility shared dress, manners, and language.

[58] Elliott, *The Revolt of the Catalans*, 69, n. 6; Le Roy Ladurie, et al., *Histoire de la France urbaine*, 193–98, 483–89, 520–29.
[59] Quoted Goldthwaite, *Wealth and the Demand for Art in Italy*, 177.
[60] Frederick Pottle, ed., *Boswell's London Journal, 1762–1763* (New York, 1950), 44.

Alternative models of gentility

Social changes like these – the nobles' urbanization, their increasingly administrative character – tended to blur differences between them and others in society. In the seventeenth and eighteenth centuries, a series of new social institutions and ideals had a similar effect. They created alternative models of social superiority, that of the educated, elegant gentleman, who stood on his own abilities and whose background was irrelevant to his standing. Increasingly, it seemed, one could be a gentleman without being born noble, and perhaps without becoming a noble either. In the 1620s the French Academy led the way in this direction. The Academy, which soon received governmental approval as the tribunal for assessing French culture and language, proclaimed in its rules its openness to all men of talent, regardless of social status, and Academy members pointed to the rule with pride, rather than anxiety. Other academies throughout Europe followed suit; the seventeenth century was the great age for founding institutions of learning, and they made the man of ability rather than the man of birth their central actor.

The literary salon adopted a similar ideal. These were gatherings of intellectuals, professional and amateur, for amusement, and critical discussion of literary and moral issues. Starting in mid-seventeenth-century Paris, they were imitated throughout Europe by the eighteenth century. Their participants too ignored formal rank, and instead mixed members of all social orders. In late eighteenth-century Berlin, probably the most snobbish of the European capitals, about 40 percent of salon participants were noble, high participation in a social institution devoted to the sharp exchange of critical views, and an institution in some degree committed to meritocratic ideals. Even more surprising, the social mixture of Berlin salons included wealthy Jews, who were hesitantly admitted to high society – before a renewed anti-semitism drove them out again after 1812.[61]

Contemporary language reflected these institutional shifts. Rather than speaking of the mere noble, thus, seventeenth- and eighteenth-century French writers increasingly offered the ideal of the "honest man," the man of taste, good manners, education. Such language implied that the critical social barrier had ceased to be that between noble and non-noble. Instead, it divided the rich and polished – noble or not – from the rest of society, poor nobles included. The antithesis to the gentleman increasingly became the boorish country squire, his attention focussed exclusively on dogs and hunting, his intellect nourished only by the study of genealogy.

[61] Hertz, *Jewish High Society*, 114 and *passim*.

Against the country squire, notions of character became increasingly central to this vision of gentility: character defined not as a purely individual quality, but as a combination of individual and social norms that demonstrated sound knowledge of the world, manners, and morals along with individual sparkle. This was the ideal that the eighteen-year-old James Boswell sought to establish for himself. "I feel a surprising change to the better in myself since I came to London," he confided to his private journal. "I am an independent man. I think myself as good as anybody, and I act entirely on my own principles. Formerly I was directed by others. I took every man's advice . . . But now I keep my own counsel, I follow the dictates of my own good sense, than which I can see no better monitor, and I proceed consistently and resolutely."[62] The gentleman in this view had precisely rejected the deference expected within a truly aristocratic society. Jane Austen likewise made this vision of character one of the central themes in her fiction, and juxtaposed the man or woman of character with the merely high-born, to show up the hollowness of the latter. In her world, men of trade might have more character and gentility than nobles themselves.

Others felt much the same. At about the moment that Boswell set out for London, the great English painter Joshua Reynolds painted the portrait of one of England's grandest ladies, the duchess of Richmond; she enjoyed not only high birth (she was the daughter of an earl) and a distinguished position by marriage (her husband's rank of duke represented the highest level in British society), but also wealth (she was an heiress in her own right). The portrait that she had Reynolds paint is therefore all the more instructive, for it presents the duchess in the guise of a simple middle-class housewife, her clothing plain, with no signs of distinction or wealth, her attention focussed on a simple domestic task, her needlepoint. Implicit in the artist's vantage point on his subject was a related idea, her privacy: Reynolds captured the duchess in an act that seemed to isolate her from the surrounding society, and situated her entirely in the household. The duchess was young (about twenty at the time of the portrait), handsome, and sociable. Her choice of self-presentation in Reynolds' portrait, then, reflected a stance toward society itself: despite her standing and wealth, she wanted the appearance of a modest bourgeois home-maker.[63] Continental artists and their clients had similar ideas. In 1748 the leading French portrait painter Jean-Marc Nattier painted the queen herself in the costume and setting of a comfortable but

---

[62] Pottle, ed., *Boswell's London Journal*, 82.
[63] *Sir Joshua Reynolds* (Paris, 1985) (catalogue of an exhibition at the Grand Palais, Paris, and the Royal Academy of Art, London), 180–81.

3 The ideal of simplicity: the duchess of Richmond, ca. 1765 (Joshua Reynolds, *Mary, duchess of Richmond*)

modest bourgeoise, her Bible open at her side; the queen had requested that she be portrayed in this manner, and the portrait proved a great success when it was publicly exhibited: the queen's choice of pose was no eccentric whim.[64]

A generation later, another English figure exemplified the same values in a complementary way – and with enormous impact on contemporaries. This was George Bryan "Beau" Brummel, who in the 1790s became the unrivalled leader of British elegance. Much of British high society followed his leadership in dress, manners, and physical carriage, and he became the intimate companion of the highest aristocrat of all, the prince regent. For twenty years (until he fled England and his creditors in 1816), aristocratic English society eagerly followed his dictates, according stylishness to the people, manners, and clothing of which Brummel approved. When a duchess offended him, he expressed his sense of his power over even the highest aristocracy: "she shall suffer for it," he boasted to an acquaintance; "I'll chase her from society." All the more significant, then, that Brummel himself was not of high birth, and indeed mocked distinctions of birth. Though educated at Eton amongst the gentry, he was the son of successful civil servant, and probably the grandson of a valet; Brummel himself sought to exaggerate, rather than conceal, his humble background, speaking of his father as "a very superior valet, [who] kept his place all his life." In Brummel, English high society found a fashion leader who not only had plebeian roots, but boasted of them.[65]

Equally important was the kind of style that Brummel called for and that so many of his highly born contemporaries wanted to imitate. For his advice almost always went in the direction of simplicity. He mocked ostentatious decoration, and in particular denounced what had once seemed the very emblems of aristocratic elegance – powdered wigs, ribbons, fabrics of delicate colors and exotic materials, elegant perfumes. In their place, Brummel championed jackets of plain blue, buff-color pantaloons, and black boots, set off by sparklingly clean white shirts and neckcloths. Fanatical cleanliness in fact marked all of his choices, and included lengthy tooth-brushing. For Brummel and his followers, personal elegance lay in the cut of clothing and the quality of its fabrics. These could still be expensive, but in ways that only a knowledgeable observer could pick up. An admiring early twentieth-century writer in fact described Brummel as the father of modern male dress, in the sense that his innovations led directly to the nineteenth-century business suit,

---

[64] Philip Conisbee, *Painting in Eighteenth-Century France* (Ithaca, 1981), 124.
[65] Ellen Moers, *The Dandy: From Brummel to Beerbohm* (London, 1960), 17–38; quotations 26, 24.

forming the decisive break with the kinds of fashion that had prevailed since the Renaissance.

In some ways opposites, Reynolds' duchess of Richmond and Beau Brummel in fact represented two facets of a single phenomenon: the disaggregation of aristocratic image in the late eighteenth century and its new openness to an undifferentiated middle class. Wealth still mattered, but distinctions of birth were less clearly relevant. In the case of the duchess of Richmond, the aristocrat had herself portrayed as middle-class housewife. In the case of Beau Brummel, an aggressively plebeian socialite came to dominate London aristocratic life – and to push its fashions in directions that undermined the visible distinction between aristocrat and commoner. Their place and time gave these examples particular sharpness. England had Europe's richest aristocracy; more pointedly, Brummel's rise to dominance of English fashions coincided with England's wars against revolutionary France, a war against egalitarian doctrines and in defense of aristocratic distinctions. Even as England led this crusade against Jacobinism, changing values were corroding aristocratic images at home.

And technology contributed to the process. Figures like the duchess of Richmond and Beau Brummel could help blur the visible markings of social standing partly because new cloths and colors reduced the differences between aristocratic and plebeian clothing. In this technology played a role, for eighteenth-century cotton fabrics brought to mass markets the most fashionable clothing. To the casual observer, it was less and less clear who was the noble, who the bourgeois or even the working man or woman in Sunday finery.[66]

At the very top of society, it seems, interchange between nobles and bourgeois might be so easy as to blur the difference between them. Lower in the social scale, among the lesser nobles of the provinces, attitudes might be harsher – not surprisingly, for such figures had little but their noble status to set them above the rest of society. We may follow the German novelist Goethe's character young Werther (1774) – a fictional character, but one who distilled many of Goethe's own bitter experiences and one who became the most intensely followed of eighteenth-century literary creations – as he attends a gathering of nobles in a small German principality. A commoner, Werther has gone to serve in the principality and has become a great favorite of the great count C. "I dined with him yesterday," writes Werther to a friend; "it never crossed my mind, nor did it ever occur to me that we subordinates do not belong in that

[66] Daniel Roche, *The People of Paris: An Essay in Popular Culture in the Eighteenth Century*, trans. Marie Evans (Berkeley, 1987), 168–74; Roche, *La Culture des apparences: une histoire düvtement, XVIIe–XVIIIe siècle* (Paris, 1989), 92–246, esp. 180, *passim*.

company . . . and afterward we walked up and down the great hall in conversation," as a group of the count's aristocratic friends gathers. But soon there is trouble, for Werther is out of place in this local version of high society. "I did not register that the women were whispering at the far end of the hall, that the whispering was spreading to the men . . . until at length the count approached me and took me aside to the bay window – 'You know how absurd things are,' he said. 'I gather the company takes exception to your presence here.'" Adding to the pain of his expulsion, rumors describing the event quickly spread throughout the entire town, and wherever he goes Werther encounters either sympathy or ridicule – both intolerable to him. Even a young noblewoman with whom Werther has begun a mild romance criticizes his appearance at the gathering. "I could plunge a knife into my heart" over the humiliation, he writes to his friend, and soon resigns his governmental position and leaves the town.[67]

Werther's humiliation reflected the complicated interactions of late eighteenth-century high society. Werther could befriend a powerful nobleman and could flirt with a pretty young noblewoman. But he could not assume acceptance by the larger aristocratic society of the area, nor could he even assume that his noble friends would defend him from humiliation – to say nothing of their possible support in the more critical areas of life, such as marriage. *The Sorrows of Young Werther* (to repeat) was among the most popular books of the late eighteenth century; the bitterness felt by its young hero at his treatment by aristocratic society must have resonated powerfully with the fears and some of the experiences of thousands of its readers. The boundary between nobles and commoners had become less visible in the late eighteenth century, but in some ways this only made it more painful to cross.

Yet *Werther* exposed a further irony in the late eighteenth century's understanding of relations between nobles and commoners. For this was, after all, a best-selling novel that mocked the social pretensions of provincial nobles, displaying them as cruel, vacuous, and conceited. Other contemporary best-sellers took the same view. The novel *Candide*, by the French philosopher Voltaire, mocked the miserable circumstances and boundless pride of Europe's country gentlemen, so ignorant of the world that they could believe their tiny homes to be grand palaces. In the same years satirical pamphlets circulated widely, depicting the courtly nobility as feeble, corrupt sexual predators, whose purity of biological descent had produced only degeneration. Popular Parisian plays showed

---

[67] Johan Wolfgang von Goethe, *The Sorrows of Young Werther*, trans. Michael Hulse (London, 1989; first pub. 1774), 83–84.

corrupt nobles seducing innocent middle-class girls, though playwrights by no means limited their satire to the nobility.[68]

Such views, of course, did not necessarily inflect actions. Eighteenth-century men and women could hear mockery of nobility without losing faith in their social order, and certainly without relinquishing their own privileges. In his last years, Voltaire himself settled happily into the country gentleman's role. He used the wealth accumulated over his career to buy an estate in eastern France, and took to warning his guests not to utter subversive ideas in front of his servants; he did not, he explained, want to be murdered in his bed. Like our own age, the eighteenth century could live happily with contradictory social ideologies. Yet the eighteenth-century critique of nobility was a powerful one, and had corrosive effects. No one in late eighteenth-century western Europe could take the grand claims of aristocratic superiority very seriously. Nobility still mattered, but it had ceased to be the most important barrier in European society.

Against such changes, official regulations offering advantages to nobles could do little. At best, they offered symbolic comfort to the lesser nobles, those who felt themselves excluded from the new money and powers of a developing society. They could at least claim exclusive access to such institutions as military schools and the higher clergy. But such claims had little meaning at the top of society, for contemporaries could see little difference between the life led by a nobleman and that of a rich financier – and they could see their easy mingling at salons and other gatherings that actually excluded the poor nobility.

Nobility – so this chapter has tried to show – had never in European history been an entirely stable social entity. To be sure, social theorists from the eleventh century on tried to give the concept biological and functional grounding. In their view, the nobles could be assigned clear social functions, those of military protection and governance; and they could be seen as a distinctive racial group, descendants of Europe's early conquerors and for this reason also deserving of a distinctive social position. They had inherited both the personal qualities – bravery, the ability to command – and the economic resources that a ruling position demanded.

Yet even during the Middle Ages such claims were difficult to sustain,

---

[68] Robert M. Isherwood, *Farce and Fantasy: Popular Entertainment in Eighteenth-Century Paris* (New York, 1986), 73–76, 106–09, 173–78; Sarah Maza, *Private Lives and Public Affairs: The Causes Célèbres of Prerevolutionary France* (Berkeley, 1993); see also below, Chapter 4.

because contemporaries could so clearly see their inadequacy. Ordinary Europeans knew about the arrival of new nobles and the disappearance of old ones; such movement became especially conspicuous in the four-teenth and fifteenth centuries. Nobles' claim to specific social functions could enjoy wider belief, because many nobles *did* fight. But here too there was potential for instability, since late medieval men and women harbored justifiable doubts about the nobles' military performance. They knew that nobles fought more for their own benefit than to protect others, and they blamed the nobles for military failures.[69]

From this starting point, the nobles' situation may be said to have changed in two fundamental, apparently contradictory ways over the early modern period. On the one hand, noble status became more elaborately defined and more difficult of access. Governments and nobles themselves both contributed to the process. They watched more irritably over the movement of newcomers into the order, and the mobility that had characterized the late Middle Ages became far more difficult. Partly as a result, nobles became scarcer over the period, while hierarchical titles became grander and more numerous. In this sense, the nobility was becoming more closed-off from the rest of society.

Yet during these same centuries, the nature of nobility itself – already uncertain in the late Middle Ages – was becoming more difficult to define and more unstable. The privileges that set nobles apart from other social groups tended to erode, dramatically in the case of fiscal exemptions, more unevenly where careers and political rights were concerned. The formation of a new administrative and urban nobility in the course of the sixteenth century undercut the order's claims to coherence of role, because it presented Europe with a nobility that did not fight; the nobility's urbanization also raised doubts about its claim to a special relationship to country life. Somewhat later, bonds within the nobility weakened and broke. Enormous inequalities had always existed within the nobility, separating wealthy from poor nobles. But in the fifteenth century wealthy and poor nobles had shared a common life and values. Poor men had moved into the nobility through service to the great; the great had needed the help of the lesser men in all manner of circumstan-ces. At some point after about 1600 – earlier apparently in England and Spain, later in France – this understanding of reciprocal service and common mode of life broke down.

This changed relationship between rich and poor nobles had large ideological implications. Lacking the social functions they had once enjoyed, the existence of poor nobles now violated images of a properly

[69] See for instance Caron, *Noblesse et pouvoir royal*, 112.

functioning social order, in which those with the highest social standing enjoyed material possessions appropriate to their rank. The poor noble was precisely a mark of inappropriateness, a disjuncture, a living image of the inadequacy of social models. His existence worried both fellow nobles and outsiders. Thus the passion that contemporaries might put into propping up the poor nobility, and thus the widespread sense late in the period of the ridiculousness of the poor noble's existence.

Two broad processes of change thus dominated the early modern period: on the one hand, a narrowing of the nobility's recruitment and numbers; on the other hand, growing uncertainty as to what exactly nobility was and where its boundaries lay. In significant ways, the two processes stood in real contradiction with each other. Some eighteenth-century governments, for instance, expanded nobles' privileges in matters of career advancement – during just the years that they sought to limit nobles' fiscal privileges. These contradictions were real, and they produced jarring moments for the individuals who encountered them, as the example of Werther suggests. Yet there were underlying linkages as well. Both reflected an increasingly prominent vision of the nobles as a ruling elite, one suited to the manifold forms of rule that characterized Europe's increasingly complex social life. Hence the order had to be pared of its poorest, most rustic, and most numerous members: however suited they might be to the nobility's military functions, they could not enjoy the respect that the order's other forms of power now demanded. The eighteenth-century nobilities were smaller than their medieval predecessors, sharing more in such matters as culture and life experiences, but at the same time more diverse in functions.

As such, they could respond with approval to a new social ideal that was becoming increasingly prominent in eighteenth-century Europe, that of the gentleman. This was a social ideal that detached social leadership from bloodlines and inheritance. It implied, at some times in muted fashion, at others more forcefully, the unimportance of nobility itself and the superior value of ability, taste, and effort. To many eighteenth-century nobles, however, these new values seemed supportive rather than upsetting, for they confirmed the nobles' own growing sense of their position as just this sort of elite.

2 Wealth, privilege, and the encounter with change

How rich were the nobles? Examples of spectacular noble wealth abounded everywhere in Europe between the sixteenth and the eighteenth centuries. In Sweden there was Magnus Gabriel de la Gardie (1622–86), whose largest castle (one of several that he owned) contained 248 rooms and whose income in a good year equalled one-fifth that of the Swedish state.[1] In the late sixteenth century, a great Spanish nobleman like the duke of Medina Sidonia, commander of the Spanish Armada, collected revenues from 90,000 vassals – another illustration of the immense economic power that high nobles could exert.[2] In France the story was the same. The early seventeenth-century duke of Lesdiguières owned a Parisian townhouse with forty-nine rooms, and built for himself an enormous country house in Dauphiné; the viscount Turenne owned rights extending over ninety villages and seven small cities, covering an area of 4,000 square kilometers. Such wealth meant that rich aristocrats towered over the rest of society. A typical seventeenth-century French duke had an income 100 times that of a well-off Parisian bourgeois, 500 times that of a substantial artisan.[3] And these were not even the richest examples. That standing belonged to those close to political power, to those whose personal charm or political acuity secured them the status of king's favorites. Such men were especially common in the early seventeenth century, and they became immensely wealthy. The Cardinal de Richelieu, the French king's chief advisor, began life as a provincial nobleman of modest means. He died in 1641 with a fortune worth at least 20 million livres, including 4 million in cash

---

[1] Bernt Olsen, "Das Verhältnis des Adels an den anderen Ständen in der Literatur der Schwedischen Grossmachtzeit," in Dieter Lohmeier, ed., *Arte et Marte: Studien zur Adelskultur des Barockzeitalters in Schweden, Danemark, und Schleswig-Holstein* (Neuminster, 1978), 221.

[2] J. H. Elliott, *The Count-Duke of Olivares': The Statesman in an Age of Decline* (New Haven, 1986), 8.

[3] Jean-Pierre Labatut, *Les Ducs et pairs de France au XVIIe siècle* (Paris, 1972), 302, 288.

– the cash alone equal to the yearly income of four thousand ordinary nobles.[4]

These examples express basic facts of early modern sociology. Nobles dominated most early modern societies as much by their wealth as by the social esteem they enjoyed. In most parts of Europe they were simply the richest people around, and other circumstances magnified their preeminence. They were expected to spend their money conspicuously, so that everyone could see it and could recognize their economic superiority; and when they lived in the countryside they towered over everyone around. The baron of Pont-Saint-Pierre was a prosperous but hardly opulent northern French nobleman. Yet in the seventeenth and eighteenth centuries his income alone surpassed the combined incomes of everyone who owned land in his three principal villages – and these included three lesser nobles.[5] Only in a few corners of Europe – Holland, a few German and Italian cities – did the commercial bourgeoisie approach wealth at these levels.[6] In any case, merchants and bankers usually wanted to enter the nobility, rather than dislodge it. As soon as their wealth permitted them to do so, they bought estates and acquired formal recognition as nobles. In most of Europe, the nobles had only one rival for economic dominance, the high officials; and everywhere, as we have seen, these officials too increasingly blended into the nobility itself. Over the early modern period, the degree of aristocratic economic preeminence might vary; but the fact remained as visible in the eighteenth century as it had been in the sixteenth. In this limited sense, the bourgeoisie had not "risen" by 1789.

Other elements in the nobles' economic situation were more complex – and have evoked more disagreement among historians. It is clear that the nobility as a whole remained wealthy throughout the early modern period, but it is less clear how different groups within the nobility fared. Did the wealthiest nobles profit most fully from the period's economic opportunities, or did the advantage lie with lesser figures, who could manage their estates more carefully? Questions of this kind lead naturally to questions about the nobles' ability to handle money. How carefully did they manage their wealth, and how well did they respond to processes of economic change? Indeed, to what extent did early modern economic changes touch the nobles at all?

Ultimately, study of the nobles' economic dealings must center on the

[4] Joseph Bergin, *Cardinal Richelieu: Power and the Pursuit of Wealth* (New Haven, 1985), 40, 248.
[5] Jonathan Dewald, *Pont-St-Pierre, 1398–1789: Lordship, Community, and Capitalism in Early Modern France* (Berkeley, 1987), 159–60.
[6] For the dramatic wealth of the Italian urban elite, Richard Goldthwaite, *Wealth and the Demand for Art in Italy, 1300–1600* (Baltimore, 1993), 59–60.

broad problem of the group's capacity to adapt to a modernizing world. The difficulty of such adaptation once seemed obvious to historians, for the nobles' orientation to warfare and their rural traditions seemed incompatible with the economic agility demanded by modern capitalism. A generation of research has dismantled these assumptions. The nobles, it has become clear, could pursue their economic interests tenaciously and effectively. But this basic discovery leaves important questions still unanswered. We need to establish the scale of the economic changes and challenges that the nobles confronted; and we need to explore the strengths and weaknesses that they brought to the confrontation. This chapter argues for the magnitude of the changes that the nobles confronted, indeed argues that in important ways the nobles inhabited a new economic world by the mid-eighteenth century. But the nobles (so the chapter also attempts to show) proved largely successful in adapting to these changes.

Hierarchies of wealth

If nobles' economic preeminence was universal, it was not everywhere equally clear-cut. In western Europe, England had a much larger number of great aristocratic fortunes than any other country. Already in the early sixteenth century, among its 6 million or so inhabitants, it counted about sixty peers and about an equal number of high-born gentry, nearly all with very substantial fortunes; a century later the numbers had doubled.[7] With twice the population, Spain in the early sixteenth century had only seventy-seven titled nobles; by 1630 the number had only doubled, to 155, and many of them were deep in debt.[8] France's population was larger still, three or four times England's, but its great nobles were less numerous. Only forty-six enjoyed the title "duke and peer" in the early seventeenth century, and perhaps 200 others should be thought of as enjoying an exalted status comparable to that of the British peerage.[9] England thus was unique in the aristocratic coloring of its social structure. It had a collection of very wealthy nobles equalled nowhere else, and these represented a far higher percentage than in any other part of Europe. They also dominated a much higher percentage of land than in any other part of Europe. The English peerage owned about one-fourth of the country; only in central Europe could comparable percentages be found. In France the whole nobility owned only about one-fourth of the nation's land, and the peerage owned only a small share of that total. In western Germany the nobles controlled still less land, only about 10

---

[7] See above, Chapter 1.

[8] J. H. Elliott, *Imperial Spain, 1469–1716* (New York, 1967), 310.

[9] Labatut, *Les Ducs et pairs*, 69.

percent of the region's arable, along with 15 percent of its forests, and in Luxembourg the percentages were similar.[10]

The great and greatly visible wealth of a few nobles did not mean that all or even most nobles were rich. In fact most enjoyed only middling wealth, and many were poor. Table 3 offers some examples of the hierarchy of wealth across Europe, and it shows how great the distances within these hierarchies might be. Incomes might vary by a factor of 100; in mid-eighteenth-century Luxembourg one-fourth of the nobles had incomes below 100 florins, while a handful had annual incomes of 10,000 florins or more. Noble poverty was common, but the middle ranks of the nobles were larger. These were families who could live well but could not afford great luxuries.

The contours of this pyramid of wealth changed visibly over the early modern period; it could hardly be otherwise, given the immense economic changes that Europe as a whole experienced in these years, as new continents and new industrial processes were discovered, and as populations rose and fell. For the nobles these broad changes had uneven and complicated effects, but in the long run the meaning of change was clear. In most places, middling nobles tended to enlarge their share of national wealth, at the expense of the very great nobles. In England the process has been called the rise of the gentry, but something similar (and less easily named) happened elsewhere. The English example remains the clearest: in the sixteenth and seventeenth centuries, so runs the estimate of one authority, the gentry doubled the share of England's land that it owned, from one-fourth to about one-half, while the great aristocracy increased its share only slightly.[11] There are indications of a similar pattern in France and northern Spain,[12] and in the Habsburg lands of central Europe, though social relations there were far more complicated. In mid-sixteenth-century Bohemia, nobles in the wealthiest category (with more than 900 serfs) held 41 percent of all the peasant subjects held by the nobles; a century later, their share had fallen to one-fourth of the total. During the late sixteenth century, 18 percent of the lower Austrian lords controlled at least 500 serfs – but by 1620 the numbers of such very wealthy lords had fallen, to only 10 percent of the total.[13]

[10] Gregory Pedlow, *The Survival of the Hessian Nobility, 1770–1870* (Princeton, 1989), 9; G. E. Mingay, *English Landed Society in the Eighteenth Century* (London, 1963), 19–22; Calixte Hudemann-Simon, *La Noblesse luxembourgeoise au XVIIIe siècle* (Paris and Luxembourg, 1985), 313. Such calculations obviously involve much guesswork.

[11] G. E. Mingay, *The Gentry: The Rise and Fall of a Ruling Class* (London–New York, 1976), 48.

[12] Dewald, *Pont-St-Pierre*, 233–38; Ramón Villares, *La propriedad de la tierra en Galicia, 1500–1936* (Madrid, 1982), 76–80.

[13] Thomas Winkelbauer, "Krise der Aristokratie? Zum Strukturwandel des Adels in den böhmischen und niederösterreichischen Ländern im 16. und 17. Jahrhundert," *Mitteilungen des Instituts für Oesterreichische Geschichtsforschung*, C, 1–4 (1992), 337–40; cf.

Table 3   *Hierarchies of nobles' wealth*

1   England, ca. 1760: 480 families, incomes 2,000–4,000 l.
        640 families, incomes 1,000 l.
        2,400 families, incomes 600–800 l.
        14,400 families, incomes 200–400 l.
2   Luxembourg, ca. 1766 (landed revenues only):
        2   families (0.5%), incomes above 10,000 fl.
        7 families (1.8%), incomes 5,000–10,000 fl.
        23 families (5.9%), incomes 2,000–5,000 fl.
        39 families (10%), incomes 1,000–2,000 fl.
        72 families (18.6%), incomes 500–1,000 fl.
        141 families (36.4%), incomes 100–500 fl.
        103 families (26.6%), incomes under 100 fl.
3   Northern France, ca. 1703 (election of Rouen, rural nobles only):
        12 percent, incomes over 15,000 l.
        47 percent, incomes 1,000–15,000 l.
        41 percent, incomes under 1,000 l.

Note: at this period, the typical "duc et pair de France" had an income of between 50,000 and 150,000 l., excluding members of the royal family and royal favorites.
4   Savoy, ca. 1700
        21 percent: revenues above 2,000 l.
        34 percent: revenues 500–2,000 l.
        45 percent: revenues below 500 l.
5   Bohemia, ca. 1656
        1.0 percent of nobles own 25.2 percent of subjects, over 16,200 groschen income
        1.5 percent own 14.5 percent, 9,000–16,200 groschen
        11.1 percent own 36.2 percent, 1,800–9,000 groschen
        86.7 percent own 24.1 percent of subjects, up to 1,800 groschen revenue

Sources: G. E. Mingay, *English Landed Society in the Eighteenth Century* (London, 1963), 22–23; Calixte Hudemann-Simon, *La Noblesse luxembourgeoise au XVIIIe siècle* (Paris–Luxembourg, 1985), 342; Jonathan Dewald, *Pont-St-Pierre, 1398–1789: Lordship, Community, and Capitalism in Early Modern France* (Berkeley, 1987), 115; Jean-Pierre Labatut, *Les Ducs et pairs de France au XVIIe siècle* (Paris, 1972), 262–70; Jean Nicolas, *La Savoie au XVIIIe siècle: noblesse et bourgeoisie*, 2 vols. (Paris, 1978), I, 277; Thomas Winkelbauer, "Krise der Aristokratie? Zum Strukturwandel des Adels in den bohmischen und niederosterreichischen Landern im 16. und 17. Jahrhundert," *Mitteilungen des Instituts fur Ostereichische Geschichtsforshung*, C, 1–4 (1992), 338.

This happened partly because of the advantages that such medium-sized landowners enjoyed during periods of rapid economic change.

R. J. W. Evans, *The Making of the Habsburg Monarchy, 1550–1700* (Oxford, 1979), 92ff., for a different interpretation, emphasizing the advantages large properties enjoyed during this period. *Small* noble properties clearly suffered in these years, and a few great fortunes arose – but the statistics suggest that in central Europe, as elsewhere, fortune favored the middling nobles in these years.

They could manage their estates more carefully than many great landowners, who had many more properties to worry about and whose attention was constantly claimed by other concerns. Middling nobles were usually also readier to grasp new opportunities, and they faced fewer pressures to spend their money: lavish expenditure was part of what contemporaries expected of a great nobleman, whatever damage this might do to his situation as a landowner. But political causes were as important as economic ones. Governments everywhere looked with suspicion on the very great nobles, who might challenge royal policy and even compete for the throne itself. Great families thus found themselves closely controlled, their properties under periodic attack. And the rise of the gentry was related to the second great process of change in early modern noble economics, the growing wealth of those directly involved with the state. This meant civil servants, whose growing numbers we have seen, and it meant courtiers, also a rising group in the early modern period. These were the men and women who lived near the prince, enjoying his gifts and supplying him with entertainment and political advice. For a variety of reasons, these were the groups that early modern economic changes favored.

Land and lordship

Until the eighteenth century, most nobles relied on landownership as their principal economic resource. Land had symbolic as well as practical functions. It was important to nobles' ideas about themselves, and it was central to the image that they wished to project to others. As conservative writers emphasized, land had a solidity that other forms of wealth lacked. It seemed permanently to attach the nobleman to his nation's past; like genealogy, it offered secure identity. And because of its seeming solidity, landowning implied virtues that contrasted with the turbulent, competitive worlds of the city and the royal court. In the countryside, nobles liked to claim, they could lead simple, quiet, decent lives, surrounded by friends, family, and loyal peasants. Thus the famous series of portraits of English nobles, showing them amidst their rural possessions. Portraits like these made an ideological point: the nobles were organically connected with rural life and with its quiet virtues. Poetry could make the same point. In seventeenth-century Holland and England, there developed a whole genre of poetry devoted to celebrating the aristocratic country house as a center of virtue, order, and intellectual activity, all of which flourished away from the distractions of the city.[14]

[14] Raymond Williams, *The Country and the City* (London, 1973).

In the fifteenth century, most nobles' landed properties represented a complex inheritance from the Middle Ages. These properties rarely took the simple form of broad acres. Rather, they typically grouped together a disparate collection of properties, rights, revenues, and powers, which historians schematize into three fundamental components. First the estate typically included a domain, land under the estate owner's direct control, that he could use as he wished. Over a second group of lands, the estate owner had only indirect control, because (at least so contemporary lawyers presented the matter) this land had been granted out for permanently fixed rents, to peasant tenants. Peasants' rights differed from place to place, but normally the peasant could sell this land, leave it to his heirs, and in most ways treat it as full property, so long as he continued his payments to the lord. Finally, the estate typically included political powers and economic monopolies within its boundaries. Its owner might have the right to try the legal cases of those who lived within it, or to try certain categories of cases; in some cases this judicial power extended to capital crimes, and the estate owner could maintain a gallows on his property, reminding all of the frightening authority that he exercised. Owners might enjoy the right to police local behavior, regulating matters like public drinking and other misbehavior and levying fines for violations. And owners might have the sole right to own mills and to require all who lived within the estate to use them for grinding their flour. Typically these rights – of justice, police, and monopoly – extended over all those who held permanent leases from the estate.

Under these arrangements, the estate owner was both more and less than a modern property owner. He was less, in that he could not fully control all the lands that he claimed to own. Over the lands that peasant tenants held by perpetually fixed leases, there was little that he could do save collect rents; the tenants could do what they wanted with these properties, including selling them and leaving them to their heirs. But in other ways the estate owner was a powerful figure, with a large sense of what his property rights meant. He was not a mere landlord. Rather, he held the dominant share of local political and judicial powers, and monopolized activities critical to the economy around him; everyone needed to use his mills and other resources.

It is in this sense that historians describe the nobleman's collection of rights and lands as a lordship, and the estate's owner as a lord rather than a mere property holder; and they describe the system of ownership itself as feudal, as a system of property distinct from those of modern societies. For this form of property intricately entwined local political powers with property in the modern sense. In fact fifteenth-century men and women probably would not have recognized the distinction between politics and property. To its owners, the estate's rights to try criminals or police local hooliganism were simply revenue sources like any others. Everyone who appeared before the estate owner's court paid for the privilege, and the owner entered their payments in his accounts alongside revenue from his livestock and fields. At the same time, the lord's economic weight gave him informal political powers. The lord collected rents from most of the villagers around him, and he usually needed servants and assistants to enforce his rights. Controlling such possibilities of employment, the estate owner could expect to exercise a loose influence over all those who lived near him. He could expect that any demands he made would receive serious attention and that his leadership in local affairs would be unquestioned.

Lordships like these could be found throughout Europe in the fifteenth century. Alongside the village, they formed one of the fundamental local units out of which European society was constituted. Yet they were rarely so coherent or so easily defined as the village, and rarely did they provide so strong a framework for local life. Some lordships were enormous, others tiny, with rights over only a handful of houses. Some lordships neatly covered entire villages, but many more held only parts of villages; individual villagers might thus find themselves under the control of two lordships, depending on the layout of fields or houses that they had inherited. Tenants' obligations even to the same lordship might vary widely, and between different lordships the differences could be enormous. Seigneurial rents might consist only of cash payments, and by the sixteenth century these were usually light. But some tenants found themselves paying rents fixed in quantities of produce, and some might have to pay a fixed percentage of what the land produced; in such circumstances, the burden could be heavy indeed. In some regions, tenants owed extensive labor service to the lordship, and almost everywhere the lordship intervened when tenants inherited property, either with taxes or with claims to purchase the property in question.

Together with his wealth, his powers to intervene in tenants' affairs assured the lord a dominant place in local life, and made his household a center of local politics. Ambitious young villagers focussed their hopes on it, for there they could rise out of farming and into careers as soldiers or officials. But lordship did not for that reason evoke warm feelings from those subject to its powers. To be sure, some historians have argued for such feelings, and have claimed (in the words of a distinguished exponent of this view) that "between the peasant and his lord . . . there was not only subjection of one to the other but also mutual loyalty," manifested in mutual aid and protection.[15] Wherever peasants' attitudes to their lords can be reconstructed, however, they prove to have been much harsher. Even during the Middle Ages peasants had used whatever means they could find to resist lords' demands, occasionally rebelling outright, more often resisting simply by performing their obligations slowly and badly. Paternalistic bonds between lord and peasant survived largely in the minds of nostalgic theorists. Even they acknowledged that most nobles paid little heed to the ideal of protection. In the words of a fourteenth-century Austrian poet, "they not only do not protect, but, as we see every day, plunder those whom they should protect."[16] In 1402 the queen of Catalonia used even stronger language in arguing that lords reduce their demands. Catalonian lordship, she wrote, involved "injust and ignominious usages, contrary to God and to justice, . . . imperilling the souls of those who levy them, . . . a source of infamy for the Catalan nation."[17]

Lordship varied widely across Europe. In the fifteenth century, it was strongest in the regions of northern France and western Germany, the regions in which feudal institutions had originated in the Middle Ages. In other regions, like southern France and Italy, Roman models of property survived, and much land remained outside the control of the lordship system. In much of Spain and eastern Europe also lordship was relatively weak, for in both regions medieval land developers had sought to attract peasant farmers with promises of advantageous conditions, and notably with freedom from impositions by estate owners. Sixteenth-century Castile, the heart of the Spanish empire, had neither serfdom nor forced labor services.[18] Catalonia offered a still more complex example. There extraordinarily brutal forms of lordship developed during the thirteenth century, allowing lords to mistreat their peasants almost at will; villagers could not move without seigneurial permission, and were subject to a variety of humiliating seigneurial taxes.[19]

England offered another complicated example. William the Conqueror had enforced the wholesale adoption of French models of property, establishing an exceptionally thorough system of lordships that stretched across the entire country. Yet England also saw the precocious develop-

[15] Otto Brunner, *Land and Lordship: Structures of Governance in Medieval Austria*, trans. Howard Kaminsky and James Van Horn Melton (Philadelphia, 1992), 215 and *passim*. Brunner's admiration for lordship clearly was related to his extremely conservative views of twentieth-century society, views that led to his enthusiastic endorsement of National Socialism.

[16] Quoted Brunner, *Land and Lordship*, 219, n. 78.

[17] Paul Freedman, *The Origins of Peasant Servitude in Medieval Catalonia* (Cambridge, 1991), 183, n. 16.

[18] Helen Nader, *Liberty in Absolutist Spain: The Habsburg Sale of Towns, 1516–1700* (Baltimore, 1990), 8.

[19] Freedman, *The Origins of Peasant Servitude in Medieval Catalonia*, 188, *passim*.

ment of centralized royal institutions, and this had reduced the political significance of lordship there. From the twelfth century on, some villagers could take their legal cases to the royal courts, and these rights expanded in the late Middle Ages. In the course of the fifteenth century, manorial power largely disappeared, a victim of economic circumstances that required landlords to offer advantageous conditions in order to retain peasant labor.

Patterns of change

This was the geography of feudal power in fifteenth-century Europe: strong at the center, in France and western Germany, weak at the margins, in most of Spain and east of the Elbe river, in central Germany. The centuries that followed brought remarkable change, above all to central and eastern Europe. Noble estate owners there succeeded in securing a series of important legal changes, all oriented to making lordship more powerful. Gradually nobles acquired new rights over the peasant farmers around them. They could demand labor services, ranging up to three and four days each week. They could forbid peasants to leave the estate, effectively tying them to the soil. They increasingly dominated local administration and justice, so eliminating any redress for peasants who believed that they had been unfairly treated. Such dramatic legal changes reflected above all the weakness of institutions that might compete with the lordship. In central Europe states were often weak, and always eager to secure the cooperation of noble estate owners; if estate owners demanded powers over the peasantry as the price of their loyalty, states in the region were ready to comply. And in contrast to western Europe, there were relatively few cities to which peasants might escape, as an alternative to their increasingly harsh judicial situation; in any case, cities often cooperated with lords and refused to admit peasant immigrants. By 1700, lordships in eastern Germany, Poland, Denmark, and Bohemia had grown enormously powerful. Symbolic of this power was the fact that lords in eastern Germany, Poland, and Hungary could sell to one another rights to the peasants who were under their lordship, their serfs, in what contemporaries described as a virtual slave trade.[20]

Spain too witnessed the expansion of seigneurial power during the early modern period. Deeply in debt, sixteenth- and seventeenth-century kings used grants of seigneurial rights as means of raising money and rewarding great nobles. By the early seventeenth century, nearly three-quarters of all law courts in Catalonia were under estate owners' direct

---

[20] Jerome Blum, *The End of the Old Order in Rural Europe* (Princeton, 1978), 41–42.

control; by the eighteenth century, lordships in some regions covered three-quarters of the territory. The crown's weakness gave to lords monopolies, extensive regulatory powers, and the right to levy rents and taxes over peasant subjects – though here villagers' personal freedom was not threatened.[21]

During the same years, however, most of western Europe saw the erosion of lordship, its steady loss of power and economic significance. In this England was an important precursor of developments that would take place across western Europe. The decline of lordship and its replacement by a different conception of property formed one of the early modern period's most important social changes, partly because the change so sharply marked the division between eastern and western Europe, as regions with radically different social and legal structures. This was the decline of feudalism and the rise of an essentially modern – what we may loosely call capitalistic – form of property. Rather than influence over men, direct and indirect, landowners increasingly wanted only money from their properties. Such matters as overseeing and regulating peasants' behavior or securing their loyalty seemed less important than securing profits from the land. Indeed, economic calculations might require the sacrifice of peasants' loyalty, for instance when landowners raised rents or expelled long-established tenants. Increasingly, landowers became ready to make such choices. Those who wanted to exercise political power did so within state institutions.

This change in the nature of property itself can be followed in the histories of individual estates. In northern France there was the barony of Pont-St-Pierre, a large lordship fairly typical of those owned by wealthy provincial families throughout France. In about 1400, 90 percent of the barony's revenues came from feudal sources. Rights of justice constituted 15 percent of the estate's worth, the milling monopoly 14 percent, fixed rents 63 percent. Only 8 percent came from the direct exploitation of the barony's domain.

For Pont-St-Pierre, decisive change came in the sixteenth century. In the early 1520s, the barony still looked much as it had in 1400, relying mainly on feudal revenues, but by the 1570s, the percentages had reversed; now three-quarters of the barony's revenue came from directly managed property, from the domain. Over the next two centuries, the disparity between feudal and capitalist aspects of the property only widened. By 1780, on the eve of the French Revolution, Pont-St-Pierre derived only 11 percent of its revenue from feudal sources, 89 percent

[21] J. H. Elliott, *The Revolt of the Catalans: A Study in the Decline of Spain, 1598–1640* (Cambridge, 1963), 98; John Lynch, *Bourbon Spain, 1700–1808* (Oxford, 1989), 227–230.

from its forests and lands. Since 1400, the shares of the two sides of the lordship had almost exactly reversed. And as it had been in the fourteenth century, eighteenth-century Pont-St-Pierre was typical of French estates: some relied heavily on feudal dues, but most were collections of large farms and forests, to which feudalism supplied a supplement that estate owners found useful but not indispensable.[22]

Table 4 presents other examples of this process of decline. As it suggests, France probably represented an extreme instance of a general phenomenon. In some regions, estate owners' success in converting their estates to market-oriented production rested on a continuation of feudal powers: this was the case in eastern Germany, Bohemia, and Poland. Elsewhere, feudal rents proved especially resilient: this was true of southwestern Germany and some parts of southern Italy. Yet even in these regions seigneurialism declined significantly.

How had this transformation taken place? A variety of large social changes contributed – forces powerful enough that estate owners had either to adapt to them or risk losing their properties to those who were prepared to exploit them more effectively. Peasant farmers themselves played an important role in the process. When estate owners in fourteenth-century England and France sought to introduce legal changes that would strengthen the lordship, their efforts were greeted by a combination of large- and small-scale rebellions. In Catalonia, years of carefully organized and strikingly sophisticated peasant protests likewise culminated in rebellion, in 1484–85; this was probably the most successful peasant rebellion in European history, and it led to the abolition of a long series of abusive powers that lords had exercised over peasants.[23] Rebellions in early sixteenth-century Germany and Switzerland were less completely successful, but they too substantially reduced the powers of lordship.

Such massive, often bloody peasant revolts against lords' authority mattered, but probably less than peasants' innumerable, individual refusals to cooperate – by failing to pay required dues and fines, by seeking better conditions on other estates, by refusing to cooperate with the lordship's officials.[24] From the sixteenth century on, villagers made use of another weapon, litigation. By the mid-eighteenth century, in

---

[22] Dewald, *Pont-St-Pierre*, 218–19.

[23] Freedman, *The Origins of Peasant Servitude in Medieval Catalonia*, 188ff.

[24] See the work of Robert Brenner, presented and discussed in Trevor Aston, ed., *The Brenner Debate: Agrarian Class Structure and Economic Development in Pre-Industrial Europe* (Cambridge, 1985); also Peter Blickle, *The Revolution of 1525*, trans. H. C. Erik Middelfort and Thomas Brady, Jr. (Baltimore, 1981); William Hagen, "Seventeenth-Century Crisis in Brandenburg: The Thirty Years War, the Destabilization of Serfdom, and the Rise of Absolutism," *American Historical Review*, 94, 2 (April, 1989), 302–35.

Table 4   *Feudal revenues as percentage of landed revenues*

1   Kingdom of Savoy, ca. 1730
      Province of Savoy: 9.2 percent
                    Genevois: 13.1 percent
                    Faucigny: 15.5 percent
                    Chablais: 25.9 percent
                    Maurienne: 0.03 percent
                    Tarentaise: 12.7 percent
2   Stavenow, Brandenburg, 1601: 28.5 percent
3   Luxembourg, 1766
      (a) Walloon regions: 31.4 percent
      (b) German regions: 52.8 percent
      (c) total: 48.5 percent
4   France
      (a) Salers, 1581–82: 45 percent
          ca. 1700: 18 percent
      (b) Pont-St-Pierre, 1398–9: 92 percent
          1521–22: 77 percent
          1570–71: 19 percent
          1740: 23 percent
          1780: 11 percent
5   The Kingdom of Naples
      (a) Aetna, 1572: 62 percent
          1625: 50 percent
          1726: 36 percent
          1776: 13 percent
      (b) Brienza, 1521–22: 41 percent
          1625: 45 percent
          1677: 43 percent
          1747: 46–50 percent
      (c) Pietrafesa, 1521–22: 74 percent
          1572: 85 percent
          1625: 39 percent
          1677: 37 percent
          1747: 33 percent
      (d) Sasso, 1521–22: 56 percent
          1625: 59 percent
          1686: 67 percent
          1726: 46 percent
          1776: 53 percent
6   Bohemia (all lords)
          1756: 18.6 percent

Sources: Jean Nicolas, *La Savoie au 18e siècle: noblesse et bourgeoisie,* 2 vols. (Paris, 1978), II, 634; William W. Hagen, "How Mighty the Junkers? Peasant Rents and Seigneurial Profits in Sixteenth-Century Brandenburg," *Past and Present,* 108 (August, 1985), 100; Calixte Hudemann Simon, *La Noblesse luxembourgeoise au XVIIIe siècle* (Paris, 1985), 309; James Lowth Goldsmith, *Les Salers et les d'Escorailles: seigneurs de Haute Auvergne, 1500–1789* (Clermont-Ferrand, 1984), 101, 173; Jonathan Dewald, *Pont-St-Pierre 1398–1789: Lordship, Community, and Capitalism in Early Modern France* (Berkeley, 1987), 218–19; Tommaso Astarita, *The Continuity of Feudal Power: The Caracciolo di Brienza in Spanish Naples* (Cambridge, 1992), 79; P. G. M. Dickson, *Finance and Government under Maria Theresia, 1740–1780,* 2 vols. (Oxford, 1987), II, 231.

France a wave of peasant lawsuits challenged the claims of lordship – often unsuccessfully, but often with sophisticated tactics that could stretch cases out for years.[25] Lordship under these conditions became increasingly expensive to sustain.

And another change made the effort to do so seem less worthwhile. For the fifteenth and sixteenth centuries witnessed a prolonged and ultimately dramatic rise in prices, the result first of rulers' manipulations of their currencies, then of population growth and an increasing money supply. For peasant tenants who held their land on permanently fixed terms, the result was a bonanza; wherever rents were fixed in money, they fell to only a fraction of their original value, and by the eighteenth century had become largely symbolic. For estate owners, the effect might be disastrous. Rents that in 1400 had been a fundamental resource became essentially worthless by 1600. In Bohemia, fixed rents lost 70 percent of their value between the twelfth century and the seventeenth, though lords there in fact enjoyed a relatively favorable position: they continued to extract valuable labor services from their peasants. In most parts of France the loss was greater still. In Galicia, in northwestern Spain, by the mid-eighteenth century seigneurial rents counted for 0.4 percent of the total charges weighing on peasants; what had once been a significant burden had become a trivial irritant.[26]

A final source of change was the state itself. In France and elsewhere in western Europe, governments were becoming stronger, more centralized, more professional – and less tolerant of the private competition that estate owners represented. In 1439 the French government established its right to tax peasants without their lords' consent, and at the same time it outlawed lords' practice of levying their own taxes.[27] In the next century it began encouraging villagers to appeal legal decisions from the estate owners' courts to the royal judicial system. The result was both expense for the estate owner and loss of local authority, since his agents were required to accompany the case to the royal courts. At the same time the king insisted on higher standards for estate courts. Judges in them were required to be full professionals, with legal educations and experience, and their salary demands rose correspondingly. A source of profits in the fifteenth century, the lord's justice became increasingly a financial burden in the sixteenth, an expensive form of public prestige.

Governments' demands on estate owners did not stop with the question of justice. In the small states of southwestern Germany,

[25] Dewald, *Pont-St-Pierre*, 148–51; Hilton Root, "Challenging the Seigneurie: Community and Contention on the Eve of the French Revolution," *Journal of Modern History*, 57, 4 (December, 1985), 652–81.

[26] Blum, *The End of the Old Order*, 163; Villares, *La propriedad de la tierra*, 32.

[27] Caron, *Noblesse et pouvoir royal*, 239.

sixteenth-century princes began to insist that all residents free themselves from any other lords' claims; the princes now claimed exclusive power over those who resided within their territories, and they viewed other lordships as unacceptable infringements on that power.[28] In seventeenth-century France the government launched a series of investigations into estate owners' rights, questioning at one time or another most of the public powers that lords claimed to exercise. Kings did not dispute feudalism in the abstract; but they repeatedly questioned individual owners' rights to the powers they exercised, examining titles and dismissing powers that lacked clear legal authority.[29] Feudalism remained vigorous in theory, but found itself increasingly under practical challenge. Kings had made an elementary calculation. What estate owners took from the peasants, kings could not take in the form of taxes. As kings became stronger after 1500, they sought to shift this balance in their own favor.

Worse was to come, for in the eighteenth century writers, lawyers, and eventually kings themselves challenged the theory of feudalism as well as its practice. For popular audiences, Mozart's opera *The Marriage of Figaro* (first performed in Prague, in 1786, and based on a play of 1784, by the Parisian playwright Beaumarchais) made the point in broad terms. It presented lordship as mere sexual predation, which accorded the lord the right to deflower his subjects' brides before their marriages; within the opera the right seems so abusive that even the lord himself can offer no reasoned defense for it. In fact this was an imaginary situation, for the right to sexual favors seems to have existed nowhere in Europe, but its place within the drama made clear the dislike with which even middle class and aristocratic audiences viewed lordship, even in relatively conservative central Europe. For Beaumarchais and Mozart had clearly touched contemporary feeling. An astute contemporary described the reception of Beaumarchais's play: "never has a play drawn such crowds to the Théâtre Français; all Paris wanted to see this famous marriage, and the hall was filled almost as soon as the doors opened to the public." Contemporaries were eager to hear about the evils of feudal power and the havoc that it brought to ordinary lives.[30]

For lawyers and administrators, the critique of lordship was less moral than economic. To these men lordship seemed to bring needless restric-

---

[28] Friedrich Lütge, *Geschichte der deutschen Agrarverfassung vom frühen Mittelalter bis zum 19. Jahrhundert*, 2nd ed. (Stuttgart, 1967), 107–08.

[29] Dewald, *Pont-St-Pierre*, 183–87.

[30] Nicholas Till, *Mozart and the Enlightenment: Truth, Virtue and Beauty in Mozart's Operas* (London, 1992), 145ff.; quotation from Francine Levy, *Le Mariage de Figaro: essai d'interprétation*, Studies on Voltaire and the Eighteenth Century, 173 (Oxford, 1978), 11.

tions, regulations, burdens, and confusions to economic activity, and as such posed a significant obstacle to economic progress. Their worries did not spring from mere altruism. All eighteenth-century administrators confronted cut-throat international competition, and all could see that rich nations were winning out. England's international power in the eighteenth century provided an especially glaring lesson. Administrators could see the simpler lesson also, that peasants who were rendered poor and apathetic by the demands of lordship provided a poor tax base for even the state's ordinary functions.

But many of these men had also been sincerely moved by the economic theories of the Enlightenment and wanted the social improvements that the theories promised. Economic freedom, so various Enlightenment writers counselled, would help nations to acquire wealth and the moral strength that accompanied prosperity. The Scot Adam Smith, among the most cogent theorists of the free-market economy, made it clear that governments had to control feudalism if they were to encourage economic development. He regularly denounced "all the violence of the feudal institutions"; and across Europe there echoed enthusiasm for Smith's ideas. In 1796 a high Spanish official, himself a member of the lesser nobility, read Smith and exulted in his diary, "How admirable!" Under Smith's influence, he successfully urged the crown to abolish advantages that large estate owners had enjoyed for centuries.[31]

In France, Italy, and Germany the response was comparable. High administrators came to see feudal property as an obstacle to development, because it seemed to reduce farmers' incentives to improve their land and seemed to guarantee the revenues of even inefficient landlords. Again, this marked a powerful shift in understanding. Seventeenth-century kings like Louis XIV had taken for granted the basic desirability of feudal institutions, and sought only to eliminate cases of abuse, in which lords exercised powers to which they had no claim. Eighteenth-century administrators came to assume the dysfunctional effects of feudal arrangements, now seen as inherently an obstacle to economic development. As one French theorist proclaimed, "the endless . . . lawsuits, abuses and injustices are sooner or later as fatal to the lords themselves, as for the cultivators and the state."[32]

Ideas like these reached even the most apparently backward parts of Europe, including those in which lordship appeared to be at its strongest.

[31] Adam Smith, *The Wealth of Nations*, ed. Andrew Skinner (London, 1982), 512; Richard Herr, *Rural Change and Royal Finances in Spain at the End of the Old Regime* (Berkeley, 1989), 77.
[32] Quoted J. Q. C. Mackrell, *The Attack on "Feudalism" in Eighteenth-Century France* (London, 1973), 144.

As a result, the later eighteenth century witnessed a series of efforts by well-read administrators and their kings to reduce lordship's burden on the peasants. Above all, this meant an attack on anything that restricted peasants' economic freedom and subjected them to the lordship's powers: an attack, in other words, on what the eighteenth century called serfdom. One after another, eighteenth-century kings legislated either the outright abolition of serfdom, or severe restrictions on its exercise: the kingdom of Savoy, in northern Italy, in 1772; Denmark, in 1701; the Habsburg empire in central Europe, in 1767 and in the 1780s; the small German state of Baden in 1783; Bavaria, through a series of piecemeal measures at about the same time. Prussia's king failed to outlaw serfdom completely, but he did end it on crown estates and denounced its practice elsewhere. When the French Revolution fully abolished what remained of feudalism in France, its efforts thus formed part of a broad movement of agrarian reform that was moving across Europe. But violent events in France gave rulers further encouragement for increasing the pace of change. Prussia, whose rulers had failed to control serfdom in the eighteenth century, abruptly undertook a series of reforms in 1807 that effectively ended serfdom. At about the same time, the kings of Spain (where serfdom was not an issue) radically changed laws governing great estates, with the same hopes of freeing the agrarian economy, enhancing prosperity, and making their state competitive as international struggle loomed.[33]

Establishing the domain

During the eighteenth century, then, lordship was everywhere under attack. In western Europe, its economic vitality had long since ebbed; by 1600 it had ceased to be a critical economic resource for most French nobles, and it had effectively disappeared from England much earlier. In central and eastern Europe, the institution survived but in a weakened state, largely because of rulers' concern to encourage economic development. Whether the causes of change were political or economic, however, in the end the result was similar. First in western Europe, then in the east, a profound change had taken place in the nature of property itself. Property was becoming detached from the explicit exercise of judicial and police power. The lord had become primarily an owner, whose income depended on what his/her land produced rather than on traditionally fixed rents. In eastern Europe, lords retained essentially feudal powers to demand labor from nearby peasants. But elsewhere labor supplies too depended on the marketplace. Though with signifi-

---

[33] Blum, *The End of the Old Order*, 216–28; Robert Berdahl, "The *Stände* and the Origins of Conservatism in Prussia," *Eighteenth-Century Studies*, 6, 3 (Spring, 1973), 305; Herr, *Rural Change and Royal Finances*, *passim*.

cant limitations and regional variations, capitalist property had replaced feudal.

For some aristocrats, this transformation of the nature of property itself was a serious blow, which damaged or even destroyed their families' economic position. But most proved more resilient in the face of change, and the aristocracy as a whole adapted well. Individual families disappeared, and specific groups within the nobility lost ground to others. But overall the group retained its economic dominance of the countryside; in some places it tightened that dominance.

This happened partly because of the nobility's political weight in most parts of Europe. Even the most powerful monarchs could not simply confiscate rights that noble estate owners had claimed for generations. If they wanted to control or eliminate serfdom, they had to listen to nobles' demands for compensation; at court they lived among the nobles and respected them, and in any event those who failed to move carefully risked serious trouble, as when Danish nobles arranged the execution of a troublesome high administrator in 1772.[34] So governments listened when nobles complained. As a result, when serfdom and other feudal powers ended, nobles usually received handsome compensation in the form of cash or even land. Even the French revolutionaries thought in these terms when they abolished the vestiges of feudalism in 1789. Nobles were to be repaid for their losses – until popular discontent brought an end to these plans and more radical leaders into power.

But the more important reasons for the nobles' resilience were economic. Sooner or later, nobles came to understand what was happening in the economic world around them. As they watched inflation blight their feudal revenues and the state compress their feudal powers, they directed their attention to sections of the estate under their direct control: that is, their domains, where they held full property rights. The decline in feudal sources of income encouraged them to look in this direction, and the economic conditions of the age made this a tempting alternative, for the early modern economy was generous to those who controlled land. In the inflation of the sixteenth century, food prices rose faster than any others. Food prices stagnated and then declined in the seventeenth century, but began rising again after 1750 – not surprisingly, since this was another era of rapid population growth. The same conditions made wood valuable. Growing populations needed fuel, and they needed building materials. Like food prices, the price of wood rose fast after 1500 – in England, so fast as to encourage the use of an alternative fuel, coal, also to be found on landowners' estates. Those who controlled the land would profit from the early modern period's most powerful economic forces.

[34] Blum, *The End of the Old Order*, 220.

For some lucky nobles, this collection of circumstances by itself assured prosperity. Like many French nobles, the barons of Pont-St-Pierre had always owned a large tract of forest, but before 1450 it had been worth very little; the barons made more money from charging villagers fees for gathering acorns than from the sale of wood. The situation changed radically in the following century, as population grew and commercial networks for selling wood became better organized. Like an oil well, the baron's forests gushed cash, and by the 1570s they supplied three-quarters of the estate's revenues. The baron had done little to deserve this bonanza, and in fact the forest deteriorated rapidly from over-cutting. Yet demand for wood was so high that his forest income continued to grow in the next century. Many nobles shared comparable experiences, for throughout France and Germany their estates often included substantial wooded areas. Early modern circumstances so favored these landowners that they could become rich without being especially careful managers.

But not everyone could follow this path, and even those who did could usually not find in it a full answer to the decline of their feudal revenues. For this, most needed to acquire direct control of farmland – to constitute, in other words, landed domains that would produce the foodstuffs so desperately demanded by early modern society. At different speeds in different regions across Europe, this is precisely what happened: lords acquired land. Nobles pursued land as vigorously in eastern Europe, where they held strong seigneurial powers, as in the west. In fact, control of peasant labor through the lordship made control of landed domains especially attractive. Lords could use forced labor to perform inexpensively the tasks that their growing estates demanded. Thus in Denmark, a region of strong lordship, the total area of nobles' domains doubled between 1525 and 1744. Across eastern Germany and Poland, the constitution of landed domains formed the central theme in the social history of the sixteenth and seventeenth centuries. By the eighteenth century, nobles' success at expanding their landholdings was so great as to evoke concern from the king of Prussia, and he attempted to outlaw some of the nobles' favored techniques for expanding their domains. In Italy, France, and England, where lordship was much weaker, there was similar expansion in lords' direct control of property. In one region of Spain, the critical moment came between the mid-sixteenth and the mid-seventeenth centuries, when middling nobles pushed to dominate landownership in several regions.[35]

[35] Blum, *The End of the Old Order*, 208. On analogous developments in eastern Germany, Hagen, "Seventeenth-Century Crisis," and his "How Mighty the Junkers? Peasant Rents and Seigneurial Profits in Sixteenth-Century Brandenburg," *Past and Present*,

Nobles had the means as well as strong motives for expanding their domains, for large amounts of land came on the market during the early modern period. Politics again played an important role. At several points states found themselves having to sell lands that had belonged to the crown, in order to finance some of their ventures. In Austria, the crown sold most of its own lands in the brief space of fifty years, between 1575 and 1625. In nearby Bohemia, the crown confiscated and sold an estimated one-half of all property in the kingdom, following the country's unsuccessful effort to throw off Habsburg rule in 1618; this land went to a handful of loyal courtiers and their friends. Most important, the sixteenth century brought sales of church lands in several parts of Europe. In parts of Germany and in England, huge land sales accompanied the establishment of the Protestant churches, as states took over monastic properties and sold them to the public. About one-quarter of England's land was thus privatized within two decades, providing domains for hundreds of gentry and aristocratic families. But Catholic countries too had their sales of church lands, justified by their rulers' expenses defending the church against heresy. In France the sales were relatively modest, but in Spain they were more important, involving seigneurial rights over hundreds of thousands of villagers.[36]

Everywhere these transfers of property favored the nobilities. Land was usually sold in large parcels, for which only the wealthy had the resources to bid. And always political connections helped would-be buyers from the aristocracy, who could know what lands were coming on the market and often bought them on advantageous terms. As usual, the nobles' only real competition in these purchases came from the high officials, who also had money and connections. But in fact these official families quickly established themselves within the old nobilities, and after a time were fully accepted among them. The state-sponsored land

108 (August, 1985), 80–116; Hartmut Harnisch, "Grundherrschaft oder Gutsherrschaft. Zu den wirtschaftlichen Grundlagen des niederen Adels in Norddeutschland zwischen spätmittelalterlicher Agrarkrise und Dreissigjährigem Krieg," in Rudolf Endres, ed., *Adel in der Frühneuzeit: Ein regionaler Vergleich* (Cologne–Vienna, 1991), 73–98; and Herbert Knittler, "Zur Einommenstruktur niederösterreichischer Adelsherrschaften 1550–1750," ibid., 99–118; for Italy, Maurice Aymard, "L'Europe moderne: féodalité ou féodalités?' *Annales ESC*, 36, 3 (May–June, 1981), 426–35; and S. J. Woolf, "Economic Problems of the Nobility in the Early Modern Period: the Example of Piedmont," *Economic History Review*, 2nd Series, 17, 2 (1964), 267–83. Cf., however Tommaso Astarita, *The Continuity of Feudal Power: the Caracciolo di Brienza in Spanish Naples* (Cambridge, 1992), 77–81, for an example of the continuing significance of seigneurial incomes in this region.

[36] Evans, *The Making of the Habsburg Monarchy*, 168; Golo Mann, *Wallenstein, His Life Narrated*, trans. Charles Kessler (London, 1976), 181ff.; Lawrence Stone and Jeanne Fawtier Stone, *An Open Elite? England 1540–1880* (Oxford, 1987), 30; Nader, *Liberty in Absolutist Spain*, 99ff.

sales of the mid-sixteenth century, whether in Protestant or Catholic countries, helped to cement this assimilation of new bureaucrats and old nobles. Old nobles could enrich themselves with the fruits of state power; new bureaucrats could acquire the landed properties that would allow them and their children to live aristocratic lives, and eventually the differences between the two groups would cease to be visible.

Lands from these sources were likely to be the best around, for the church had been richly endowed by medieval donors. But nobles could also take control of some of the less rich lands, waste lands that had been used as common pasturage or for gathering wood. The process was most dramatic in England, where nobles and gentry took over large tracts of commons and the process stimulated wide public debate. But something similar happened in France and Spain as well. There too estate owners claimed that waste lands essentially formed part of their property, and that they were under no compulsion to share these lands with villagers. Instead, they could enclose them for their own use: in other words, turn common properties into private ones.

But the most important source of land for nobles seeking to constitute domain properties lay elsewhere: not in the large properties seized from Europe's monasteries, but in the small properties of Europe's peasants. After 1500, peasants who owned land faced increasingly difficult times all across Europe. Wages dropped and food prices rose – important for all but the wealthiest peasants, the small minority who controlled enough land to feed themselves without recourse to working for others and buying food at the market. Taxes and rents rose as well, so that each year most peasants needed to come up with substantial amounts of cash. Even the lordship's permanently fixed rents might be a significant burden, though often they had shrivelled to insignificance.

These were all pressures leading peasants into debt and eventually into selling the small plots of land that they held. The buyers, again, were nobles, old and new; officials eager to establish themselves as full nobles found buying peasant properties especially appealing, for these could form the basis of a landed estate. The inhabitants of one Burgundian village typified the situation of most French peasants, when they complained in 1667: "In earlier times, nearly all residents owned the properties they worked on, and at present they are only share-croppers and mere laborers" on the properties of others. Statistical studies from throughout France have confirmed their assessment.[37] In Spain there

---

[37] Quoted Hugues Neveux, Jean Jacquart, and Emmanuel Le Roy Ladurie, *Histoire de la France rurale, 2* (Paris, 1975), 276; for discussion of peasant expropriation, 259–75. See also Jonathan Dewald and Liana Vardi, "The Peasantries of France, 1400–1789," in Tom Scott, ed., *The Peasantries of Europe* (London, forthcoming).

were similar comments. "The countryside is deserted, the [farmers] having fled their poverty, overburdened with debts and foreclosures."[38] Despite differences in property laws, the same patterns prevailed in German lands. During the second half of the sixteenth century, the Fugger family – once Europe's greatest bankers, but by the 1550s increasingly concerned with establishing themselves as landed aristocrats – bought land from hundreds of indebted peasants in southwestern Germany; these lands formed the core of the vast estates that the family established. In upper Austria the story was the same. As early as the fourteenth century, nobles there too began a systematic policy of buying peasant farms and establishing these as the chief resource of their estates. Between the 1520s and 1750, nobles increased their holdings by at least 50 percent.[39]

England too had its own laws and circumstances, and these allowed nobles to expropriate peasant farmers from direct control of the land more completely than anywhere else in Europe. Striking anecdotes accompanied the process. In one seventeenth-century village, the land-lord expelled 340 people in one day; in another, the landlord consolidated what had been fifteen farms into a mere three, all under his control. These were matters of conscious economic strategy. English advice books urged landowners and their agents to watch for any peasant property that came on the market, and pointed out how the landlord could use his legal advantages to hasten the process.[40]

As the richest and most powerful landed elite in Europe, the English nobles and gentry took the process of reshaping their estates farther than any continental nobility. Their success was the more striking in that it often involved qualitative as well as quantitative changes. Unlike most continental nobles, English landlords sought to rearrange landholdings as well as increasing their share of village acreage. Through private agreements and often through parliamentary legislation, English land-owners exchanged parcels with one another so as to create compact blocs of property, thus maximizing farming efficiency. Such exchanges often entailed the destruction of village houses, and they were usually accom-panied by expensive efforts to separate the newly created farms from one another, with hedges and fences. Together, enclosures and the dismant-ling of villages made English agrarian change the most dramatic in Europe, as well as the largest in scale.

[38] Quoted David Vassberg, *Land and Society in Golden Age Castile* (Cambridge, 1984), 205.
[39] Robert Mandrou, *Les Fugger propriétaires fonciers en Souabe, 1560–1618* (Paris, 1969), 48–49; Herman Rebel, *Peasant Classes: The Bureaucratization of Property and Family Relations under Early Habsburg Absolutism, 1511–1636* (Princeton, 1983), 26–27.
[40] Mingay, *The Gentry*, 41–44; Charles Wilson, *England's Apprenticeship, 1603–1763* (London, 1965), 250–53.

But the English experience was different in degree, rather than in kind. In France, Spain, Germany, central Europe, and elsewhere, nobles' domains grew, and they grew at the expense of peasant landholders. French and German nobles' farms were usually smaller than the English; in seventeenth-century France a farm of 50 acres was large, whereas in England one three times as large counted as only a middling property. And vestiges of feudal ownership remained on the continent long after they had disappeared from England. Many nobles preserved real powers over villagers who lived nearby, and they held impressive symbols of that power: in France and Germany, the gallows that denoted lordships' judicial power reminded villagers of the lords' claims. In some areas, feudal revenues themselves remained important; in the eastern half of eighteenth-century Luxembourg, for instance, they continued to supply nobles with half their landed incomes.[41] Despite all of these differences, however, the main lines of change remained the same across Europe, and so too did their principal result. By the eighteenth century, most families drew the bulk of their landed revenues from domain properties. As a result, the decay of feudalism represented for them an irritant rather than a lethal challenge. The essence of the estate had come to lie in what it could produce, rather than in its authority over people.

Administering the estate

These facts gave special importance to the attitudes that underlay estate management. In the Middle Ages, the owner of a feudal estate had few choices about administration, for tradition governed most aspects of the estate's economic life. Her/his rents were set at fixed levels, and most other income rested on monopolies of important services like milling. In the early modern period, most owners of large domain farms faced an entirely different situation. They had to find markets for what their estates produced, and they had to respond to both changing demand and new conditions of production. Knowledge became far more important and so too did possibilities for technological innovation.

What probably remained unchanged in these years was the basic fact of nobles' greed. Despite their ideals of chivalry and their occasional claims to rise above mercantile calculation, medieval nobles were normally grasping and calculating in their approach to economic matters. Already in the thirteenth century English nobles had manuscript books of advice counselling them to manage their estates closely and urging them not to trust their officials. At one time or another, the mid-fifteenth-century

---

[41] Hudemann-Simon, *La Noblesse luxembourgeoise*, 308–10.

knight John Fastolf jailed half of his estate officials for falling behind in their payments; by the early sixteenth century at least one very distinguished nobleman had begun keeping lists in his own handwriting of debts that were owed him.[42] "At the reverence of God," wrote the late-fifteenth-century English gentlewoman Margaret Paston about one of her sons, "advise him yet to beware of his expenses and guiding, that it be no shame to us all."[43] For Margaret, failure to watch one's money was not just unfortunate – it was shameful. In France the situation was similar. The great fifteenth-century nobleman Gaston de Foix perused his accounts every few weeks and took great care with his money.[44] No one thought that it was beneath the dignity of a gentleman to try to grasp as much money as possible, whatever the circumstances.

There was nothing new, then, about the bare fact of economic calculation in the early modern period. What was new was the range of calculations that now had to be made and the range of circumstances that now had to be taken into account. Even in the early modern period, of course, conservative responses to economic conditions appealed to many nobles. In large areas of Castile, for instance, middling nobles usually chose to recreate a form of seigneurial rent in the domains that they created. They established long-term leases with the peasants who actually worked the land, usually set in quantities of wine and wheat, and concerned themselves only with maintaining the steady flow of these inflation-proof rents. If they played a direct economic role at all, it usually was limited to marketing the products that their rental contracts brought them.[45]

But economic conditions favored a more daring approach. We have already seen how population growth over the early modern period brought value to nobles' woodland properties. The same growth brought rising food prices, making farming profitable, and especially favoring producers of the most basic foodstuffs, grains. The advantage was especially great around cities, and in areas that could easily trade with cities. This was the lucky situation of the German nobles who held estates along the Baltic sea and the rivers that drained into it. These nobles of Prussia and Pomerania (the Junkers) and their cousins in Poland could easily transport their grain to the booming cities of Holland; and as the Dutch in the seventeenth century expanded their commercial networks,

[42] K. B. McFarlane, *The Nobility of Later Medieval England* (Oxford, 1973), 50.
[43] Norman Davis, ed., *The Paston Letters: A Selection in Modern Spelling* (London, 1963), 206.
[44] Jonathan Dewald, *Aristocratic Experience and the Origins of Modern Culture: France, 1570–1715* (Berkeley, 1993), 151–53.
[45] Villares, *La propriedad de la terra en Galicia*, 76–118; Vassberg, *Land and Society in Golden Age Castile*, 105.

east German grain found its way even into the Mediterranean. Here aristocratic estate and international capitalism developed in mutually profitable accord.

On a smaller scale, comparable linkages emerged throughout Europe. As cities grew they needed supply networks, and these extended over large areas. Already by 1650 Paris needed 3 million bushels of grain each year to feed its inhabitants, and it drew these from throughout northern France; still more distant regions met the city's needs for livestock. By modern standards, early modern Europeans had only primitive means of transporting foodstuffs to these markets, but after about 1600 their means of transport improved dramatically; new roads and canals were built, and better government made shipment along them more reliable. As transport improved, even nobles on once remote estates could sell their grain and livestock on urban markets.[46] One of the richest nobles in Saxony, in central Germany, typified the new situation in a 1625 letter to his business agent: he wanted regular reports on grain prices in the regional capital Erfurt, in order to make more profitable decisions.[47]

In the long run, these circumstances promised success to noble estate owners who had made the transition from feudal to domain property. Some periods, of course, were better than others. The crisis-torn fifteenth century posed difficulties, as depopulation made labor expensive and weakened demand for food. Between 1500 and 1660, in contrast, there stretched a golden age for owners, in which growing population made labor cheap and food production profitable. Conditions were more sluggish during the later seventeenth and early eighteenth centuries, but after 1750 prosperity returned. The later eighteenth century brought landowners rapidly increasing incomes: in France farm rents typically doubled between the 1750s and the 1780s. At least for some parts of Europe, there were further farm profits to be had from the great age of war that lasted between 1792 and 1815.[48]

But long-term success often came with short-term anxieties, even crises – more worries than the owner of a medieval lordship could have imagined, as he tranquilly collected his permanently fixed rents. Some of the estate owner's problems were those of any agricultural enterprise. There might be localized harvest failures, or dropping prices caused by

[46] Jan DeVries, *The Economy of Europe in an Age of Crisis, 1600–1740* (Cambridge, 1976), 159; cf. E. A. Wrigley, "A Simple Model of London's Importance in Changing English Society and Economy, 1650–1750," repr. in Wrigley and Philip Abrams, eds., *Towns in Societies: Essays in Economic History and Historical Sociology* (Cambridge, 1978), 215–43.

[47] Harnisch, "Grundherrschaft oder Gutsherrschaft," 77.

[48] Robert Forster, *The House of Saulx-Tavanes: Versailles and Burgundy, 1700–1830* (Baltimore, 1971), 227–29.

over-production. Early modern Europeans had trouble storing grain, which had to be kept dry and safe from rodents, so estate owners could not always hold back from the market when prices were low. Governments tried to control the food trade and might limit estate owners' access to distant markets, precisely in hope of keeping down prices. If improved transportation made new markets available, it also sharpened competition for them, likewise driving down prices. Nobles shared these problems with any substantial farmer, but they also confronted more specific problems. No noble could accept working with his hands, or even becoming too involved in business of any kind; to do so meant relinquishing noble status, and thus nobles could involve themselves directly in agricultural production to only a limited degree. Many nobles, and especially the richest among them, sought to play a public role away from the estate, at court, in the army, or in the civil service; thus they could not always be present to manage their estates. And large estates might spread over miles of territory, with fragments in many villages; keeping track of production was no easy matter.

For all of these reasons, nobles usually played a secondary role in administering their properties. Some might oversee their lands directly, using hired workers or (east of the Elbe) the enforced peasant labor that serfdom provided to do the actual work. In lower Austria, a mid-seventeenth-century noble advised the estate owner "to believe that his presence is necessary in every field, vineyard, forest . . . and in everything he owns; never believe that another, whoever he might be, could be as faithful . . ."[49] The same advice had been offered in sixteenth-century northern Italy: "It is necessary that [the estate owner] always, or as often as possible, be personally present in every major matter and that he understand everything, see everything, touch everything, trusting as little as possible, especially the peasants, who because of their vile nature are enemies of their masters."[50]

Direct management of this kind, however, probably best suited remote areas, where there was least need for staying sharply attuned to market changes and where much of the land's produce might be consumed at home. Elsewhere, the more common choice was to confide estate management to one or several agricultural entrepreneurs, tenant farmers who would take on the risks of running the property for part of its profits. For nobles distracted by public careers and the complexities of managing several properties, this was a wise economic decision.

---

[49] Quoted Otto Brunner, *Adeliges Landesleben und Europaischer Geist: Leben und Werk Wolf Helmhards von Hohberg, 1612–1688* (Salzburg, 1949), 44.
[50] Quoted James S. Ackerman, *The Villa: Form and Ideology of Country Houses* (Princeton, 1990), 116.

Such arrangements varied widely across Europe. In England, tenant farmers were very substantial figures, who took on large properties and could command flexible arrangements. They held a large capital in livestock, tools, and financial backing. The scope of their investments made them difficult to replace, and both they and their landlords assumed that they would retain their leases for long periods, to the benefit of both sides: for stable leasing arrangements encouraged tenants to invest in the land, with the knowledge that they would not lose the profits of investment to a new tenant. Across northern France, in contrast, leases normally lasted only nine years before owner and tenant renegotiated their terms. French tenant farmers were usually not such substantial figures as their English counterparts, but they did not entirely lack weapons in negotiating with landowners, for they too brought a significant array of livestock and tools to the arrangement; nobles could not easily find men with the capital and skill to manage a large property successfully, and thus faced some pressure to renew leases on favorable terms. But French tenant farmers paid the owners a higher share of the land's produce than did the English, and they had less incentive to invest in the properties they rented, by applying costly fertilizer to the land or improving barns and fences, for any improvements would benefit the owner once the lease was up. To the south, conditions were still harsher and tenants had still fewer incentives for improvement. Southern France and Italy were regions of share-cropping, arrangements which usually could be ended year by year and in which estate owners held all the agricultural capital, livestock, and tools, as well as the land itself. Here the farmer was little more than a laborer, and, bringing little to the bargaining table, he could be easily replaced. Most share-cropping arrangements testified to the unequal bargaining that ensued, by according the owner at least half of the land's produce, and often more.

The wide diversity in these arrangements reflected some of the sharpest differences in social practice across Europe, and in turn produced other differences. From the fifteenth century on, English observers professed themselves shocked by the poverty of the continental peasantry and by the lack of socializing between nobles and farmers. In the late eighteenth century, the agronomist Arthur Young marvelled that his aristocratic French hosts failed to introduce him to their tenant farmers, whereas he would have naturally encountered such men in any gathering of English landed society. By this point the English tenant farmer had acquired forms of gentility. In turn, the differing visions of leasing arrangements helped to produce wildly differing agricultural results. Partly because its tenant farmers could invest in their farms knowing that they would benefit from the effort, agriculture probably improved faster in sixteenth- and seventeenth-century England than on the continent. Elsewhere, owners offered their tenant farmers fewer incentives for investment. Tenants had shorter leases than in England and paid higher rents in relation to what the land produced. Probably the vestiges of feudal lordship added to these disincentives, by adding to the financial burdens and pointless regulations that weighed on all farmers. Continental agriculture suffered because estate owners proved too ready to grasp at its immediate profits; in this case nobles' greed stood in the way of capitalist rationality.[51]

Alongside these important differences in estate administration across Europe, however, were important similarities – and recent studies of continental agriculture have made these increasingly apparent. Despite the difficulties that many encountered, continental tenant farmers tended to become increasingly wealthy and powerful figures, some of them with attachments to the world of urban commerce. Farmers in the chief grain-producing regions of France in fact compared well with their English counterparts. They dealt with huge sums of money, and their farms were as productive as those of their English rivals.[52] Northern Italy too experienced important agricultural improvements in the mid-seventeenth century, despite years of terrible warfare in the region. Here progress involved agricultural diversification as well as improvements in traditional crops: landowners and their tenants introduced vines, rice, clover, and mulberry trees, for raising silkworms, while at the same time cereal production improved.[53] In central Germany, there appeared during the seventeenth century an analogous but still more striking entrepreneur: farmers and merchants from Holland took to renting properties and herds there, from which they could draw substantial profits by applying Dutch expertise in dairy management.[54] With his huge investment and large-scale enterprise, the early modern tenant farmer needed to market his products in distant places. He brought to the

[51] Historians have recently tended to reduce differences between English and continental agricultures: see Philip Hoffman, "Land Rents and Agricultural Productivity: The Paris Basin 1450–1789," *Journal of Economic History*, 51, 4 (December, 1991), 771–805; cf. Dewald, *Pont-St-Pierre*, 74–88, for stress on obstacles to agricultural development.

[52] For emphasis on the wealth, education, and wide prospects of tenant farmers near Paris, Jean-Marc Moriceau, *Les Fermiers de l'Ile de France, XVe–XVIIIe siècle* (Paris, 1994), *passim*; see also the literature on French agricultural development summarized in Dewald and Vardi, "The Peasantries of France, 1400–1800."

[53] Domenico Sella, *Crisis and Continuity: The Economy of Spanish Lombardy in the Seventeenth Century* (Cambridge, MA, 1979), 120–23.

[54] Hermann Kellenbenz, "Die wirtschaftliche Rolle des schleswig-holsteinischen Adels in 16. und 17. Jahrhundert," in Lohmeier, ed., *Arte et Marte*, 15–32.

management of his rural enterprise methods and assumptions of the city. Such figures, with their heavy investments of capital and their need for careful market calculations, were the crucial actors in Europe's agricultural development.

During the eighteenth century, these changes in the nature of aristocratic property produced a flurry of cultural and political activity; public discussion now made clear just how dramatically economic life had changed. In the years around 1750, French and German translators made available English texts on agricultural improvement; and governments across the continent sought to stimulate interest in them. Royal agricultural societies appeared, not just in capitals like Paris but also in provincial cities and in relatively backward states like Spain and Savoy. Many of them published periodicals in which members could learn of recent experiences and new methods. Some nobles participated actively in these institutions, and nobles formed the leadership of the physiocratic movement, an effort to bring free-market economics to French agriculture. Whether oriented to farming techniques, as in the agricultural societies, or to abstract economics, as among the physiocrats, eighteenth-century nobles encountered doctrines that encouraged them to manipulate nature and eschew tradition. Not always, it should be added, with positive results, for the proposed innovations were often expensive and unproductive. "Sooner or later this mania for getting rich will land us in the poorhouse," complained the son of one enthusiastic agricultural improver, in late eighteenth-century Savoy. In this period, short-term improvements mattered less than nobles' newly utilitarian attitude to their land.[55]

Such doctrines probably had a serious influence on only a minority of the nobles. Most noble landowners, however, felt the full impact of a broader change, in ways of seeing and treating property itself. For the eighteenth century brought new techniques of visualizing landed properties. Surveying and map-making techniques developed enormously in the second half of the seventeenth century, and by the eighteenth century reached fully modern standards. Having one's estates surveyed and mapped became something of a fashionable mania in the eighteenth century, and the profession of estate surveyor boomed. The German novelist Johan Wolfgang von Goethe described the impact late in the eighteenth century: "Eduard saw his possessions taking shape on the paper like a new creation," wrote Goethe of his estate-owning hero, as he has his estate surveyed and mapped. "It seemed to him that only now was

---

[55] Blum, *The End of the Old Order*, 249–51; Jean Nicolas, *La Savoie au XVIIIe siècle: noblesse et bourgeoisie*, 2 vols. (Paris, 1978), II, 807, 808–10; Richard Herr, *The Eighteenth-Century Revolution in Spain* (Princeton, 1958), 154–63.

he coming to know them, only now did they really belong to him.''[56] A new sense of property derived from new ways of seeing; in the novel, this sense of ownership leads in turn to a new readiness to manipulate the landscape – in other words, to a new view of nature itself.

At the same time, nobles became increasingly ready to buy and sell their properties, and steadily less attached to them by ties of sentiment or tradition. Such ties, it must be emphasized, had never been so strong as would be claimed in the nineteenth and twentieth centuries, when Europe witnessed a renewed emphasis on aristocratic tradition and attachment to the land. But estates probably did sell with increasing speed over the early modern period, testifying to their owners' growing readiness to view property as a purely economic resource, to be kept or sold as economic interest might dictate. Certainly contemporaries believed this was happening, and they worried about the consequences. Thus a Prussian writer in 1801: "The noble estates are viewed as a ware in which one deals, for many buy estates, not in order to keep them, but in order to sell them again for a profit." "The uninterrupted progress in the buying and selling of estates," wrote another anxious German, in 1810, "naturally tears the moral connection, built over years of inheritance, between the subject and his lord."[57]

In their turn, the land market's growing activity and breadth produced further perceptual changes, new ways of describing property, for the eighteenth century had begun employing modern techniques of real-estate marketing, with printed advertisements describing the attractions of properties for sale and newspapers printing classified advertisements for them. Like the new maps, the new advertising brought to nobles' consciousness a quantitative vision of property, setting out its acreage and revenues, and encouraging comparisons with alternative investments. Property had become a thing, fully detached from person and family.

The country house

A final set of developments accompanied these changes in the way nobles managed their landed properties. Beginning in the sixteenth century, nobles across Europe began to view their country residences in new terms. The country house lost most of its military role and much of its significance as a center of political leadership. In exchange, it took on new functions as a site of elegant comfort and as a retreat from the pressures of

---

[56] Johann Wolfgang von Goethe, *Elective Affinities*, trans. R. J. Hollingdale (London, 1971), 40.
[57] Both quoted Berdahl, "The *Stände* and the Origins of Conservatism in Prussia," 318.

public life. As new aesthetic ideals spread, the country house came to play an additional role, that of demonstrating to the world its owners' good taste, familiarity with advanced ideas, and wealth.

Together, these changing values and changing social needs meant that building went on almost everywhere in the sixteenth- and seventeenth-century countryside. Ideas about what a country house should be changed so completely in these years that few families indeed could avoid building. The ideal medieval country house had offered protection and hospitality. It gave security from the violence that often prevailed in the medieval countryside, and it afforded its owners political power, by giving them control of strategic points. No one demanded privacy in such a house. Most medieval men and women wanted to live surrounded by attendants and servants, and nobles' houses included few private spaces; even beds were set up within the large halls, rather than in bedrooms set off for the purpose. Nobles seem to have had equally little interest in separating the house itself from its neighbors. Gardens around the house were small, farm buildings might adjoin it, and villagers' own houses were nearby.

Standards of aristocratic housing began to change in the sixteenth century partly because the country house began to lose its military functions. This was a slow process. England was probably the best governed country in Europe, but country houses there retained defensive functions into the 1550s; in France fortified country houses remained a worry in the first decades of the seventeenth century. But thereafter violence diminished in the countryside, and defensive strength ceased to seem a primary architectural need. At the same time, powerful new aesthetic aims had begun to shape country house design. Rather than solidity, owners began to want beauty, light, privacy, and comfort. They sought these in new technology and in new design models. Glass became widely available for construction, and blank fortress walls were replaced with windows. Ancient Rome and contemporary Italy supplied models for how one might live elegantly in the countryside. Private bedrooms and corridors – so that one could move through the house without intruding on others – came to be widely used. Architectural fashion itself became a significant concern. Families no longer accepted outmoded designs. They wanted their houses up-to-date, and by the eighteenth century publications made them aware of new styles.[58]

All of these impulses made building seem necessary to even old noble families, who had long owned substantial country houses. New families

[58] Stone and Stone, *An Open Elite?*, 379ff.; for an example, Boris Ford, ed., *The Cambridge Cultural History of Britain*, IV (Cambridge, 1989), 228. Styles of building are discussed in more detail below, Chapter 4.

had of course a further need, to establish their presence in the countryside as estate owners, and house-building answered this desire as well. A large house made visible to all the family's success and its local standing. As a result, a mania for building swept across seventeenth-century Europe, followed by a somewhat smaller wave of building in the eighteenth century. In England even minor gentry participated in the process; the period brought what one historian has called the "rebuilding of rural England." Contemporaries spoke often of the infatuation that house-building seemed to produce, leading owners to spend more than they could afford and distracting them from other duties. But even the wisest seemed to agree that this was an uncontrollable urge, with little hope of cure. Grievous expense did not end once the house had been built, in fact. The costs of setting up and decorating the house's interior might exceed these for the exterior shell, especially since contemporaries believed that new buildings required new furniture.[59]

As significant as this new conception of the house itself was a new conception of its spatial relationship to other houses. Increasingly after 1600, nobles sought to create large private spaces around their houses, separating themselves physically from ordinary villagers. Separation of this kind served ideological ends. It emphasized the distance in rank between the estate owner and the humble villagers around him/her, and it displayed the elegant leisure that the owner enjoyed, by removing farmland from his/her view; seventeenth- and eighteenth-century owners wanted to see only "natural" land around them, rather than scenes of agricultural toil. During the Middle Ages, aristocratic houses had sat easily among the farm buildings that supplied their needs. As new ideals of comfort and elegance developed, this proximity became less and less acceptable. Instead, estate owners wanted uninterrupted vistas over the space around them, and to assure privacy within this space they walled it off. The fashion for creating "parks" (as they were known in England) around country houses went farthest in England. Parks there might extend for hundreds of acres. Usually the cost included giving up valuable farm land for an essentially recreational use, and in a few cases it included the destruction of whole villages, which were removed to assure the estate owner's privacy. "Ten miles around," Jane Austen's fictional heroine Elizabeth is proudly told when she asks about the size of the park she is visiting in northern England. For others, this appropriation of useful land to serve the recreational needs of wealthy nobles signified social trouble: in the words of an eighteenth-century English poet, "the man of wealth and pride/ Takes up the space that many poor supplied;/

[59] W. G. Hoskins, "The Rebuilding of Rural England, 1570–1640," *Past and Present*, 4 (November, 1953), 44–59; Stone and Stone, *An Open Elite?*, 329–94.

Space for his lake, his park's extended bounds,/ Space for his horses, equipage and hounds."[60]

Matters rarely went so far in France, another sign that eighteenth-century England in fact remained the most aristocratic country in Europe. But continental nobles had the same impulses as the English, and when they had the cash they acted in the same way. In about 1660 Nicolas Fouquet, Louis XIV's first finance minister and a very wealthy man, had three villages removed to make way for the walled park at his home Vaux le Vicomte. Like the English, eighteenth-century French nobles sought to create a sense of wilderness within their parks, by building false ruins and summerhouses for isolated revery. Such building projects took the ideal of privacy a step further. They implied that the estate owner would want a place for retreat from all others – not just from villagers and other social inferiors, but even from social equals. The same impulses prevailed in eighteenth-century Germany: the estate-owning heroine of Goethe's *Elective Affinities* designed a pavilion within her park so small that only two people could enter it.[61]

The walled park thus carried numerous meanings in the seventeenth- and eighteenth-century countryside. It expressed a lofty distance from the rest of rural society and from the work carried on within it. Medieval estate owners had sought the presence of lesser figures, but after 1600 estate owners sought to make these others invisible, uprooting nearby villages and establishing a barrier of uncultivated space between themselves and such villages as remained. The park made insistently visible ideals of privacy and linked these to ideas of class: ordinary villagers were to be excluded from view. At the same time, the park expressed a refined enjoyment of nature, for it sought to contain a properly governed nature. It suggested preference for leisured enjoyment over mere cash returns, for in many instances usable farm land had been sacrificed to create the park. Yet at the same time its walls gave an alternative message, of absolute control over property and an ability to reshape the earth itself – as the park itself had been reshaped to suit the owner's desires. Even as the park demonstrated distance from certain forms of capitalist calculation, it made visible the absolute property rights that the decline of feudalism had created.[62]

---

[60] Goldsmith, "The Deserted Village," quoted Williams, *The Country and the City*, 96.

[61] On the diffusion of the park as a landscape ideal in Germany and Austria, Brunner, *Adeliges Landesleben*, 135–37.

[62] Chandra Mukerji, "Territorial Gardens: The Control of Land in Seventeenth-Century French Formal Gardens," in Thomas Haskell and Richard Teichgraeber III, eds., *The Culture of the Market: Historical Essays* (Cambridge, 1993), 66–101.

Alternative forms of wealth

The decline of feudalism was especially important because it coincided with a broader process of change: after about 1600, nobles focussed their economic attention less exclusively on land, and increasingly involved themselves in other forms of economic activity. Even in the fifteenth century, of course, land was not the whole story. Nobles owned other properties, and landowning itself shaded easily into certain forms of commerce. Nobles owned forests, mines, mills, breweries, all of which depended on their control of the land, but all of which drew them away from purely agricultural pursuits. Fifteenth-century nobles also expected profits from war, directly from the kings who paid them, indirectly from the booty they picked up on the battlefield and from ransoming hostages, until the practice died out in the sixteenth century. A few, like the Englishman John Fastolf, became rich from war; a great many earned from it a handsome supplement to what their lands supplied.

Well into the sixteenth century, however, nobles who moved beyond this range of economic enterprises encountered a series of powerful ethical and social inhibitions. The Greek philosopher Aristotle himself had taught Europeans to view commerce and banking with suspicion; the Catholic church had adopted many of his teachings, and condemned lending money at interest with particular vigor. In France and Spain, nobles who worked with their hands or involved themselves directly in commerce might lose their titles of nobility, and the tax exemptions that went with them. The essence of nobility was military service and social leadership, so ran contemporary ideas – and no one could perform these if sordid commercial interests constantly claimed his attention. Nobles who turned away from the land to follow more commercial pursuits thus risked a threefold loss. They relinquished the powerful moral qualities that contemporaries associated with the land; they placed at risk the image of disinterested service that served as the basis of their order; and they encountered the church's censure of many business practices.

In the years after 1600, however, both ideas and practices changed. This happened partly because an increasing range of investments became available to nobles, investments that were especially tempting because land offered low returns throughout the early modern period. In the sixteenth century, land offered a yearly return of about 4 percent of its cost. In contrast, money could be loaned for returns of 8 or even 10 percent, and this with some degree of security. Private borrowers needed cash, but governments needed even more, as warfare became more expensive and larger in scale. Starting in the sixteenth century, thus, governments established appealing mechanisms to draw funds from conservative investors. Even richer rewards beckoned for those with insider connections and a taste for financial adventuring. Seventeenth-century banking served the interests of the state as much as those of commerce, and here nobles enjoyed special advantages. Bankers might seek to use their influence – in exchange for participation in the profits. In France, where aristocratic participation in any commercial venture was frowned upon and the "bourgeois gentleman" provoked snobbish laughter, nobles found indirect ways to invest in state banking. They placed their money with tax farmers, often men of humble backgrounds, and reaped huge but discreet rewards. Similar machinations characterized the Kingdom of Naples in the early seventeenth century.[63]

Comparable disparities between returns from land and those from money-lending persisted through the eighteenth century, though interest rates declined, and they supplied a steady enticement for nobles to look to non-landed forms of wealth. By the mid-eighteenth century, both English and French nobles placed substantial parts of their money in these government bonds, often in preference to land. Nobles quickly became involved in such lending when they had cash to spare, and by this point no one seemed to mind the religious problems that it raised. "I am beginning to think like all the rich people of Paris," wrote a provincial nobleman in 1736. "There is not one of them who wants land. Most of them have only [stock market] shares or government bonds." Eighteenth-century England witnessed a similar shift, as nobles enthusiastically bought the 3 percent bonds offered by the Bank of England.[64]

Another option lay in a special form of landed property, urban land. The years after 1600 witnessed important transformations of Europe's urban geography, as new neighborhoods opened in the largest cities and new standards of urban elegance emerged. Elegant row houses, geometrically symmetrical squares, straighter streets, entirely new neighborhoods – these marked urban development in seventeenth-century Madrid, London, Prague, and Paris, and in dozens of provincial cities as well. Nearly everywhere, nobles played an important role in these efforts at urban rebuilding. In some cases they held the original properties on which these speculative ventures were built. More often, they benefitted from their connections with kings and administrators, who handed over direction of the projects. However they managed it, nobles became

---

[63] Daniel Dessert, *Argent, pouvoir, et société au Grand Siècle* (Paris, 1987); Astarita, *The Continuity of Feudal Power*, 221–24, on both the availability of high-interest government bonds and aristocratic networks behind government financiers.

[64] Quoted Robert Forster, "The Nobility during the French Revolution," *Past and Present*, 37 (July, 1967), 82 n. 40; for clarity, I have slightly changed this translation.

tightly involved in many of these real-estate developments; and all could see the new kind of wealth that such ventures might offer.[65]

Nobles moved easily into both money-lending and urban real estate developments during the sixteenth and seventeenth centuries. They hesitated much more before involving themselves in commerce. But after 1600 new commercial institutions made even this step an easier one. The advent of the Amsterdam stock market, in 1611, and the development of public banks (in Venice and Amsterdam by the early seventeenth century, in England in 1694) offered a new kind of economic opportunity. Those with money but without commercial expertise could place their funds with those who had the necessary commercial skills, while at the same time enjoying some security on what they loaned. By the end of the eighteenth century, stock markets boomed in many parts of western Europe.[66]

Europe's increasingly profitable colonial empires offered yet another alternative to investment in the land. Spain here set the model, with its colonial arrangements based in Seville. A contemporary observed in 1587 that "the discovery of the Indies had presented such wonderful opportunities to acquire great wealth that the nobility of Seville had been lured into trade."[67] English gentlemen followed their example in the next century. Nearly one-fifth of those investing in English overseas trade during the early seventeenth century were drawn from the gentry, partly because the risks were so high as to dissuade the more calculating merchants. But if the risks were high so were returns. A series of huge new fortunes in the eighteenth century made the situation clear: the Indies East and West were the source from which several aristocratic fortunes were constructed or reconstructed.[68]

Attitudes limped haltingly after these changing practices, but by the eighteenth century they too had decisively changed. As more nobles found themselves enjoying the profits of commerce, ethical doubts about its pursuit receded. In fact governments sought to encourage the change, and their propaganda sought to link patriotic service to commerce. In 1682 the Spanish crown formally decreed that factory ownership would no longer be incompatible with noble status, and in 1770 it widened this

[65] Lawrence Stone, "The Residential Development of the West End of London in the Seventeenth Century," in Barbara Malament, ed., *After the Reformation: Essays in Honor of J. H. Hexter* (Philadelphia, 1980), 167–212; Anthony Blunt, *Art and Architecture in France, 1500–1700*, 4th edn (London, 1980), 159–65, 367–68; David Buisseret, *Sully* (London, 1968).

[66] DeVries, *The Economy of Europe in an Age of Crisis*, 226–32.

[67] Quoted Ruth Pike, *Aristocrats and Traders: Sevillian Society in the Sixteenth Century* (Ithaca, 1972), 22; for examples, 22–52.

[68] Mingay, *The Gentry*, 104–06, quoting the work of T. K. Rabb.

permission to include all forms of economic activity. A similar change occurred in France. Since the 1660s French officials had worried about their nobles' resistance to commercial enterprise and had sought to encourage commercial investments. In the eighteenth century, at least some pamphleteers began calling for a "commercial nobility" in France, a nobility that would contribute its capital to French commerce and raise the total level of wealth in society. In part their efforts derived from patriotism, for commercial successes would be needed if France was to stay even with its British and Dutch competitors. And at least some nobles listened. Seventeenth-century France had seen the nobles make only secretive investments with bourgeois front-men, for fear of the disdain in which commerce was viewed; but in the eighteenth century a series of well-publicized ventures involved nobles in the sugar business, in iron manufacturing, and in stock-market speculations.[69] Such men remained a small minority, but their example mattered; it taught a revisionist ethic, one that assimilated commerce and citizenship. This was a message that the government sought to reinforce. "Commerce has always been viewed as one of the most solid and fruitful sources of the strength and power of States," it proclaimed in 1756; "the Nation should know that it can find in [commerce] honor as well as profit."[70]

The English employed similar rhetoric to more practical economic effect. There a series of famous nobles undertook important and expensive investments in mining, canals, and roads. By the mid-eighteenth century English aristocrats regularly glorified commercial life, as a principal source of their nation's wealth. "Our trade," wrote one, ". . . is so much the vital breath of this nation that the one cannot subsist whenever the other is long stopped."[71] The great aristocrat here expressed more than acceptance of commerce as a legitimate pursuit, in itself an ethical stance that would have startled the sixteenth century. Rather, he made it essential to national life, a patriotic duty that concerned landowning aristocrats just as much as city merchants. Such ideals found surprising echoes in other parts of Europe. "I hope to God," wrote a Danish noblewoman about her sons, "that they become useful and happy men, in whatever position they come to hold. It is all the same to me what they become, and I would rather have a son who is an admired

---

[69] Herr, *The Eighteenth-Century Revolution in Spain*, 97; Guy Richard, *Noblesse d'affaires au XVIIIe siècle* (Paris, 1974); for similar changes in Italy, Daniel Klang, "Reform and Enlightenment in Eighteenth-Century Lombardy," *Canadian Journal of History*, 19 (April, 1984), 39–70.

[70] Quoted Patrice Higonnet, *Class, Ideology, and the Rights of Nobles During the French Revolution* (Oxford, 1981), 47.

[71] Quoted Lewis Namier, *England in the Age of the American Revolution*, 2nd edn (London, 1961), 33.

physician, an intellectual, or a businessman, than an idler at court or some other useless member of the human race."[72]

Here was a fundamental transformation in European culture: the assimilation by landowning and military nobles of an ideal of commerce as a dignified and important activity. The change was not absolute. Restrictions on aristocratic commercial activity had always allowed for exceptions, and nobles' devotion to their lands had never been so absolute as propagandists wanted. Nobles had always been ready to sell ancestral estates when the opportunity warranted. But the change was real and important nonetheless. It meant the full integration of some nobles into capitalist culture, and the acceptance by most of that culture's basic elements. Full results of the process would be evident in the nineteenth century, as nobles moved easily into boards of directors of industrial enterprises – in other words, as they involved themselves in the management as well as the profits of capitalism.

Serving the state

In the seventeenth and eighteenth centuries, we have seen, nobles found the range of economic activities permitted to them widening. Starting somewhat earlier, the economics of state service also began to change, ultimately bringing wider economic opportunities in this domain as well. Increasingly, states offered their nobles well-paid employment, both as soldiers and as bureaucrats.

This was an uneven process, partly because the state took away some economic opportunities even as it offered new ones. Into the sixteenth century, warriors could hope to get rich by ransoming captives. But by this time new conditions of warfare were beginning to restrict chances for ransom. Battlefields had become too big and (especially with the advent of firearms) too violent; and more disciplined forms of combat made such private enterprise increasingly inappropriate, an interference with generalship. Collecting booty from the battlefield or from conquered civilians retained its legitimacy longer. But in the seventeenth century this too receded as a source of real profits. By this time, medieval ideas of the economics of warfare had become largely irrelevant.

In their place, however, came new and glittering sources of profit. Armies grew rapidly during the sixteenth and seventeenth centuries, and they offered positions for nearly all nobles who wanted them. As

---

[72] Quoted Dieter Lohmeier, "Der Edelman als Burger: Uber die Verburgerlichung der Adelskultur im dänischen Gesamtstaat," in Lohmeier and Christian Degn, eds., *Staatsdienst und Menschlichkeit: Studien der Adelskultur des späten 18. Jahrhunderts in Schleswig-Holstein und Dänemark* (Neuminster, 1980), 139.

bureaucracies expanded, they too offered numerous positions, though many of these required substantial investments in education. And there were positions at court, attending the king, serving his needs, and in most cases enjoying the gifts and pensions that he could bestow. Across Europe, seventeenth- and eighteenth-century nobles increasingly relied on positions like these as sources of income. Eighteenth-century Prussia probably represented an extreme instance, for there both army and bureaucracy took much larger shares of national resources than in most of Europe. One result was that a full third of nobles in Brandenburg, the region around the capital city of Berlin, had no significant landed incomes, and instead relied entirely on incomes from their service to the state. In France and England there were few cases of such complete dependence on the state, but French and English nobles also avidly sought the state's resources. In seventeenth-century France, state salaries might easily count for one-quarter of the income of even a substantial landowner, and for lesser landowners they could constitute the outright majority of income. Such dependence had political consequences, which we will consider below, in Chapter 3. At the economic level, nobles' reliance on such sources of income meant that by the eighteenth century they were not an exclusively landed group – and in some regions, land was not even their primary resource.[73]

Spending

Across Europe, nobles' incomes remained generally buoyant during the early modern period – despite regional variations and despite momentary crises, individual and collective. Yet during these years many nobles ran into severe economic problems. A few great families and many lesser ones faced bankruptcy; many more found themselves needing to sell some of their lands in order to overcome temporary difficulties. Such financial disasters received wide publicity. In early seventeenth-century Spain, there was the duke of Sesa, a great nobleman who died (as it was said) "from melancholy at being ruined and not having received from His Majesty gifts that would allow him to pay his debts." In mid-seventeenth-century France there was the duke of Elbeuf, "the first prince whom poverty had degraded," in the words of a contemporary nobleman. In England at about the same time, the earl of Arundel was so hopelessly in debt that he had to hide from his creditors: "I dare not be seen or suffer it to be known where I am," he wrote. Difficulties resulted not from declining incomes, but from expenditures. The early modern period

[73] See for instance Deborah Hertz, *Jewish High Society in Old Regime Berlin* (New Haven, 1988), 31–32; Dewald, *Pont-St-Pierre*, 178–81.

placed on nobles steadily greater pressures to spend money, and it made the control of expenditures especially difficult. Most nobles rationally and successfully adapted their estates to the changing economic world around them. They had much more difficulty managing their spending.[74]

Varied forces contributed to making expenditure so intractable a problem. Individual weaknesses played a role. The English earl of Arundel thus spent himself into trouble as the greatest art collector of his era. Other problems reflected the particularities of national culture. Most Spanish nobles felt obliged to spend large sums on the increasingly elaborate religious practices of the sixteenth and seventeenth centuries, endowing religious orders and elaborate religious ceremonies. But other pressures for expense were more universal. Building country houses and arranging the gardens around them formed one enormous expense. To enclose a substantial park could be ruinously expensive. Along with the walls themselves there were the costs of relocating villagers and the sacrifice of productive land. These were followed by new expenses, as owners shifted large quantities of earth to create new vistas, built walks, and created waterways and fountains, along with the complex machinery needed to work them; the first James Watt steam engine sold in France powered the fountains at the duke of Orléans' estate. The turn to more natural gardening styles in the eighteenth century brought no financial relief, for estate owners insisted on reworking nature in expensive ways, by relocating large amounts of earth and water. Some families spent themselves into bankruptcy through building; a great many families suffered serious financial strains because of it.

The need to serve the state likewise weighed on nobles' finances everywhere in Europe. In mid-seventeenth-century Spain, monarchs pressed for cash asked the high nobility to raise and equip units for the army; three leading nobles each found themselves paying the enormous expenses of 3,000–man regiments. At the other end of Europe, the Bohemian magnate Wallenstein found himself in a comparable situation, using his own resources to raise troops for the emperor. In the long run such arrangements might lead to vast profits, but the short-term expenses were such that Wallenstein's banker eventually drowned himself, in despair at the financial pressures such levies created.[75]

But the central problems of nobles' spending lay elsewhere, in the demands of an increasingly exchange-oriented society and in an increasing need to buttress social status with purchased goods. Nobles increasingly found themselves entering the market economy as consumers, just

---

[74] Quoted Antonio Dominguez Ortiz, *Las clases privilegiadas en la España del Antiguo Regimen* (Madrid, 1973), 106; Dewald, *Aristocratic Experience*, 154; Stone, *Crisis*, 520.

[75] Dominguez Ortiz, *Las clases privilegiadas*, 93–94; Mann, *Wallenstein*, 515–17.

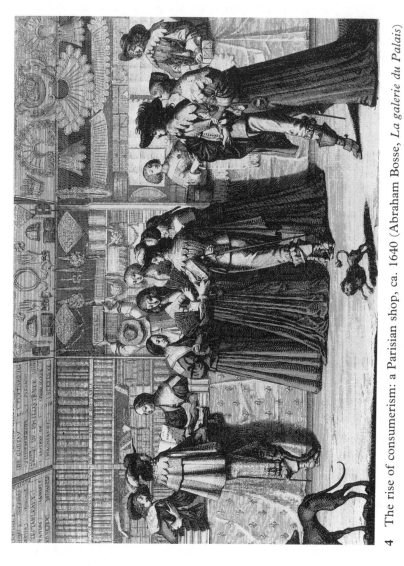

4　The rise of consumerism: a Parisian shop, ca. 1640 (Abraham Bosse, *La galerie du Palais*)

as they entered it as producers. The change involved both ideals and practices. Through the sixteenth century, nobles had deployed a powerful ethic of self-sufficiency, in keeping with the suspicion of the marketplace that medieval Europeans had learned from Aristotle and a long succession of scholastic theologians. As landowners, they claimed, they should supply themselves from what their properties produced. Obviously some goods could only be acquired outside the estate; medieval lords had always purchased weapons, cloths, and spices. But into the sixteenth century basic food supplies had come from the estate itself. Peasant tenants paid some of their rents in grain and poultry, and these supplied the basic needs of most lords' kitchens. Noble estate-owners established vineyards to supply their own wine, even in unlikely areas such as northern France. "I hold it . . . a happy thing to have no need to send for necessaries to the city," wrote the sixteenth-century Italian Torquato Tasso in his advice book *The Householder's Philosophy.* "I have abundance of everything ministered unto me upon mine own ground," abundance sufficient, the text makes clear, for a gentleman, not just for an ordinary man. Tasso's advice seemed sufficiently pertinent that an English translation appeared in 1588, and numerous estate owners echoed it in their private writings.[76] The advice made practical as well as moral sense, given the wide-open hospitality estate owners were expected to offer and the large number of servants they maintained; they needed quantity, not quality, of goods.

But already as Tasso wrote these ideals were becoming obsolete, and in the seventeenth century they lost all moral force. The new country houses were oriented more to private life than to public hospitality. New consumer goods appeared on the market, and the commercial networks that provided old goods became more reliable and efficient. What once was produced on the estate now could be purchased at urban shops, which themselves became more numerous and more abundantly stocked with goods.

The history of food and drink supplies an especially clear example of this transition from self-sufficiency to the market. In sixteenth-century France, thus, most nobles drank the product of their own vineyards, although a limited number of wine-producing regions had acquired some reputation. By the mid-seventeenth century, however, nobles had become more demanding. Specialized wines came to be increasingly prized; by the early eighteenth century all the major French wines valued today had been established. Other local delicacies had also acquired renown.

---

[76] Torquato Tasso, *The Householders Philosophie* (London, 1588; facsimile repr. Amsterdam-Norwood, NJ, 1975), fo. 3 v. (spelling modernized); for examples of these attitudes in practice, Dewald, *Pont-St-Pierre*, 198–99.

Wealthy consumers expected their meats to come from certain regions, their fruits and vegetables from others, regardless of distances. By the early eighteenth century a daily service supplied Paris with oysters, though the city lay over 200 miles from the Breton coasts where they were harvested. By the end of the century, the high French nobility would accept no less than the most refined cuisine. The Parisian duke of Saulx-Tavanes had his olives from Marseilles, his chicken patties from Rouen, his sauerkraut from Strasbourg, his prunes from Tours, his spiced bread from Reims. Local consumption, of the products of his own estates, had by this point become inconceivable. No estate could produce the range of goods available in eighteenth-century city shops; even in small cities these offered an increasingly varied range of goods. With specialized products came also specialized preparers: the duke's cook was his highest paid servant, with a cash income (he was also fed, lodged, and clothed by the duke) exceeding that of many provincial nobles. Other noble families replicated the Saulx-Tavanes' dependence on the market economy.[77] It is the depth of that dependence that is important. The Saulx-Tavanes and these other families had come to rely on a national market for goods that they could easily have acquired locally – indeed, for goods that they could have produced themselves, on their own estates. Local poultry, meat, and wine had seemed perfectly adequate to fifteenth-century nobles. By the opening of the eighteenth century, they no longer sufficed.

Many developments contributed to this turn to the marketplace. Improved roads and vehicles made national markets of this kind possible, and stronger governments made them reliable; eighteenth-century buyers could count on goods arriving safely from distant producers. But technological possibility supplies only a partial explanation for nobles' readiness to buy such basic goods as Rouennais chickens or Scottish beef, for transporting heavy goods like these remained expensive. More important than technological possibilities were the social needs that consumption served. Buying offered nobles means of displaying both their wealth and their ability to make elegant use of it. The marketplace allowed them to establish clear social boundaries, and they increasingly mocked those who pretended to high status but failed to keep up with elegant fashion – by serving bad wine or stringy chicken, or falling behind fashions in clothing, furniture, and architecture.

Pressures of this kind rose in the seventeenth century partly because

---

[77] Forster, *The House of Saulx-Tavanes*, 121, 122; Dewald, *Pont-St-Pierre*, 193–96. For general discussion of the increasing complexities of European dining, Roger Chartier, ed., *A History of Private Life*, III, trans. Arthur Goldhammer (Cambridge, MA, 1989), 277–307.

competition was becoming increasingly visible. Far more than in earlier times, nobles could see one another's purchases, because they encountered one another at the king's court or in the increasingly aristocratic cities of the era. They could read about fashions in the increasing number of newspapers and – starting at the end of the eighteenth century – even from fashion magazines. Having up-to-date food, drink, and clothing mattered in a world where (as in the seventeenth-century city and court) what one wore and ate was regularly seen and evaluated.

Fashion mattered more for a further reason: in the sixteenth and seventeenth centuries, new groups increasingly claimed high social standing, and elegant expenditure represented an aspect of that claim. Newly rich officials, courtiers, and even soldiers built for themselves splendid new houses to affirm their arrival in high society. They offered their wives beautiful clothing and their guests splendid meals. Even the grandest noble families, those who ought to have been most secure in their own social position, had to respond to this kind of social challenge in order to maintain their own standing. Their expenditures on clothing, houses, and other goods thus mounted too. In the later eighteenth century, the very aristocratic duke of Saulx-Tavanes spent about one-quarter of his income each year on clothing and other adornments; in one case the family spent 10,000 livres – the yearly income of a well-off provincial nobleman – on a single dress. Cumulatively, the effect was to overturn budgets and absorb resources. Despite an enormous income (ten times that of a solid provincial nobleman, 100 times that of a prosperous craftsman), thus, the Saulx-Tavanes family saved and invested little, and gave almost nothing to charity; they spent almost all the income that came their way. Provincial nobles, with less money to waste than the Saulx-Tavanes, repeated the same history. The Roncherolles family, prosperous Norman landowners, found themselves hopelessly indebted in the 1760s because of long years of heedless spending. English nobles and gentry could better afford such expenditures, but they felt the same enthusiasm at what the marketplace offered them. Jane Austen's novels of country life in late eighteenth-century England present as a predictable figure the gentleman unable to control his expenditures, and as a result forced to rent out his ancestral home or undertake other economy measures. The spendthrift nobleman had become a social type.[78]

These temptations were the more threatening to familial fortunes because they coincided with an easing of credit mechanisms. Over the early modern period, it became steadily easier for nobles to get them-

---

[78] Forster, *The House of Saulx-Tavanes*, 125–27, *passim*.

selves deep in debt in their pursuit of consumer goods. Interest rates fell by about one-half in the century after 1580, and they continued to fall in the eighteenth century. In Prussia, the government itself established banks especially oriented to the nobles, allowing them to mortgage up to half their estates. In Catholic countries, reforming governments tacitly undermined restrictions on lending money at interest. Everywhere, nobles had growing opportunities to get themselves into financial trouble.[79]

Here was the most threatening economic transition that early modern nobles faced: from self-sufficiency within the estate to choosing among the increasingly tempting goods offered for sale by the market economy. The availability of so many goods had an unsettling effect on many nobles, leaving them apparently unable to limit their expenses or think in long-range terms. The market's limits and the need for local supplies had protected noble families in earlier times, for most well into the seventeenth century. Such protections fell away in the course of the seventeenth century.

Many families proved simply unable to make this transition, and spectacular bankruptcies marked their failures – spectacular partly because these families brought others down with them. All nobles usually bought on credit from shopkeepers, and many fell far behind in paying their servants. Yet most wealthy families could recover with surprising speed. The timely sale of property or of timber rights might suffice, as it did for the Saulx-Tavanes on the eve of the French Revolution. Other families turned their affairs over to business managers or trustees, who put the family on an allowance and budgeted sums to repay creditors; this was a typical pattern in England, and it also served the Condé family in seventeenth-century France: confronting enormous debts, the family put its affairs into the hands of an astute banker, and was able to resume its expenditures within a very few years.[80] In Spain as in England, property laws protected familial interests in these cases, by prohibiting the sale of the family's chief properties. Though debts might accumulate, families could thus count on passing their ancestral properties and status on to the next generation. As with the other transitions that they confronted, the wealthy nobles proved astoundingly resilient in the face of over-expenditure.

For lesser nobles, however, the story could be different and sadder. After about 1660, such figures confronted a merciless combination of pressures. Standards of elegance had risen, so that they could maintain their noble status only by expenditure; and even heavy expense might not

[79] Berdahl, "The *Stände* and the Origins of Conservatism in Prussia," 316–17.
[80] Forster, *The House of Saulx-Tavanes*, 138; Dewald, *Aristocratic Experience*, 153–54.

spare them the mockery of the more fashionable. By the mid-seventeenth century, it had become normal to make fun of the backward tastes of nobles who lived in the country, far from the influence of court and city. Their tastes in clothes, food, and wine, their manners, even their reading habits – all were subjects of mockery in the increasingly urban realm of high aristocratic society. This widening difference between rich and poor nobles' habits of consumption further strained the feudal attachments that had once held together the nobility as an order. Increasingly viewed as unpolished and out of touch, poor nobles received less hospitality and support from the rich. And with all this, their modest estates could not support high levels of debt. With so little room to maneuver and facing strong pressures to spend money to maintain their standing, the lesser nobles tended to fail much more easily than the greater. The result could be clearly seen in France. In upper Normandy, the number of nobles declined by about one-half over the eighteenth century – but average incomes of the region's nobility rose. Very simply, the poorest nobles were being forced out of existence. In 1500 such families could afford the mode of living that contemporaries expected of the nobility, because expectations were low and refinements few. After 1650 standards rose, and could only be met with large amounts of cash. For the lesser nobles, the result was a relentless drift into bankruptcy and eventual disappearance.[81]

The European nobles confronted a series of economic transformations in the early modern period, changes that can be loosely summarized as the full arrival of capitalism in the European countryside. They found themselves with wider ranges of economic choice as the period advanced. In 1500, land had offered the only form of investment that most could have imagined; by the mid-eighteenth century, many invested heavily in commercial and financial ventures, and new institutions like stock markets and state banks made these easy and relatively safe choices. By the mid-eighteenth century, nobles in many parts of Europe voiced ideologies that glorified commerce and economic development. By that point, large numbers of nobles were not landowners, and many treated their land as a pleasant adjunct to more important sources of income.

As important, the nature of landowning itself changed during these years. The late medieval estate (and in many parts of Europe this form of ownership lasted well into the sixteenth century) consisted mainly of rights and fixed rents. Most of its profits were not directly linked to agricultural production, but came instead from taxes on those who did

[81] Dewald, *Pont-St-Pierre*, 113–15.

produce. Peasant farmers paid fees for holding land within the estate, and they paid for services that the estate monopolized, such as milling and judicial protection. In most cases the estate owner directly controlled some land as well, but his principal revenues came from lordship over people rather than from the possession of things. Lordship in this sense weakened in the early modern period, a victim of both economic and political changes, but most nobles proved adaptable to the change. They constituted estates of a new kind, centered on domain lands that they controlled directly, a process helped by sixteenth-century seizures of church lands and by the growing debts of Europe's peasants. Resiliency in the face of external shocks remained a dominant theme in the nobles' history, even as the economic world around them began to function in new ways.

The new estates that emerged in the sixteenth century demanded new kinds of estate administration, indeed a new vision of what the estate was. Nobles needed to be more flexible in dealing with their properties, readier to manage them with an eye to market conditions, and they had to be more detached from the people living on or around the estate. The estate's economic setting ceased to be primarily local, and became instead regional, in some cases international: estate owners in eastern Germany were selling their grain to feed cities in Holland and contracting with Dutch experts to manage their dairy herds. With the development of the market-oriented estate came a new preoccupation with its owner's privacy, the separation of his house and land from his neighbors, if possible within a large walled park. The final change that nobles confronted followed naturally. Just as estate production increasingly oriented itself to the market, the market became increasingly the normal source of the estate owner's needs. Nobles wanted products that could only be bought in city shops, and increasingly they insisted on specialized, higher-quality versions of even goods that could have been acquired locally. This consumer revolution posed serious problems for nobles of all economic levels, yet for many resiliency again predominated. Despite close brushes with bankruptcy, they managed to control expenses and rearrange their resources.

But ultimately the consumer revolution proved the least forgiving of the changes the nobles faced, for it implied a change in the nature of the group itself. An important share of a family's status now rested on its ability to buy elegant goods, and the widening array of consumer goods made differences painfully obvious. This was not a matter of conspicuous consumption alone, though certainly the nobilities presented numerous examples of expenditure designed only to assert social superiority. More important was the growing sense that an individual's choice of material objects expressed important facts about her/his character and sensibility. As a result, economic differences counted for far more in the eighteenth century than they had earlier. In the sixteenth and early seventeenth centuries there had been a social place for poor nobles, especially in the countryside, as dependants on the wealthy. After 1660 or so, rich nobles wanted fewer dependants, and the impoverished nobleman seemed increasingly a contradiction in terms; he was someone who could not validate his claim to high status with the purchases that constituted a part of that status. As the eighteenth century opened, poorer nobles were beginning to drop from the group.

As a social group, the nobles were not necessarily weaker for the change. On the contrary, their cohesiveness as a group probably became stronger, as economic disparities within the order diminished. Certainly they fitted better within eighteenth- and nineteenth-century assumptions about how social elites ought to look: they had begun to look more like a class, that is, a group with a common economic position and common sources of wealth. At the same time, an important loss came with these changes. Nobles' control of people in the countryside radically diminished over the early modern period. This was the cost of replacing lordship with property, and the cost of their growing interest in privacy; even the decline and disappearance of the lesser nobles played a role, by removing from the scene intermediary figures who had served the great nobles' interests in local life.

3   Nobles and politics

In 1559 the French king Henry II arranged a series of spectacles to celebrate an important peace treaty. At the center of the festivities were several days of jousting by armored knights, held in the streets of Paris. An athletic warrior, Henry himself participated in the jousts, and there met his death. After tilting successfully against several members of his court, a last opponent's lance shattered against his helmet, and a splinter pierced his eye. His opponent, a young courtier, fled the scene, fearing arrest for the king's death, but returned after the king (dying slowly in a room near the scene of the joust) made clear his forgiveness.

Henry's death encapsulated important facts about power and politics in mid-sixteenth-century Europe. It demonstrated the continuing force of medieval ideals: gunpowder had appeared on European battlefields more than a century earlier, but kings and nobles continued to take seriously the armored knight, along with the skills and equipment he needed. The event also made clear the role violence played in the lives of king and nobles alike. They found in personal combat, in the public display of strength and physical skill, an appropriate image for the head of state. The king, contemporaries believed, should participate personally in warfare and should shine in hand-to-hand combat. Finally, Henry's death displayed the familiar interchange of king with nobles, the expectation that he and they should compete with one another and that they shared common ideals and amusements. When he jousted, Henry played the part of first nobleman in his kingdom, one knight among many, willing to be buffeted about by his subjects.

Henry's jousting produced extraordinary consequences, for his death helped to bring on thirty years of civil war, but the event itself was not at all unusual in sixteenth-century Europe. Other kings jousted and suffered occasional injury. Charles V, Holy Roman Emperor and king of Spain, had himself portrayed on horseback, charging an enemy, lance in hand, and the English king Henry VIII was seriously injured in a joust in 1536.[1] Kings were still expected (as they had been throughout the Middle

[1] Neville Williams, *Henry VIII and His Court* (London, 1971), 141, 156.

108

Ages) to lead their troops into battle and to share the dangers, discomforts, and excitements of camp life. In 1525 the French king Francis I (father of the unfortunate Henry II) was captured in battle and held for an enormous ransom. The event represented another disaster in French political life, but did not discourage later monarchs from entering combat. French kings gave up the habit only after 1643. The Swedish king Gustavus Adolphus died in battle in 1632; like Henry II's, his death had grave consequences for his kingdom.

Before the seventeenth century ended, however, a transformation had taken place in the nature of European kingship and in nobles' relations with their kings. The values and practices symbolized by Henry II's fatal joust had largely disappeared from the European scene. New ideas had emerged as to what the king was and how he should relate to his subjects, nobles and commoners alike. Kings now set themselves higher above their subjects, precluding the violent play that cost Henry II his life, and (though there were notable exceptions) personal participation in warfare ceased to be a normal aspect of kingship; Louis XIV only once came close to leading his troops in battle, and his successors never did. Warfare itself, of course, remained central to kings' understanding of their duties. Louis XIV was at war during most of his reign. But kings now fought mainly as planners, not as soldiers. They had become too important to risk death in battle.

Violence had lost some of its allure for nobles as well, and new conceptions had arisen as to how one might live as a nobleman. Large numbers of nobles now lived peacefully as administrators or country gentlemen; Europe's richest nobles, the English, had little experience of warfare through the seventeenth and eighteenth centuries, despite a handful of famous exceptions. This change too constituted a revolution in political values and practices, a revolution that touched personal as well as political life.

Between them, these twin changes – kings' efforts to distance themselves from their nobles, nobles' declining interest in violence – gave noble politics a surprising intensity in the early modern period. Nobles felt themselves dislodged from traditional intimacy with their kings, and they found themselves having to adapt, often awkwardly, to new social roles. The result could be a sense of insecurity that easily boiled into anger, occasionally into violence. Such anger helps to explain a paradox that surrounds the nobles' politics. They formed a ruling class that enjoyed increasing wealth and important privileges – yet for much of the period they were a rebellious group, ready not only to oppose their kings, but to encourage the lower classes to revolt as well.

Regional communities

at first power begins at home

For most European nobles, politics began in local settings, in the communities where they held their lands and lived most of their lives. This was where they competed for power and the material benefits that power could bring. Here they had to defend their households and properties, securing themselves against physical and economic attack. And here they confronted the struggle for esteem, to early modern men and women just as important a motive as the pursuit of economic advantage. Great families struggled for local preeminence, lesser families for mere respect – but for both the politics of honor formed a constant preoccupation. Local politics thus combined issues of status and respect with those of hard material calculation. As a result, no noble family could stay aloof from regional politics. Too much was at stake.

In the fifteenth and sixteenth centuries, local politics might involve outright force. In 1469 the English gentlewoman and landowner Margaret Paston described the difficult situation of one of her sons, holed up in one of the family's properties against the men of the duke of Clarence. The duke, she wrote, "hath sent for all his tenants from every place . . . to be there at Caister [the Paston property] on Thursday next coming, that there is then like to be the greatest multitude of people that came there yet. And they purpose then to make a great assault, for they have sent for guns to Lynn and other places by the sea's side, that with their great multitude of guns, with other shoot and ordnance, there shall no man dare appear in the place" on the Pastons' side. She reproached her son for his lack of energy in the matter. Loss of the castle, she wrote, would bring "the greatest rebuke to you that ever came to any gentleman, for every man in this country marvelleth greatly that you suffer them to be so long in so great jeopardy without help or other remedy."[2]

Margaret Paston's letter described the central elements of local politics as they functioned across much of Europe in the fifteenth century. First, there was the fact of violence, here used to settle a dispute over property rights. Closely related, there was the availability of the latest military technology for even private quarrels like this one; like the duke, the Pastons used artillery, and Margaret complained that the fort was running short of gunpowder. Third, there was the question of mobilizing followers. The duke's properties supplied him with men as well as income; when trouble arose, he could send "for all his tenants" in the confident expectation that they would risk their lives in his disputes. The

[2] Norman Davis, ed., *The Paston Letters: A Selection in Modern Spelling* (London, 1963), 184.

Pastons could not match the duke's range of followers, but they had their own loyalists, some of whom had already been killed in the fighting. Fourth, watching over the whole chain of events was the community of gentlemen, extending over what Margaret called "this country" and, later in the letter, "this shire of Norfolk, this troublous world" – what we would call the region.[3] As Margaret explained to her son, the community would follow and judge the events taking place, admiring honorable behavior and condemning sloth. At stake in the conflict, in other words, was status in the community as well as material interest. Finally, there was a striking silence in Margaret's letter. She made no mention of seeking the intervention of king, army, judges, or police. No clear public power stood above this struggle between noble families or could immediately bring local peace. The Pastons were not for that reason entirely alone. Margaret urged her son to negotiate for help with other great nobles and with the archbishop of York, and told him to seek legal advice in London. Outright battle represented only one step in a complex series of negotiations, but the king did not participate significantly in any stage of the process. The Pastons sought powerful political allies who could stop their enemies' advance, not protection from the monarchy.

With some variations, the Pastons' situation might have been encountered anywhere in Europe during the fifteenth century, and in many places during much of the sixteenth. Local violence could flare for basic technological and social reasons. Military technology remained readily available to all, even after the development of gunpowder began to increase the complexities of warfare. Great nobles were expected to maintain large arsenals of weapons; the government had no monopoly on the means of violence, even on its most technologically advanced forms. All nobles were expected to have had military experience, so that states had no monopoly on military skills either. Violence was so normal an experience in the Pastons' England, in fact, that 46 percent of fourteenth- and fifteenth-century dukes died violent deaths; even in the more peaceful sixteenth and seventeenth centuries, 19 percent of the dukes died this way, signs of how normal it was to use arms.[4] Eventually gunpowder would change this balance between private and public power. Weapons (and adequate fortifications to defend against them) eventually became too expensive for even great nobles to afford; and new military techniques enlarged the distance between royal and private armies. But

---

[3] Ibid., 185.
[4] T. H. Hollingsworth, "A Demographic Study of British Ducal Families," in D. V. Glass and D. E. C. Eversley, *Population in History: Essays in Historical Demography* (London, 1965), 359.

Europe only slowly absorbed the implications of gunpowder for the sociology of war. Until about 1550, great nobles could assemble arsenals that rivalled those of the state. Local conflicts quickly turned violent, then, partly because nobles had the means of violence so ready to hand, and because they could fight effectively even against the power of the state itself.[5]

But the political and social conditions of local conflict were just as important. During the late Middle Ages, kings and nobles alike took for granted the legitimacy of private warfare. In 1318, for instance, the king of France ordered his nobles to suspend all private wars – but only temporarily, so as to allow them to join his military campaign in Flanders; and even his ban acknowledged that the "customary laws of the region and [royal] privileges" allowed for private war.[6] Practical politics likewise demanded fighting. The Pastons lived in what was probably the best-governed corner of fifteenth-century Europe, yet even they knew that the central government would not settle their differences with the duke of Clarence: Margaret Paston urged a search for aristocratic allies, not the intervention of governmental police forces. Elsewhere, governments might be weaker still, leaving whole regions prey to warlords. A chronicler described conditions in mid-fourteenth-century France: "Sir Eustace d'Aubrecicourt maintained himself in Champagne," the prosperous region to the east of Paris; "he was [its] virtual master. Whenever he liked he could assemble at a day's notice seven hundred to a thousand fighting men," which set out on almost daily raids, enriching both Eustace and his followers.[7] In areas farther from the centers of law and order, conditions like these persisted through the sixteenth century. In northern Spain, early seventeenth-century nobles still sponsored gangs of bandits, and a visitor from Madrid voiced his amazement at a region where nobles "cannot go out of town without a large number of men" to protect them.[8]

To function in this way as private warlords, nobles needed troops as well as weapons. They found them in institutions that we have already examined. Rich nobles, we have seen, expected to live surrounded by hordes of servants, many of them drawn from the lesser nobility itself. Lower in the social scale, farmers too might find themselves called upon to support the nobles whose land they worked; the disloyal risked losing

---

[5] Lawrence Stone, *The Crisis of the Aristocracy, 1558–1641* (Oxford, 1965), 217–23.
[6] Marie Thérèse Caron, *Noblesse et pouvoir royal en France, XIIIe–XVIe siècle* (Paris, 1994), 40.
[7] Jean Froissart, *Chronicles*, selected and trans. Geoffrey Brereton, (London, 1968), 161.
[8] J. H. Elliott, *The Revolt of the Catalans* (Cambridge, 1963), 75.

the lands they rented or positions they held. An early seventeenth-century Polish nobleman summed up the feelings of his fellow nobles across Europe: "whoever takes a lease from me becomes my serving man."[9]

Nobles could usually find followers for their political ventures. At the same time, to preserve these patronage connections required that nobles be politically venturesome. Leaders who failed to provide for their followers' material needs could not hope to sustain loyalty; even in the late Middle Ages, the relationship rested partly on material rewards, rather than on abstract fidelity. Patrons had to show their power, by defending their followers' material interests and securing new resources for them. These facts gave a twofold instability to the system of fidelity and service. There was the steady movement of followers from one leader to another, often with violent resentments on each side. As important, there was the constant pressure on leaders to find the resources that would keep their followers loyal. To preserve the loyalty of dozens of followers – and really great nobles might have hundreds of such men to provide for – required a constant flow of resources, constant demonstrations of the leader's ability to help. Leaders needed dependants if they were to act effectively, and they needed to act if they were to secure the resources that would preserve their dependants' loyalty.

Just as fidelity between rich and poor nobles covered contradictory practices and ideals, so also the regional community within which nobles acted posed contradictions. For nobles thinking about the regions within which they lived, the community of those who mattered was a small, even intimate place: those who mattered socially and politically numbered only in the dozens, for the mass of non-nobles (it was assumed) could be safely disregarded. Men and women within these limited boundaries knew one another and carefully followed one another's affairs. Everyone knew who were the richest and most powerful families, and these figures expected to dominate local institutions. Well into the seventeenth century, for instance, elections to the English House of Commons showed this expectation at work. In theory candidates might compete for election as county representatives to Parliament; in fact, the leading families in each county needed to do little more than express their desires, in order for voters to follow their directions.[10] Nowhere else were

---

[9] Quoted Andrzej Pośipech and Wojciech Tygielski, "The Social Role of the Magnates' Courts in Poland (from the End of the 16th up to the 18th Century)," *Acta Poloniae Historica*, 43 (1981), 84; Stone, *The Crisis of the Aristocracy*, 214–16.

[10] Mark Kishlansky, *Parliamentary Selection: Social and Political Choice in Early Modern England* (Cambridge, 1986), 13–14, 22–31, 54–72.

parliamentary institutions so powerful as in England, but many regions had more modest equivalents. In France, Spain, Scandinavia, and Germany, parliaments, usually known as estates, were expected to give their consent before taxes could be levied, and they had the right to propose legislation; nobles usually had their own chamber in these institutions, an institution that required collaboration and encouraged friendships within the order. In some regions, like Brittany in western France, the annual meeting of the estates became one of the primary social events of the year, with a round of feasting and dancing. But such institutions only gave clear expression to a basic social reality: nobles spent much of their political lives within local communities that were small, clearly ranked, closely followed, intimately known.[11]

Yet these very qualities might produce silent tensions or open conflicts within the regional community of nobles. Closely aware of one another's claims and rankings, nobles inevitably competed with their neighbors. Belief in social hierarchy might make competition extraordinarily bitter – for in so hierarchical a world, a world in which each noble family had a slightly different status, any man or woman's gain could come only at another's expense. During the sixteenth and seventeenth centuries, nobles typically expressed this understanding of the world in a constant awareness of precedence, a concern with rights to march first in processions, occupy honored offices, hold the best seats in church. Struggles over such matters – often preposterously trivial in themselves, but terribly important to those involved – might last for generations and divide loyalties across entire regions, as when the two greatest families in seventeenth-century Brittany struggled over leadership of the provincial estates. Whatever common interests and experiences united the provincial community balanced uneasily against these sources of competition. Provincial unity was fragile. Nobles within a region found themselves united around certain basic assumptions, rather than on specific political choices. Other conditions further restricted provincial unanimity. Regional communities changed continually, we have seen, as new nobles moved in and old families declined. Inevitably, hierarchies of status and wealth were reshuffled as a result, and painful conflicts might ensue. More important, concrete interests might diverge substantially. Noble families might find themselves in very different economic circumstances, and their relations with the centers of power might be very different.

[11] For examples of these institutions, J. R. Major, *Representative Government in Early Modern France* (New Haven, 1980); Manfred Orlea, *La Noblesse aux Etats Généraux de 1576 et de 1588* (Paris, 1980); James Collins, *Classes, Estates, and Order in Early Modern Brittany* (Cambridge, 1994); R. J. W. Evans, *The Making of the Habsburg Monarchy, 1550–1700* (Oxford, 1979), 166–67; F. L. Carsten, *Princes and Parliaments in Germany from the Fifteenth to the Eighteenth Century* (Oxford, 1959).

The regional community and political change

Events like the Pastons' encounter with the duke of Clarence illustrated one of the driving forces of early modern political change. Substantial families like the Pastons wanted stronger central government, for provincial communities were too unstable and too ineffectual to provide orderly settlement of disputes. Violence was always costly, even when (as with the Pastons and many others) families knew how to combine violence with litigation and political string-pulling; when the contest involved well-armed opponents like the duke of Clarence, who could bring both superior weapons and stronger political alliances to the contest, the method proved especially inadequate. Middling nobles had much to lose from violence; at the same time, they could afford the costs of alternative methods of conflict settlement, such as litigation. Such families represented a sizable constituency in favor of strong government.

They had another interest in seeing violence brought under control. Crime by those lower on the social scale seemed especially threatening in the fifteenth and early sixteenth centuries. A French edict of 1431 described the mood of fear there: "The nobles like others have suffered personal injuries and financial losses; their tenants have been kidnapped and killed, and they dare not leave their homes . . . for fear that these will be pillaged and that their wives and daughters will be raped."[12] In England there were comparable anxieties: "I should send you money," wrote Margaret Paston to her son, in 1471, "but I dare not put it in jeopardy, there be so many thieves stirring."[13] Less frequent but still more frightening were rebellions by the lower classes. Dramatic peasant rebellions had touched much of western Europe in the late fourteenth century, and in the early sixteenth century the Lutheran Reformation brought new movements to western Germany. Later experiences only confirmed this fear of the lower orders. France witnessed numerous serious rebellions in the century after 1590, and so too did the Habsburg lands of Austria, Bohemia, and Hungary. Families like the Pastons had good reason to want stronger government, because only government could control the varied sources of violence that seemed to threaten them. Many nobles remained convinced of their right to exercise private violence, but the usefulness of governmental order increasingly seemed more important. In the end, their demand for strong government outweighed other values.

States responded to this political demand first by expanding their

[12] Quoted Caron, *Noblesse et pouvoir royal*, 279–80.
[13] Davis, *The Paston Letters*, 206.

judicial apparatus. The later fifteenth and sixteenth centuries saw the establishment of numerous new law courts and the creation of an abundant personnel of jurists and lawyers to work in them. We have already seen the example of France, with its fiftyfold increase in the number of courts between 1450 and 1550, and still more dramatic increase in numbers of jurists. This was not only an era of expansion in the legal professions, but of elaboration in legal codes. In France traditional laws were codified, reviewed, and published, and a series of great law codes from the king codified legal practices. In Germany the story was similar. Official codes, usually based on Roman law, were written out and published, and new courts of law enforced them.[14]

By the 1550s, litigation had begun to replace violence in the settlement of local disputes. For nobles with any significant property holdings, this meant incessant litigation and constant interchanges with the legal system. Nobles could have no doubt about the growing power of the state in the sixteenth and seventeenth centuries, for they had constantly to deal with the state and its agents; decisions by the state's judges could entirely overthrow a family's economic circumstances. Faced with this potential power, nobles had to be deferential. They found themselves waiting as humble petitioners before even minor judges and officials.

With these increasingly powerful judges there appeared another, closely related figure: the governmental commissioner, sent by governments to investigate local situations and further the state's aims. Such interventions began as responses to local demands for conflict settlement, but they soon took on a more autonomous quality, as governments sought out and tried to solve local problems. We have already seen what such efforts might mean for estate owners. Nobles found their property rights subject to close inspection by government commissioners, on the grounds that the estate owner might have usurped crown rights. They found the state's commissioners defending peasants' rights, since the peasants paid most of the state's taxes.

Other developments accompanied and reinforced this rise of litigation. Above all, there was a slow and uneven decline in nobles' readiness to use violence for settling disputes. Historians have charted the process by tracing the history of duelling and the histories of other violent crimes. In France, the judicial duel – in which legal right was established in physical combat between the two litigants – remained a living reality in the mid-sixteenth century: king Henry II presided over the last such event in French history, a dozen years before his own death by jousting, and

---

[14] On the implications of the spread of Roman law, John P. Dawson, *The Oracles of the Law* (Ann Arbor, 1968), 176–232, 266 ff.; James Q. Whitman, *The Legacy of Roman Law in the German Romantic Era: Historical Vision and Legal Change* (Princeton, 1990), 4ff.

watched as one of the litigants killed the other by a tricky piece of swordsmanship. Thereafter state-sponsored fighting between nobles died out, but in compensation private bloodshed developed rapidly. During the early seventeenth century, a historian has estimated, about 350 French nobles died each year in duels. The French count Montmorency-Bouteville, from one of the country's grandest families, seems to have had no other real object in life than duelling. Starting at age fifteen, he had fought twenty-two duels by the time he was twenty-eight.[15]

But careers like his contributed to a growing revulsion at pointless bloodshed and led toward a drop in duelling's popularity. In 1627 Montmorency-Bouteville figured in a widely publicized episode that showed the dawning readiness of government to control such private violence. Having been forgiven for his previous killings, Montmorency was warned not to try the king's patience further. Instead, he and several young friends fought in one of the most elegant squares in Paris, effectively daring the king to take action. To general amazement (and to Montmorency's own) the king and his chief advisor the Cardinal Richelieu took up the challenge, arrested Montmorency, and had him tried and beheaded. To contemporaries this seemed an extraordinary event, defying conventional ideas about both behavior and high birth. The king had asserted his right to judge even the greatest aristocrat, and his right to control practices that had at least wide acceptance. It implied a still broader idea, that the state had a monopoly on violence itself; the king determined when violence could be exercised. Montmorency-Bouteville's trial opened a prolonged and eventually successful campaign against duelling. By the 1660s it had lost much of its luster. Private violence like this had ceased to be a social norm, even a proud obligation, and had become instead something of an aberration. Spanish rulers acted in similar ways, arresting those who fought and proclaiming intolerance of the practice.[16]

Other forms of private violence diminished at about the same time. Increasingly, nobles found themselves being taught the virtues of self-control. A wave of behavior manuals, more or less directly imitating Baldesar Castiglione's 1528 *The Courtier*, taught the message; so did humanist schoolteachers, influenced by the Dutch writer Erasmus, whose best-selling books made fun of the violent and boorish nobleman. Ideals of romantic love were encouraged at court, and likewise led to control of violence. As more nobles moved to the cities, they found closer controls over their behavior and additional pressures for good manners.

---

[15] François Billacois, *Le Duel dans la société française des XVIe–XVIIe siècles: essai de psychologie historique* (Paris, 1986), 83–93, 115, 247ff.

[16] Billacois, *Le Duel*, 247ff., 381; Elliott, *The Revolt of the Catalans*, 125–26.

All of these pressures worked slowly, but by the later seventeenth century their effects were obvious. "I could travel from Madrid to Almazan [the site of his estates]," wrote a Spanish nobleman in 1613, "alone or with a single servant, without being afraid of anybody." In this region of Spain, at least, the dangers of feuding and brigandage had largely ended – though the story was different in outlying areas. In France crime statistics tell a similar story. England had been largely pacified by the early seventeenth century, and by 1660 such private violence had largely disappeared from Austria, Bohemia, and Germany. Early modern societies remained violent by modern standards. Nobles continued to carry weapons and occasionally used them. Duelling even enjoyed a renaissance in the nineteenth century, now usually carried out with pistols rather than swords. Yet the quantity of blood spilled had diminished enormously. The eighteenth-century state could claim with some reason that it controlled violence, and that citizens could receive from the state protection of their interests.[17]

Community within the country changed as well. Nobles could no longer rely so easily on their neighbors' support after about 1650. The change has been documented for English elections: whereas in 1600 leading gentlemen and peers could expect unanimous support from the gentry community, since everyone agreed on the community's natural leadership, after 1660 dissent became the norm. Electoral contests became more common and more hard-fought, as gentlemen ceased to accept the natural leadership of the most eminent local landowners.[18] Status, in other words, ceased to guarantee a following. At the same time, as we have seen the great made fewer efforts to keep lesser figures loyal. There was less hospitality in great houses, fewer opportunities for employment with great men.

Revolution at the center: kings, administrators, subjects

Rising demand for the kinds of order that government could supply, growing willingness to accept the peaceful settlement of disputes – these formed the first element in states' relations with the early modern nobilities. There was a second element in these relations, states' increasing need to organize themselves for new conditions of warfare. These changes were already apparent by the mid-sixteenth century, despite the

[17] Elliott, *The Revolt of the Catalans*, 75; Iain Cameron, *Crime and Repression in the Auvergne and the Guyenne, 1700–1790* (Cambridge, 1981), 119, 197–203; Stone, *The Crisis of the Aristocracy*, 199–242; Evans, *The Making of the Habsburg Monarchy*, 107.

[18] Kishlansky, *Parliamentary Selection*, esp. 225–30.

continuing eagerness of kings like Henry II to present themselves as chivalric heroes. By this time, warfare was becoming increasingly complex and expensive. Armies had grown, and the new gunpowder technology required better training; new systems of fortification demanded vast sums of money and encouraged a new profession, that of specialized military architects. States could not remain aloof from these developments, for significant parts of Europe were at war throughout the early modern period. Those that refused to arm themselves risked losing out to stronger neighbors. Thus everywhere armies grew. The process continued with few interruptions into the eighteenth century. In France the wartime army had numbered at most 50,000 soldiers in the early sixteenth century; by 1700 it had grown to about 340,000, with another 200,000 men involved in some form of occasional armed service. Early eighteenth-century England was less populous and less bellicose than France, yet it too had enormous armed forces: 70,000 soldiers and 50,000 sailors.[19]

All of this had to be paid for, and their need for funds encouraged monarchs to pursue two, interrelated policies. They needed of course to tax their subjects, on a scale that medieval rulers had never dreamed of. And they hoped to make their subjects richer, so as to enlarge their tax bases and reduce the tensions that heavy taxes produced. The two aims converged in a single governmental strategy, that of a closer, more attentive, often more interventionist administration of society's resources. The strategy demanded new administrators, both to collect taxes and to compile the mass of information that efficient collection would require. Under the efficient prodding of fiscal greed, governments began compiling increasingly careful listings of population, property, and economic activity. Bureaucracies grew everywhere in sixteenth- and seventeenth-century Europe, often in brief bursts that made growth especially traumatic to conservative nobles. Sweden, which only acquired an important place in European power politics in the 1620s, offered a striking example: its fiscal and judicial administrations were essentially created between 1618 and 1634, bringing into existence a whole range of positions that had never before existed in the country.[20] Nowhere else was the process so rapid. Yet the Swedish example captures a fact of wider relevance. Sixteenth- and seventeenth-century governments expanded in revolutionary leaps, rather than by small additions.

[19] John A. Lynn, "Recalculating French Army Growth during the *Grand Siècle*, 1610–1715," *French Historical Studies*, 18, 4 (Fall, 1994), 881–906; William Wilcox and Walter L. Arnstein, *The Age of Aristocracy, 1688–1830* (Lexington, MA, 1992), 38–39. On the causes, character, and results of military expansion, Geoffrey Parker, *The Military Revolution: Military Innovation and the Rise of the West* (Cambridge, 1988).

[20] Michael Roberts, *Gustavus Adolphus*, 2nd edn (London, 1992), 76–77.

Such changes struck contemporaries the more sharply because other forces too encouraged government's expansion. There was more litigation, hence more need for lawyers and judges. An expanding commerce required its own forms of officialdom, to regulate disputes, control international trade, build roads and bridges. New officials seemed to be appearing everywhere.

Inexorably, these changes affected relations between king and nobles. Often desperate for tax revenues, kings could not afford complete respect for nobles' tax exemptions, no matter how iron-clad these might be in theory. In one country after another, thus, kings demanded increasing levels of taxation from their nobles. Nobles continued to pay less than other subjects, but the difference ceased to be so great as it once was. Nor could kings afford to be patient with representative assemblies – the estates that brought together nobles, bourgeois, and churchmen to consent to taxation and present grievances to the king. To kings these seemed only to impede the urgently needed work of government. Some kings might be more tolerant than others, or at least better at disguising their impatience. The enormously popular Swedish king Gustavus Adolphus preserved his nation's estates, while manipulating their consent to a series of burdensome tax increases. The inept English king Charles I failed to persuade his Parliament to approve any of his ventures, then sought to rule without it – only to call it back into session in 1640, its members in a revolutionary fury. The German state of Saxony illustrated another possibility: in the 1690s its prince made a number of important political and fiscal decisions without the estates' approval, but reached a compromise with them, assuring their continuing political voice. French kings followed a more forceful strategy, succeeding where their English rivals failed. After 1615 they refused to convene their estates, and ruled successfully without them for the next 175 years. Thus liberated from the need to secure consent, the French kings succeeded in 1695 in imposing significant taxes on the nobles. The fiscal revolution of the early modern years thus had consequences for Europe's political institutions. Rulers challenged both nobles' exemptions from taxation and their longstanding right to consent to any taxes that they did pay.[21]

Just as important, kings found their own role changing in these circumstances. As war came to involve hundreds of thousands of soldiers, often spread over vast areas, their responsibility lay increasingly with making war possible and with directing its broad strategies, more than with personally leading its execution. However sympathetic they were to the military enterprise, few kings could combine this role with life as one

[21] See above, Chapter 1, for the narrowing of nobles' tax exemptions throughout Europe.

soldier among many. Now kings lived mainly among bureaucrats and increasingly shared their concerns. Already in the mid-sixteenth century, the Spanish king Philip II exemplified this role. Philip was at war through most of his reign, but (unlike his father and his French rivals) he directed war from his office, rather than at the head of an army. In keeping with this approach, he established a permanent court in Madrid to be the administrative center of these efforts. Reports reached him from throughout his empire, and through his responses he attempted to direct strategy on several fronts. Philip, in other words, detached statecraft and power politics from chivalric individualism. He fought as an administrator, and other kings increasingly did the same. Louis XIV fought wars throughout his long reign, but like his Spanish ancestor Philip II he fought them from a fixed administrative center, his palace at Versailles, outside Paris. In Germany, kings gave up their active military role more reluctantly. Frederick II of Prussia led his troops in battle and made provision for his possible capture by the enemy; even the unglamorous George II of England led one notable military advance in defense of his German possessions. Despite their example, an important change had taken place in relations between king and nobles. He had ceased to be their companion in arms.

The administrative needs of increasingly complex states thus placed nobles at a widening distance from their kings – and in uncomfortable proximity to ordinary people, whose fiscal burdens they increasingly had to share. Still more difficult for the nobles, kings' beliefs about the significance of royalty were also changing. Though with many complicated nuances, early modern kings tended to attach increasing grandeur to monarchy, to stress the holiness of their functions and the distances that this created from even aristocratic subjects. Louis XIV emphasized that all rewards came from him, not from the merits of those who received them; the needs of royal policy might in fact require rewarding the less rather than the more deserving. Ceremonies surrounding the king made the point in a public way. At Louis XIV's Versailles, the king ate alone, separated from all others by railings and by servants – a sharp contrast to his father's practice of living informally among his friends. Violent physical contact with his subjects, of the sort that Henry II had so enjoyed, now seemed unthinkable. Coronation services increasingly stressed the king's distance from other mortals and the special qualities of royal blood. Political theory followed suit, and suggested that the king's need superseded any rights of his subjects no matter how reasonable or lawful they might appear. Jean Bodin initiated this line of thought in the later sixteenth century, arguing that monarchs had absolute powers to legislate, and seventeenth-century theorists developed his ideas at length.

From the sixteenth century on, then, nobles confronted a change in the nature of monarchy itself. Henry II had presented himself as like other nobles, had shared their ideals, and had interacted with them on relatively equal terms. A century later, Louis XIV permitted no one to feel such likeness. His reign stressed instead the distance between king and all subjects, nobles included.

The court

Relations between king and nobles were chiefly hammered out within one of the period's most important institutions, the royal court. This was the collection of servants, suppliers, leading officials, and favored nobles who lived around the king. The court provided the king with both the pleasures of companionship and with practical services; here critical political decisions were arrived at and important appointments were made, often on the basis of the personal relations that developed within the court. The court thus exemplified the nearly universal overlap in early modern society between the political and the personal spheres of life. At court, the distinction in fact lost all meaning. Kings sought advice from those they felt comfortable with, from their friends, mistresses, and spiritual advisors, as well as from officials.

Kings had always had courts around them, for they had always needed service and entertainment, and they had always had resources to give out. Just like nobles on their estates, they had no desire to live alone; they wanted crowds of people around, even in what we would view as private moments. During the fourteenth and fifteenth centuries, in fact, kings' courts differed little from those of their richest subjects; at several points in these years, the leading French nobles had larger and more elaborate courts than the king. But in the sixteenth and seventeenth centuries this balance changed. Kings now had more money at their disposal, and they were becoming more intent on asserting their powers and placing themselves at the center of national culture.[22] In effect, the court could serve as a propaganda machine, advertising national glory and demonstrating the prince's command of his leading subjects.

Hence the first systematic efforts to make full political use of the court came in small and peripheral states, rather than in the great powers, and in fact grew from political weakness. Rulers of small states like the fifteenth-century duchy of Burgundy – a collection of territories carved from eastern France and the Netherlands – used the glamor of their courts to establish authority and legitimacy. By attracting their nobles

---

[22] See Caron, *Noblesse et pouvoir royal en France*, 188–90, 256–57.

with the pleasures and excitement of court life, the dukes established practical authority within their lands, and they also attracted international notice; their court helped the dukes in their claim to a place among Europe's leading states. The dukes spent accordingly, on festivals, elegant food and dress, and literary patronage to glorify their doings, and they encouraged refinement of manners. "As for the duke's court . . .," wrote an English visitor in 1468, "I heard never of none like to it save King Arthur's court." His comment illustrated the connection contemporaries perceived between the grandeur of court life and a government's claim to share in Europe's monarchical traditions. Power and legitimacy, it was believed, manifested themselves in the grandeur that surrounded the prince. Similar efforts occurred in the small Italian states of the fifteenth and early sixteenth centuries, which likewise deployed substantial resources in order to make court life glamorous and attract important men to it.[23]

Fashions from Burgundy and Italy spread to the great powers of western Europe in the sixteenth century, and by 1600 courts there too had come to play a dominant social role. As late as 1550 wealthy French nobles had spent the bulk of their time at home in the countryside, coming to court only when they had to. The same was true of England. Early in his reign Henry VIII occasionally complained about the small number of nobles who attended him, and lists had to be drawn up to ensure that the king had a suitable number of dinner companions. By 1600, however, nobles were all too eager to be at court. Their numbers produced occasional rowdiness and repeated efforts to drive them back to the countryside; in 1632 and 1634 the English king Charles I actually prosecuted nobles who came to London without specific royal invitation, on the grounds that their presence led to excessive spending and the neglect of rural duties. But the pleasures of court life were too strong for even the king to resist, and legal action had little effect.[24]

What exactly did these people seek at court, and why did its pleasures seem so tantalizing? In part of course they sought power, and government remained sufficiently personal in 1600 that much power could only come from direct contact with the king. Like modern lobbyists, nobles came to court as petitioners for jobs, favorable rulings in judicial matters, direct financial help. For a tiny number, success at court meant still more. The

---

[23] Quoted A. G. Dickens, ed., *The Courts of Europe: Politics, Patronage and Royalty, 1400–1800* (New York, 1977), 70; the collection offers excellent sketches of the leading European courts and their political functioning.

[24] Lucien Romier, *Le Royaume de Catherine de Médicis: la France à la veille des guerres de religions*, 4th edn, 2 vols. (Paris, 1925), I, 160–62; G. R. Elton, *The Tudor Revolution in Government: Administrative Changes in the Reign of Henry VIII* (Cambridge, 1952), 42–43; Stone, *The Crisis of the Aristocracy*, 397–98.

sixteenth and seventeenth centuries formed the great age of the court favorite, young men and women who attracted the prince's attention and became his intimate friends or even his lovers. In early seventeenth-century England, thus, there was the duke of Buckingham, handsome enough that he aroused the sexual interest of king James I and ingratiating enough that James's successor Charles I relied on him as an intimate advisor; both kings lavished wealth on Buckingham, making him one of the richest nobles in the country. Such affections were something of a royal fashion in the early seventeenth century, with exactly similar situations in Spain and France. Many of the lucky beneficiaries had begun life in modest circumstances, in the lesser nobility, but royal favor raised them to positions among the very high nobility. Only a few won such prizes, but the stakes were high enough to draw numerous hopefuls to court.

cultural

But the court had a deeper appeal than such hopes for wealth and power. It seemed to meet important cultural and psychological needs, by offering a model of life that contemporaries could find deeply appealing, even thrilling. The appeal was so great that a series of best-selling books described the ideals and experiences of life at court for eager readers who might never see it themselves. Baldesar Castiglione's *The Courtier* appeared in Italy in 1528; a Spanish translation appeared six years later and an English version in 1561. A French imitation, much of it wholesale plagiarism, appeared soon after and became one of the most frequently reprinted books of the early seventeenth century. Readers' enthusiasm suggests the power that the court exercised over sixteenth-century imaginations. Princes had practical motives for making their courts more inviting and glamorous, but their efforts also responded to desires in society at large.

We can understand some of these desires by examining Castiglione's vision of the court and its people.[25] *The Courtier* presented itself as an historical record, a depiction of several evenings' conversations at the court of Urbino, a small duchy in Italy. Conversation in fact formed part of the ideal of life that the book proposed. There was the glitter of quick-witted interchange among the court's residents, as they lightly debated ideas about what the courtier and the court should be like. There was also the format's implied skepticism: as each character presented his/her ideas, the reader became aware that there was no single truth in

---

[25] Citations here are taken from Baldesar Castiglione, *The Book of the Courtier*, ed. and trans. Charles Singleton (Garden City, NY, 1959). For discussion of the book's contexts, see Dickens, *The Courts of Europe*, 33–53; for insightful discussion of its themes, Robert Hanning and David Rosand, eds., *Castiglione: The Ideal and the Real in Renaissance Culture* (New Haven, 1983).

these issues, that multiple ethical readings were possible on even important issues. *The Courtier* appealed partly because of its message about the relativity of truth.

This conversation occurred within a space that Castiglione described as enclosed and protected. The duke had furnished his new palace so well, Castiglione wrote, "that it seemed not a palace, but a city in the form of a palace."[26] The court thus envisioned promised material comfort, then, but also something more: it promised to be a space closed off from the cares, disruptions, and inconveniences of ordinary life, a world of its own. The court was a place of delight also in the more specific sense, that it included beautiful women and sexual excitement. Castiglione's women participated with the men in the debates about the courtier's qualities, joked with each other, and repeatedly raised questions about love. It is important to recognize this affirmation of relative sexual equality and of the presence of sexual feeling itself, for these made the court nearly unique in early modern life. Nearly everywhere else, women were resolutely excluded from social life and from power. Schools, universities, and learned academies excluded women altogether; the learned professions not only excluded women, but dressed their members in dark clerical costumes that symbolized affinity with the priesthood and rejection of sexual feeling. Unlike these other centers of early modern learning, the courtier's world admitted women and love, and even displayed moments of women commanding men. Castiglione's world presented a combination of protective enclosure and lively freedom.[27]

It was a world that was also open to outsiders, even to non-nobles. Castiglione's conversationalists assumed that many of those who appeared at the court would be newcomers, who would establish themselves by virtue of their own abilities; newcomers were inevitable, given the court's function as a center of power and status. This fact led the characters to debate the further question, does the courtier need to be noble? They concluded that noble birth was desirable in the courtier, for it created an initial good impression among those who met him; but they also assumed the possibility that he would be a commoner, who needed to rely on other qualities to make his way. One of the speakers, in fact, argued for the superiority of the non-noble, as someone making his way more by virtue of ability than of birth.

At the center of the court and of the courtier's life, as Castiglione presented the matter, stood the figure of the prince himself. "I would

---

[26] Castiglione, *The Book of the Courtier*, 13.
[27] For reflection on this point, Marc Fumaroli, "Le 'langage de cour' en France: problèmes et points de repère," in August Buck et al., eds., *Europäische Hofkultur im 16. und 17. Jahrhundert*, II (Hamburg, 1981).

have the courtier devote all his thought and strength of spirit to loving and almost adoring the prince he serves above all else, devoting his every desire and habit and manner to pleasing him."[28] *The Courtier* thus offered a strongly monarchical vision, according to which the courtier had no rights against the prince, but only the duty of complete subordination – inward as well as outward, for the courtier was to bend not just his actions but even his private feelings toward serving the prince. Yet the book also nuanced this ideology of subordination by its depiction of actual relations between courtiers and prince. For the prince of Urbino as Castiglione presented him was a weak figure. Gout-ridden since the age of twenty, he could barely move; his political plans had mainly failed; and his infirmities prevented him from taking part in the lively discussions that made up most of the book. These took place in his wife's chambers, after he had gone to bed; and the duchess had apparently transferred her interest from the impotent prince to a lively young courtier. In theory the courtier was to subordinate his own identity to that of the prince; in practice, Castiglione displayed a life free of princely intervention. Again, the vision was extraordinarily appealing, combining theoretical devotion to the ruler with depictions of the courtier's actual autonomy, even superiority.[29]

Finally, Castiglione presented the courtier's life as one of activity and engagement in the affairs of the world. Ideally the courtier was to be a soldier, and he was to spend much of his time preparing for that role by learning the skills of war. But he was also to be a political participant, whose function was to advise his prince, and for this task he needed to be educated, with sufficient literary knowledge that he could speak persuasively before the prince and his other counsellors. More than education, however, the courtier needed charm if he was to be an effective advisor, for he had to secure the prince's good will before he could supply effective advice. Thus the courtier needed to study and control all his actions, if he was to play the proper political role. He had to move gracefully, with an easy lightness. He should undertake nothing that he could not carry off gracefully and without strain. *The Courtier*, in other words, presented the body and even the inner feelings as malleable, capable of being trained to elegant and pleasing actions. The courtier was to discipline his habits, thus in some sense remake himself in a form that would attract and impress others.

As *The Courtier* presented it, then, life at court offered more than material rewards and chances to mingle with the great. Castiglione's

[28] Castiglione, *The Book of the Courtier*, 110.
[29] For a somewhat different reading of these issues, Thomas M. Greene, "*Il Cortegiano* and the Choice of A Game," in Hanning and Rosand, *Castiglione*, 1–15.

court appealed to a powerful combination of ideals: it was orderly yet free, enclosed yet open to able outsiders, a field for masculine action yet one marked by the presence of women and of sexual feeling. Bringing together so many apparently contradictory qualities, the court not surprisingly attracted all who could have a claim to join it. For many others, the court provided a powerful image of contemporary life. Most of those who read Castiglione and his imitators had no hope of actually enjoying the festivities they read about; nor did most of those who watched the plays of Shakespeare and Racine, which were so often set in court contexts, have any direct knowledge of courtly life. The playwrights set their dramas at court because it supplied such powerful ideals of human life.

Ideals and realities

Castiglione's images of court life appealed to readers all across Europe because they offered a vision of personality flowering within a political setting. Princes had no need to force nobles into the court setting thus imagined; on the contrary, courtliness had enormous appeal. But of course other images circulated of the court, many of them less delightful. Shakespeare's *Hamlet*, from around 1600, displayed the fears that contemporaries had about court life. At the court of Denmark as Shakespeare imagined it, the perils of life at court are more apparent than the delights; most of its residents have hidden interests in the events of court life, and few are exactly what they seem. Dissimulation is here central to court life.

Hamlet proposes a series of themes about court life that had powerful resonance in the sixteenth and seventeenth centuries. The court appears in this instance as a world of falsehood, which requires of its members a special stance toward relations with others. Surrounded by self-interested calculations, Hamlet can turn only to his intimate friend – or to himself. Castiglione's characters had moved in a world of social pleasures, in which conversation delights and fulfills the individuals who participate. In *Hamlet* conversation mainly traps the unwary, and individuals are essentially alone. Other playwrights and novelists took up this image of the court's isolating effect; everyone understood that court life demanded careful self-control, the ability to conceal one's inner thoughts. European nobles regarded the court with a mixture of excitement and anxiety. But fear did nothing to weaken people's readiness to come to court and join in its pleasures. In fact Hamlet's vision of the possibilities of court life was not so distant from Castiglione's. Both stressed the courtier's need for self-control and inner discipline; both made life at court a scene for individualism, a setting in which the individual needed to preserve his/her private thoughts from others' scrutiny. *Hamlet* merely brought to the fore the frightening sides of individualism.[30]

Where did real courts fit between the images of Castiglione and those of *Hamlet*? In some ways the distance from Castiglione's ideals remained enormous, even at the most glamorous courts, for they all were crowded, bustling, often uncomfortable places. Ordinary people had easy access to most courts until the early seventeenth century, so that crowds of petitioners, beggars, suppliers, and swindlers mingled with the courtiers and high officials. Life at court might seem more a chaotic free-for-all than the gracious elegance Castiglione described. In addition, most courts moved about, partly following the whims of rulers and their favorites, partly for solid political reasons. Subjects' obedience depended on personal feeling for their rulers; rulers knew that they had to be seen. For courtiers this meant the discomforts of travel and the chaos of finding lodging when the court reached its new site. A few courts settled down in the mid-sixteenth century, most dramatically the Spanish court, which established itself in Madrid in 1561, but some continued travelling into the 1660s; this was the case with Louis XIV, before he decided on Versailles as a permanent capital. Numbers compounded the discomforts of travel. Thousands of people might follow an important court, and they quickly overwhelmed whatever locality had to house them. In 1577 about 8,000 people were officially attached to the French court, along with the mob of suppliers and hangers-on that the court attracted. When the Spanish king Philip II moved his court from Toledo to Madrid, 25,000 people moved along with him. Early in the eighteenth century, the miniature German state of Württemberg had a court of 1,800 people – roughly one person for every 300 who lived in the duchy. Thus crowded, courtiers needed to push if they were to be noticed and given the rewards they had come hoping for. They could not afford too much dignity, nor did they worry unduly about delicate hygiene. Life at court might be a rough and tumble business.[31]

Yet that life also moved closer to Castiglione's ideals over the sixteenth and seventeenth centuries. *The Courtier* (like *Hamlet*) made it clear that the successful courtier needed to train him/herself, so as to perform

---

[30] Rebecca West, *The Court and the Castle* (New Haven, 1957), offers a brilliant analysis of *Hamlet* in these terms.

[31] Jacqueline Boucher, *La Cour de Henri III* (Rennes, 1986), 39; M. J. Rodrguez-Salgado, "The Court of Philip II of Spain," in Ronald G. Asch and Adolf M. Birke, *Princes, Patronage, and the Nobility: The Court at the Beginning of the Modern Age, ca. 1450–1650* (Oxford, 1991), 215; James Allen Vann, *The Making of a State: Württemberg, 1593–1793* (Ithaca, 1984), 265.

effectively in the difficult circumstances of court life; and already in the sixteenth century institutions began responding to this demand. Schools developed in mid-sixteenth-century Italy to teach young men the manners and skills that life at court would demand, skills in riding, dancing, and swordsmanship, and they attracted a steady stream of northern European youth. Imitation soon followed, and around 1600 comparable academies had been established in Germany and France; young men could learn the techniques of courtly grace while staying home. Those for whom the academies were inaccessible could find something similar closer to home: across Catholic Europe the Jesuit colleges concerned themselves with teaching young men elegant manners and forms of speech, as well as more bookish subjects.

In other ways also court life was changing so as better to fit Castiglione's models of it. Monarchs responded to the image that Castiglione presented of the court as a separate world, detached from the cares of urban life. Thus an important political shift of the seventeenth and eighteenth centuries, the movement to create new settings for court life, spaces that removed courts from cities. Few sixteenth-century princes had felt this urge very strongly. Nearly all had some properties in the countryside, like the French kings' string of palaces along the Loire river, places for hunting and rural relaxation; but most also spent much of the year in the city. The French king Henry III (1574–1589) had more reason than most kings to fear the Paris mob, but during most of his reign he spent at least half the year in Paris – and in the other years he spent at least two months in the capital.[32] Kings could do this because they liked the city itself, and also because of the court's mobility. Even Louis XIV, who disliked Paris, seriously considered making it his principal home and commissioned famous architects to draw up plans for modernizing the Louvre palace.[33]

Ultimately, of course, Louis decided on an entirely different plan. He would establish a permanent court, ending the monarchy's mobile habits, and he would settle about twenty miles outside the city, at Versailles. Beginning in the 1670s, he enlarged and beautified one of his father's favored retreats, adding spacious gardens and waterways for pleasure to the hunting grounds that had so appealed to his father. Louis brought his entertainments as well, sufficiently so that during the next forty years he visited Paris only rarely. During these years, Versailles replaced Paris as the cultural center of the country. Louis established playwrights,

[32] Boucher, *La Cour de Henri III*, 45.
[33] Victor-L. Tapié, *The Age of Grandeur: Baroque Art and Architecture*, trans. A. Ross Williamson (New York, 1960), 110–31; Irving Lavin, *Past-Present: Essays on Historicism in Art from Donatello to Picasso* (Berkeley, 1993), 139–200.

5　The court of Lorraine, ca. 1625 (Jacques Callot, *Parterre du Palais de Nancy*)

6 A French courtier, ca. 1570 (Monogrammist LAM, *Portrait of a Courtier in White*)

painters, and musicians there. Providing entertainment for the court had become in some ways the focal point for French cultural life. In fact Louis had realized on a grand scale Castiglione's vision: the court had become an alternative to the city, so well supplied with every luxury that the city itself could be dispensed with. Versailles proposed itself as a world apart – though in fact the great palace needed far more services than it alone could house, and the town of Versailles (nearby, but clearly separated from the palace) quickly became a thriving city serving the court. Within this enclosure, Louis's court could acquire a more orderly, ceremonial texture, with clothing, eating, and entertainments all more closely regulated.

As the greatest king of his day, Louis's example resonated through Europe; even petty princes wanted to imitate the court he had created. Like Louis, these princes established their palaces outside the principal cities of their realms: Lunéville in the duchy of Lorraine, Caserta in the Kingdom of Naples, Potsdam in Prussia, Schönbrunn outside Vienna. Even Louis's great English adversaries William and Mary imitated his choice, devoting much energy to expanding and beautifying the Tudor palace Hampton Court, outside London. The separation of court from city had become the predominant model of court life. These years – the last quarter of the seventeenth century and the first years of the eighteenth – in some ways marked the apogee of court life in early modern Europe. Kings spent large sums to make their courts attractive, building fine new palaces and encouraging cultural life in them. No nobleman would want to stay away from Versailles or the courts that imitated it. In the words of a Spanish nobleman who had been exiled from court in 1634: "To leave the court is . . . to go to the extreme poles of the earth, away from all warmth and light, to live alone in an uninhabited, sterile and despoiled world."[34]

Yet the apparent strength of court life in the years of Louis XIV was deceptive, and in fact the court's influence had already begun to wane. By the late seventeenth century, rich nobles had begun to find the court stuffy and its formal modes of behavior burdensome. The problem was partly personal and specific to France: after a lively youth, Louis himself became pious in his old age, and life at Versailles ceased to be much fun. But there were also deeper causes for alienation. The court's very success in regulating behavior and in glorifying the king made it oppressive. Versailles and its imitators had acquired a bureaucratic feeling very different from what Castiglione had described. Hesitantly in the seven-

[34] Quoted R. A. Stradling, *Philip IV and the Government of Spain, 1621–1665* (Cambridge, 1988), 156.

teenth century and rapidly thereafter, the aristocratic salon offered an
alternative source for one of the court's pleasures, the chance for men and
women to converse in relative equality. This was one of several ways in
which the court's distance from the city also reduced its appeal, for urban
life was taking on a new elegance in the late seventeenth century. Nobles
bought townhouses to take advantage of these new pleasures, and their
attendance at court became simply an occasional burden, which they
undertook for political interest more than for pleasure. With the king's
most glamorous subjects living much of their lives elsewhere, the court in
turn lost much of its luster. Eighteenth-century visitors found even
Versailles unimpressive. Its rooms were poorly kept up, and tourists and
hawkers wandered unimpeded through its halls, even into the king's own
chambers. Court life remained more vigorous in Berlin and Vienna, yet
there too cultural primacy passed from court to city. Indeed, the late
eighteenth-century emperor Joseph II largely broke down the distinction
between court and city. He opened his palace grounds to strollers of all
social classes, and on occasion even opened the palace ballroom to the
public; and he vigorously supported the development of public theater in
Vienna. In such circumstances, the court could no longer function as a
closed world, nor could it dominate contemporary culture. Courts had
lost much of their exclusive glamor, and too much was happening outside
them.[35]

Across Europe, then, the eighteenth century completed a complex
process of change in nobles' relations with their monarchs. The distance
between nobles and monarchs grew dramatically over the early modern
period. Seventeenth-century kings withdrew from the battlefield and its
rough familiarity with aristocratic soldiers. After about 1670 they
withdrew further, to the world of enclosed palaces like Versailles. For a
time these courts could claim a position as focal points of national culture,
but by 1700 this claim had weakened. Nobles found themselves drawn to
the more lively urban culture that had grown up away from the court, and
travelled to Versailles and other rural palaces only out of duty. As
monarchs used ceremony to separate themselves from their nobles,
nobles themselves increasingly turned to cultural worlds that had little
relationship to monarchy.

[35] Descriptions in Christopher Hibbert, *The Grand Tour* (London, 1975), 61–62, 192–97;
Nicholas Till, *Mozart and the Enlightenment: Truth, Virtue and Beauty in Mozart's
Operas* (London, 1992), 94–95.

The problem of rebellion

Relations between kings and nobles thus involved complicated tensions. Nobles wanted, indeed needed, the stronger government that kings offered, yet at the same time they were dismayed by some of their rulers' new powers. They enjoyed and admired life at court, but they also disliked their kings' growing aloofness. Nobles were losing the habit of private violence, but the process was slow and uneven; in most of Europe it was still incomplete in the mid-seventeenth century. All of this proved an explosive mixture. As a result, from the fifteenth century through the late seventeenth Europe's political history was marked by recurring aristocratic rebellions. These were rebellions of Europe's wealthiest and most privileged inhabitants.

We have seen that nobles long retained the means for violent resistance to the state. Advanced military technology remained cheap enough that nobles had access to it, and they could mobilize large numbers of followers. More important than the technological means to wage war, however, were ideologies that justified nobles' resistance to the state. These ideologies were an inheritance from the Middle Ages, and they focussed on law as a central fact about government. The law – so nobles had argued for centuries – bound rulers as well as subjects. Rulers had to obey the fundamental obligations of the kingdom just like everyone else, or risk losing their subjects' obedience. These were the terms in which a high nobleman addressed an English king in the mid-thirteenth century: "It would not be for the king's honour if I submitted to his will against reason, whereby I should rather do wrong to him and to the justice which he is bound to observe toward his people. I should set all men a bad example, in deserting law and justice out of consideration for his evil will."[36] Similar language characterized the oath that the nobles of early modern Aragon took to their kings: 'We who are as good as you and together are more powerful than you, make you our king and lord, provided you observe our . . . liberties, and if not, not."[37] When the king failed to fulfill his duties, in other words, subjects had a positive duty to disobey, and the duty became even stronger when the king seemed under the control of ill-intentioned advisors, when the king was a child or simply weak-willed. Subjects owed obedience to kings but not to tyrants, and tyranny began when rulers failed to obey fundamental laws. Political ideas like these had particular force for the nobility, though in some

[36] Quoted Fritz Kern, *Kingship and Law in the Middle Ages*, trans. S. B. Chrimes (New York, 1956), 87; for skepticism about such statements, Susan Reynolds, *Fiefs and Vassals: the Medieval Evidence Reinterpreted* (Oxford, 1994), 29–31, 35–38.

[37] Quoted Angus MacKay, *Spain in The Middle Ages: From Frontier to Empire, 1000–1500* (New York, 1977), 105.

circumstances they might concern other social classes as well. The nobles were presumed to form the wisest part of society, that most accustomed to governing. Feudal law in fact required nobles to advise their leaders, and it established a fundamentally equal relation between leader and follower: feudalism joined them by a contract, which spelled out obligations on each side, and it established ample grounds for followers to break with their feudal superiors. Insofar as nobles defined kings' superiority in feudal terms, they accorded themselves rights to disobey.

Such claims to legitimate disobedience accorded well with nobles' loose sense of attachment to the states in which they resided. National identity mattered relatively little to men and women who might have familial attachments throughout Europe. For the mid-fourteenth century, we have the account of the chronicler Froissart: "At that time Sir Godfrey of Harcourt [an important French noble] having been banished from France, arrived in England. He went straight to the King and Queen . . . was received with open arms and was immediately made a member of the King's household and council. A large estate was assigned to him in England to enable him to maintain himself and his followers on a lavish scale." His landed base thus reestablished in a new country, Godfrey's political loyalty shifted accordingly. He urged the English to invade France, promising easy conquest and "enough wealth to make [the English] rich for twenty years to come."[38] Godfrey's choices typified national politics in the late Middle Ages. He and his large retinue of followers moved easily across national boundaries, quickly acquiring land and influence in the new setting. Linguistic and cultural differences posed few problems, for in England nobles spoke French and shared in French culture. Once settled, Godfrey had no hesitation about initiating an attack on his former homeland; the rich pickings there made invasion a matter of simple good sense. Even more striking, Godfrey managed to change sides a second time; after helping the English in battle, he returned to France, where the king forgave him his treachery and restored him to possession of his estates.[39]

Godfrey's example continued to find imitators over the next three centuries, though his vision of greed as the basis of warfare lost some of its appeal. As late as 1652 there was the example of the Grand Condé, a cousin of the French king and one of the greatest generals of his era. As leader of a failed rebellion, the Fronde, Condé chose exile over submission to the crown; he fled to the Spanish Netherlands, and stayed for seven years – years in which he led Spanish armies against the French. Condé's resettlement in France became an important issue in the treaty

[38] Froissart, *The Chronicles*, 68, 69.
[39] Caron, *Noblesse et pouvoir royal en France*, 103.

that eventually ended the long war between the two countries, and he was quickly restored to full honor in France. Louis XIV spoke publicly of Condé as the brightest ornament of his court, and within a decade he received high military commands. He spent his last years lavishly rebuilding his palace near Paris and became a notable patron of French writers. Like Godfrey of Harcourt, he had succeeded in reclaiming his place at the top of French society and politics.

Probably Condé was the last to manage such reinstatement after outright treason, but even in the eighteenth century many nobles found themselves in a complicated relationship to the states where they resided. Especially in Europe's numerous small states, nobles who wanted governmental or military positions might have few opportunities at home; they had to move in order to advance. In the southwestern German state of Württemberg, nearly all the prince's aristocratic courtiers during the early seventeenth century were drawn from outside the duchy. Probably such movement was especially common in Germany; the region's combination of fragmented politics and unified culture allowed nobles to move from one state to another without losing contact with their native language and customs. But there might also be movement across linguistic and cultural boundaries. Ottavio Piccolomini was born to a distinguished Tuscan family, in 1599; through the Thirty Years War he alternated between serving the Spanish and their allies the Austrians, changing sides when he felt his services were insufficiently appreciated, and ended life as an estate owner in Bohemia, with palaces in Prague and Vienna. Early in the eighteenth century, one-sixth of the nobility of Savoy (a small state that combined regions now belonging to Italy and France) was serving in a foreign army, and one-third of the duchy's retired military nobles had spent some part of their careers in foreign armies. Most served the French kings, but many served in Germany; it was not uncommon for aristocratic brothers to find themselves fighting in opposing armies.[40] Royal marriages could have similar consequences. Two marriages allied the French monarchy with the Medici family of Florence; each brought to the French court swarms of Italian nobles, eager to make their fortunes in a new setting.

In some respects, circumstances after 1500 actually made national loyalty and obedience *more* difficult than they had earlier been. For in the sixteenth century kings and subjects might often find themselves in disagreement about the most important of all laws, those to do with

---

[40] Vann, *The Making of a State*, 69; Thomas M. Barker, *Army, Aristocracy, Monarchy: Essays on War, Society, and Government in Austria, 1618–1780* (Boulder, 1982), 72–110; Jean Nicolas, *La Savoie au XVIIIe siècle: noblesse et bourgeoisie*, 2 vols. (Paris, 1978), I, 231–36.

religion. Sixteenth-century rulers had to choose whether to follow or to outlaw the teachings of Protestant reformers; whatever their choice, in northern Europe they were left confronting a substantial minority who believed that God's laws – the foundation of any legitimate government – had been violated. The situation again brought to the fore the duty of disobedience, now tinged with the colors of crusade. Luther, Calvin, and other religious leaders did not invoke such talk of disobedience lightly, for they had a horror of disorder and they took seriously biblical injunctions to render unto Caesar what was Caesar's – in other words, to obey even unjust rulers. Yet they could not accept the persecution of their followers, and they quickly came to see resistance to tyrannical kings as a basic political right. Basic, at least, for the nobles, whose special position (so argued Luther, Calvin, and several of their most articulate followers) gave them special duties within the state. Unlike other social groups, they held the right to evaluate kings' behavior, urge amendment, and ulti-mately take action when talk failed; they had a right to resist. A series of widely read sixteenth-century pamphlets justified and popularized these positions, and they found an audience among Catholics as well as Protestants; when governments in England and France seemed to be favoring Protestants, Catholics explained the right of resistance in print and acted accordingly.[41]

Sixteenth-century nobles thus confronted their rulers with powerful ideologies and with practical weapons; they had the capacity to resist government effectively, and widely held ideas justified their doing so. They had, finally, a psychological impetus to rebel, in their feeling that government was drifting out of their reach. Kings, they could see, had become more aloof, and had surrounded themselves with growing numbers of officials. Even nobles whose affairs prospered could feel irritation at these changes; nobles who found their revenues shrinking could feel intense anger.

The result was a spectacular series of aristocratic rebellions, stretching from the fifteenth to the mid-seventeenth centuries. Nobles acted as a group, and they also found themselves leading into action rebels from other social classes, peasants and townsmen. In the fifteenth century, great princes – many with close familial ties to the monarchs they challenged – played the leading role in these movements. In the next century, religion became the central issue for rebellion. Religion receded

[41] Theories of resistance are summarized by Quentin Skinner, *The Foundations of Modern Political Thought*, 2 vols. (Cambridge, 1978), 189–238 and *passim*. For nobles' broader belief in their right to rebel, Arlette Jouanna, *Le Devoir de la révolte: la noblesse française et la gestation de l'Etat moderne, 1559–1661* (Paris, 1989); Jean-Marie Constant, *Les Conjurateurs: le premier libéralisme politique sous Richelieu* (Paris, 1987).

somewhat as a political motive after 1600, but new waves of rebellion nonetheless arose, now mainly fought against tax burdens and over the intrusiveness of government officials. The culmination came in the 1640s, a decade that saw nobles in revolt across much of western Europe. Catalonia and Portugal exploded in 1640, over the Spanish king's effort to impose taxes equal to those prevailing in the central province of Castile. A few years later there were rebellions in Naples and Sicily, likewise dominions of the king of Spain. The English Civil War had begun in 1642, and in 1648 there was the Fronde in France. Only in the 1650s did political confusion come to an end, in most regions with the restoration of monarchical order.[42]

Much divided these rebellions from one another, but all of them showed nobles' readiness to oppose the state. In France the rebels included the very highest nobles, including in the end a cousin of the king's, the prince de Condé: immensely wealthy, widely admired as the greatest general of the age, and the beneficiary of numerous grants and positions from the crown. Likewise in Spain: in 1641 the very wealthy duke of Medina Sidonia, a cousin of the king's principal minister, conspired against the crown, with the idea of establishing an independent kingdom for himself. Elsewhere such leading figures tended to remain on the sidelines, and lesser gentlemen played the leading roles. Yet even these men did not act simply because of poverty or a sense of having been disregarded by the state. By and large they too were substantial figures, who could mobilize neighbors and dependants. Their example showed the continuing force of belief in nobles' right to resist. But this was to be the last such manifestation. A few instances of noble rebelliousness recurred in the 1650s and 1660s, notably in France, and nobles led the 1688 Glorious Revolution in England. But like duelling, large-scale disobedience had lost its standing as an aspect of political normality.

This happened partly because the technology of war had now accorded decisive advantages to governments. Royal armies had become too well armed, too large, and too carefully organized to allow effective resistance by nobles, even by a great general like Condé. Warfare in the age of firearms required trained soldiers, who could patiently stay in formation despite the dangers and chaos of the battlefield; few aristocratic rebels

[42] For interpretive overviews of these events, Trevor Aston, ed., *Crisis in Europe, 1560–1660* (Garden City, NY, 1967); J. H. Elliott extends a similar analysis to sixteenth-century rebellions in "Revolution and Continuity in Early Modern Europe," repr. in *Spain and Its World: Selected Essays* (New Haven, 1989), 92–113. A recent case study is offered by Karen McHardy, "The Rise of Absolutism and Noble Rebellion in Early Modern Habsburg Austria, 1570–1620," *Comparative Studies in Society and History*, 34 (1992), 407–38.

had the resources to recruit troops of this quality or the time to train them.

More important, however, ideas about proper political behavior had changed. The very success of the rebellions of the 1640s encouraged the change, by suggesting the disorders that rebellion might produce. The English example seemed especially frightening. In England, much of the gentry and peerage supported early resistance to the king, and enthusiastically joined efforts to control his advisors. As resistance to the king became more direct, however, noble and gentry support diminished; the king's execution in 1649 and the development of popular radicalism narrowed gentry rebelliousness still further. Abroad, nobles found these events equally shocking, a demonstration of the chaos that rebellion could bring. Nobles found their successful rebellions frightening. Failure, of course, could be equally frightening, or at least humiliating. Condé and his followers spent long years in exile following the Fronde, and many others found their hopes for careers ended.

Instead of justifying rebellion, nobles after 1660 gave increasing allegiance to an alternative vision of the state, one that emphasized order and utility over the strict attention to individuals' rights. Contemporaries continued to believe in a contract between rulers and subjects, but they understood the contract in new terms. Rulers' paramount obligation, it now came to seem, lay in preserving society as a whole, rather than in respecting every individual's rights. Obviously the good ruler should try to respect those rights, and should listen attentively to complaints about injustice. Theorists continued to distinguish between legitimate monarchy and tyranny. But they denied to individual subjects, no matter what their status, the right to determine when that line had been crossed and the right to withdraw obedience. The danger of disorder was too great, and so was the king's responsibility: only the king in fact could see issues whole, could see the complex factors that lay behind his individual decisions and the collective good that individual subordinations might produce. No individual nobleman could attain a comparable vision of the commonwealth. These were not new ideas in the seventeenth century. They had circulated in administrative circles since the late Middle Ages, for they reflected the assumptions of the Roman law that administrators had learned at the universities. If the ideas themselves were old, though, they acquired new relevance in the seventeenth century. They proposed a solution to the problem of disorder. After a century of revolutions, even the most bellicose nobles were prepared to listen.

The absolutist compromise

This was the political philosophy of absolutism, a view that kings had higher responsibilities than merely respecting the specific rights of their subjects, or even the laws of religion itself: the ardently Catholic French king Louis XIII and his advisor the Cardinal Richelieu, a high official of the Catholic church, allied with Protestant Germans, Swedes, and Dutch against the Catholic king of Spain and the Catholic Holy Roman Emperor, because French national interest seemed to require this violation of religious loyalties. For them the state was more important than any alternative law, no matter how sacred. Events seemed to demonstrate the wisdom of these policies: the Spanish and Austrian monarchs clung to more strictly religious ideals, and suffered defeat in the Thirty Years War and after. As nobles came to accept this vision of the state, they had to relinquish their age-old conception of their own political rights. They had now less right to political dissidence in the new order, and no right at all to violent disobedience. Both Richelieu and Louis XIV unhesitatingly jailed nobles who offered even mild criticism of their policies. One side of absolutism was a straightforward police state.

But nobles gained as well as lost from the new order. They gained partly because even the most powerful kings could not govern without cooperation from their most powerful subjects. Apparently so indifferent to subjects' voices, ministers like Richelieu and kings like Louis XIV in fact listened carefully, and often acquiesced to subjects' wishes – at least to subjects who were sufficiently important. "Nothing must be overlooked," Richelieu counseled his king, "in sustaining the nobles in the great virtues of their fathers, and neither should anything be omitted to help them enlarge the landed estates which they have inherited."[43] Such solicitude was occasionally visible in the realm of high policy, but it appeared above all in matters of local action. For even the most absolute early modern rulers needed aristocratic support in order to govern effectively. The limited technology and communications of the early modern period meant that every government needed to rely on the cooperation of local figures, and governments remained small by modern standards. Every exercise of governmental power ultimately resulted from negotiation between central and local interests – from alliance with local ruling groups.[44]

---

[43] Henry Bertram Hill, ed., *The Political Testament of Cardinal Richelieu* (Madison, 1968), 21.

[44] For a well-documented example of this argument, William Beik, *Absolutism and Society in Seventeenth-Century France: State Power and Provincial Aristocracy in Seventeenth-Century Languedoc* (Cambridge, 1985); see also Evans, *The Making of the Habsburg Monarchy*, 169–80.

Governments needed nobles' cooperation, and they had tempting rewards for those who went along. As the absolutist state grew, it could offer a growing range of political employments, with significant chances for making money. Most visibly it needed soldiers, for the major states of Europe were at war during most of the sixteenth, seventeenth, and eighteenth centuries, and their armies were steadily growing. Nobles could feel confident that the state needed them and their military traditions and skills; innovations in military technology did nothing to change this. Even the conditions of nobles' service changed slowly, so that they continued for a long time to enjoy many of the powers and pleasures of feudal warfare. Through the seventeenth century, military commanders everywhere had to recruit their own companies, and typically they filled these with personal dependants.[45]

And the new forms of military organization paid well. Seventeenth-century warfare did not offer the spectacular profits of medieval plundering, but successful officers could make their way very nicely, and some became rich. Even the medieval practice of ransoming prisoners ended slowly. Holding captured civilians for ransom remained normal practice through the mid-seventeenth century; for captured soldiers, the practice remained sufficiently normal that in the mid-seventeenth century tables of ransom rates were set out by the authorities in Denmark, Sweden, Holland, and Spain. Plunder too remained an acceptable mode of military behavior. But the commander remained an entrepreneur in a more general sense, for he recruited his own troops and contracted for reimbursement from the state; often he received powers of taxation for the purpose. This of course was the case with the great German and Bohemian commanders who dominated central Europe during the Thirty Years War.[46] In theory French commanders were under closer control, but they too often enriched themselves by the tax revenues they were granted for support of their troops.[47] Early modern war (like its medieval predecessor) remained a business. As in any business, participants risked losing money, but many prospered. Warfare lost its business quality only in the eighteenth century, as central governments became

---

[45] The opposite view – that nobles lost their military functions with the state's development – was presented by Alexis de Tocqueville in the mid-nineteenth century: *The Old Regime and the French Revolution*, trans. Stuart Gilbert (Garden City, NY, 1955); for a recent restatement of this view, Ellery Schalk, *From Valor to Pedigree: Ideas of Nobility in France in the Sixteenth and Seventeenth Centuries* (Princeton, 1986).

[46] Fritz Redlich, *De Praeda Militari: Looting and Booty 1500–1814* (Wiesbaden, 1956), 34–36; *The German Military Enterpriser and His Work Force: A Study in European Economic and Social History* (Wiesbaden, 1964).

[47] Jonathan Dewald, *Pont-St-Pierre, 1398–1789: Lordship, Community, and Capitalism in Early Modern France* (Berkeley, 1987), 178ff.

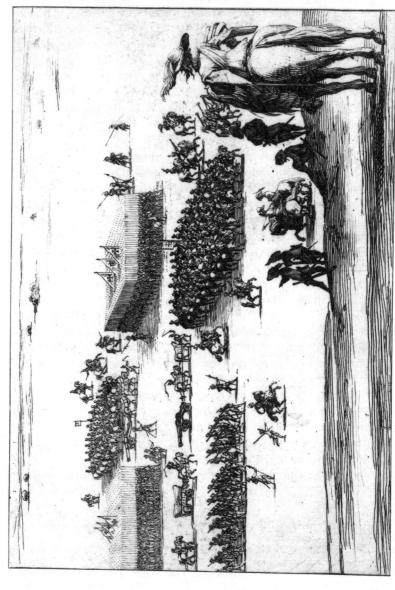

7 A new ideal of warfare: the Spanish army, ca. 1635 (Jacques Callot, *The Review*)

stronger and better organized. They no longer had such need of the military entrepreneur; governments now began to recruit troops, to supply them with food and other necessities, and to house them in barracks – a late seventeenth- century invention that finally ended the practice of imposing troops on unfortunate private householders. There was less need for the military entrepreneur and less opportunity for enormous profits from warfare. Looting ceased to be acceptable, and increasingly the state's interests came to predominate over those of the individual commander: the point of war, the eighteenth century finally decided, was to defeat the enemy as a whole, not to enrich individuals. In fact commanders ended looting for just this reason: not out of humanitarian concern, but because it reduced military effectiveness, leaving an army vulnerable and disorganized as its members scrambled to acquire and hold their loot. But the change also brought benefits. Nobles could now enjoy more secure rewards from military service, by and large comparable to those of leading bureaucrats.[48]

The state offered other rewards as well. Kings awarded revenues directly to large numbers of gentlemen. In early seventeenth-century France, several hundred nobles received funds every year from the crown, and in most cases these added significantly to family incomes – perhaps 40 percent for middling provincial gentlemen. For a handful of great nobles, much more was at stake: with salaries and pensions on the order of 100,000 livres, the great French nobles in the mid-seventeenth century received enough from the crown to support several middling families. In southern Italy the situation was similar: seventeenth-century nobles enjoyed offices and financial privileges from the government, and responded by offering the government its support.[49]

Finally, there were administrative positions. Embarked on its breathtaking growth, the early modern state needed large numbers of civil servants and magistrates, and many of these positions brought honor as well as income. To be sure, such positions diverged sharply from what many nobles saw as their appropriate social function, that of fighting, and most such positions demanded university educations, usually in the law. Initially, then, nobles might find themselves handicapped in the competition for positions, by both lack of education and by the group's warrior traditions. But these hesitations ended very soon – a part of the larger merger (discussed above, pp. 36–40) between the new bureaucrats and the warrior nobilities. Already in the early sixteenth century, old noble

[48] Redlich, *De Praeda*, 62ff.
[49] Dewald, *Pont-St-Pierre*, 180–81; Robert Harding, *The Anatomy of a Power Elite* (New Haven, 1977), 138–42; Tommaso Astarita, *The Continuity of Feudal Power: The Caracciolo di Brienza in Spanish Naples* (Cambridge, 1992), 221–32.

families began sending their sons in large numbers to universities, precisely to acquire the educations that government service would require. In the first decades of the sixteenth century, about one-quarter of the students at the University of Paris were drawn from the nobility, and in the following years the percentages rose still higher at English and Spanish universities. Nobles began urging their sons to follow this career path, as a more certain avenue to riches than warfare, with its risks and discomforts, could ever be, and they lobbied governments to make positions available for their sons.[50]

These efforts succeeded. Large numbers of nobles, usually from the order's middling and lower ranks, entered the bureaucracies and law-courts of most European states. In the small southwestern German state of Württemburg, about half of the leading administrators during the late sixteenth and early seventeenth centuries were noble. In the Habsburg states of central Europe, from the 1620s on, virtually all administrators with any power were nobles. In early seventeenth-century Spain, 70 percent of the members of the Council of State were from the old nobility, and the percentage rose even higher in the 1640s. By this point, nobles had come to dominate the universities from which most bureaucrats were recruited, and they used the connections thus established to fill lesser official posts as well. French nobles probably were among the least equipped in sixteenth-century Europe to compete for positions, yet they too succeeded to a striking degree: in one region about one-fifth of the high court magistrates were nobles. Their presence gave added strength to a movement that had already begun, the civil servants' increasingly successful effort to establish themselves as a special form of nobility. The recruitment of old nobles into official careers strengthened these claims, by adding further dignity to the bureaucracy.[51] At the highest level of government, nobles' success was even more complete. Though there were exceptions, kings tended to select their principal advisors from the nobility. The chief architects of early seventeenth-century absolutism, thus, were men like Richelieu in France, Strafford in England, Olivares in Spain, Oxenstierna in Sweden – all of them members of the high nobility. Most had military backgrounds, and most of them also became rich through state service.

Nobles thus succeeded in gaining a substantial share of the state's civil

[50]   See below, Chapter 4.
[51]   Vann, *The Making of a State*, 78ff; Evans, *The Making of the Habsburg Monarchy*, 179–80; Ignacio Atienza Hernández, *Aristocratia, poder y riqueza en la España moderna: la Casa de Osuna, siglos XV–XIX* (Madrid, 1987), 51; Richard Kagan, *Students and Society in Early Modern Spain* (Baltimore, 1974); Jonathan Dewald, *The Formation of a Provincial Nobility: The Magistrates of the Parlement of Rouen, 1499–1610* (Princeton, 1980).

benefits

offices, and they dominated the army and the court. In important ways, then, the state's development worked directly to the nobles' benefit, supplying them with new forms of power, dignity, and wealth. Indeed, nobles derived far more from the powerful states of the seventeenth century than the medieval system of local powers and allegiances could ever have permitted. Directly profitable to many nobles, the state's development offered indirect profits to many more, through the security and order that it brought. In achieving these ends, to be sure, the early modern state also exacted costs from the nobles. It required that they relinquish some forms of violence, and it suppressed some forms of political action. For many nobles, the benefits of strong government far surpassed its costs.

But such benefits did not flow equally to all nobles. Some groups found their chances for profits reduced for geographical reasons. The nobility of Luxembourg lived far from the centers of political power. The Habsburg emperors in Vienna controlled their region, but allowed them few official positions; and at such a distance there was little hope of the personal connections that would attract financial support.[52] Religion and class posed other barriers. In the seventeenth century, the Habsburgs systematically favored Catholic over Protestant nobles, according them positions and monetary help as well as social advantages.[53] Many positions required high initial investments. There were the costs of legal education, which many nobles could not afford, and the costs of residence at court in pursuit of high positions; in the glamorous atmosphere of the seventeenth-century courts, even a few months' residence might be extremely expensive. Even the highest born nobles might have trouble making their way in these circumstances. Most English peers in the early seventeenth century either held no royal offices, or held only minor and ill-paying ones.[54]

In a variety of ways, then, the state's growing influence and the economic possibilities that it offered accentuated divisions within the nobility. Some nobles benefited, others fell further behind. Seventeenth-century nobles in many countries could see examples of meteoric success, in the handsome or able young men who managed to make their ways in court society and to accumulate large fortunes. Even poor nobles, such stories seemed to suggest, might hope to become rich serving the king.

But such great success stories did not change the basic fact that benefits tended to flow in one direction: toward the nobles who had the closest

---

[52] Calixte Hudemann-Simon, *La Noblesse luxembourgeoise au XVIII siècle* (Paris-Luxembourg, 1985), 153–55.
[53] Evans, *The Making of the Habsburg Monarchy*, 91ff.
[54] Stone, *The Crisis of the Aristocracy*, 385ff.

connections with the prince himself, because their birth gave them
chances for friendship with the prince and because their wealth allowed
them easy residence at court. The rich, by and large, became richer, for it
became harder for young outsiders to break into the world of the court
after 1650, as ceremonial became more elaborate and court residence
more expensive. Military office became difficult to acquire, and might
require substantial investment of the officer's own resources. And there
was more pressure from longstanding official families that their descendants be named to high positions. In all, nobles' financial dependence on
the state reinforced a trend seen elsewhere in this study, a paring away of
the nobility's poorest elements. The poor nobleman had less and less
place in these political systems, and steadily fewer chances to enjoy the
system's material benefits. But for the leading nobles the balance was
positive: they gained more than they lost from service to the state. They
gained in a variety of indirect ways as well. They gained support in
lawsuits, and they often gained advantages in their efforts to buy
property. Here ultimately was the bargain struck between nobles and
governments. Nobles relinquished their habits of violence, both public
and private. They accepted the idea of kings' authority over their lives,
and gave up belief in their right to an autonomous political stance. They
ceased to support the dozens of followers who had been the foundation
for political power in the fifteenth century. In exchange, they received the
vague benefits of civic peace and the more concrete advantages of
government service. State service became an important economic resource.

The bargain was clearest in continental Europe, where bureaucracies
grew most abundantly and most states maintained large, permanent
armies. In a variety of important ways, England evolved differently
during these years. Its kings found their powers limited by Parliament,
which brought together not representatives of the whole nation, but its
leading citizens – mainly the high nobles and the gentry. There was only a
weak army, a smaller bureaucracy than in most continental states, and the
English nobles retained a stronger landed base than most nobles on the
continent.

For all the clear differences, however, something like the continental
bargain between states and nobles took place in England as well. Despite
all the limitations that Parliament placed on it, the English state too grew
during these years. It grew especially fast after the Civil War, so that
eighteenth-century England, like other European countries, had large
numbers of fiscal officials, judges, and other civil servants; England's
colonial successes offered new opportunities. Like its continental rivals,
the English state absorbed a high percentage of its country's product in

tax revenues – in fact perhaps a higher percentage than the French state. And as in France, most of this revenue went to the nobles. This fact accounted for the special qualities of eighteenth-century English politics. Whereas there had been little competition for seats in Parliament before 1640, after 1660 competition became the norm – precisely because the financial stakes of politics had dramatically risen. Gentlemen who wanted shares in the profits of power had to fight for them. As on the continent, though with slightly different means, government functioned with aristocratic power, not against it.

In the course of the sixteenth and seventeenth centuries, the European nobles experienced a series of dramatic political changes. In many ways, government became less personal, less accessible – and less tolerant of longstanding aristocratic values. Nobles could no longer treat their kings as near equals, nor could they expect acceptance of their rights to political independence. Nobles lost their rights to private violence as a means of settling disputes, and they lost their right to rebel when they thought the government had violated fundamental laws. They lost some tax exemptions, and in many areas they lost their right to a real voice in the legislative process. These were painful changes, for some nobles painful enough to spark armed rebellion. Rebelliousness, it seems, derived above all from the nobles' sense of cultural and psychological threat, rather than from concrete material losses, for on many occasions rich and successful nobles proved as ready to rebel as their poorer neighbors.

Ultimately, however, the nobles as a group profited from the state's development. They could no longer wage private war, but they could fight for the king, often for substantial rewards. They could benefit from serving the king in other ways, at court or in his bureaucracies, and as landowners they profited from the peace and stability that stronger royal government provided. If there were cultural losses, there were also powerful cultural gains. Nobles responded with passionate enthusiasm to the ideals of courtliness that Castiglione propounded and Louis XIV sought to realize. They developed a keen sense of the state's great work, its contributions to social welfare and its achievement of order. Most willingly participated in the state's military efforts, despite the direct burdens that these placed on them both as tax-payers and as soldiers.

Many of these benefits touched all nobles. But the state's most concrete rewards went to only some. The poorest nobles received the least, and probably lost the most. They had the fewest hopes of positions at court or in the civil service, for the necessary education cost money. Military service itself often required a substantial investment in horses, armor, weapons, and training. At the same time, the state worked hard to dismantle that system of local solidarities that into the sixteenth century offered positions and esteem for the poor nobles. Like the early modern period's economic changes, then, the state's development contributed to making the nobles a different kind of group, one more coherent in its wealth and status, one that had less room for relative poverty. The nobles were becoming something more like a ruling class.

4   Lives and cultures

Early in the twentieth century, the French novelist Marcel Proust described a vacation encounter between his autobiographical hero and a group of pretty, giggly teenage girls. One of them (so the novel recounts) worries about her upcoming school examinations, and so her friend offers answers to the most likely questions, including the following: "You are to imagine that after the first performance of [Jean Racine's play] *Esther*, Madame de Sévigné writes to Madame de Lafayette to say how sorry she was to have missed her." The student is to write the appropriate letter, employing her knowledge of seventeenth-century aristocratic society, language, and literary tastes.[1]

Schoolchildren throughout nineteenth- and early twentieth-century Europe had to answer essay questions like this. They testify to a surprising fact. Six generations after the Revolution, in a staunchly Republican France, educators demanded that middle-class students immerse themselves in the lives and thoughts of seventeenth-century aristocrats. In a world that already had automobiles, telephones, airplanes, and elevators (all of them vividly present in Proust's novel), high aesthetic experience was to be sought through reentering the world of Louis XIV and his favorite writers, following their debates, and imitating their language. Aristocratic culture remained alive, and Republican scholastic authorities saw in it the values they wanted children to acquire. To some extent it remains alive today. Schoolchildren in France continue to learn the verses of Racine and Molière, written to please Louis XIV's courtiers. Our ideas about proper manners have their origins in courtly settings, and some of our ideas about personality as well. For after all, some of our most vigorous explorations of the nature of personality (in Anglo-Saxon literature, say, Shakespeare's *Hamlet*) unfold in court settings and concern aristocrats.

Here is yet another paradox in the history of the European nobles. These were intensely conservative men and women, who inherited a

---

[1] Marcel Proust, *A l'ombre des jeunes filles en fleurs* (Paris, 1954), 581.

reverence for the past. Yet these same men and women produced and enjoyed a culture that continued to dominate the bourgeois Europe of the nineteenth and early twentieth centuries. In part the tenacity of the nobles' culture reflected adaptation, the fact they showed themselves remarkably receptive to new cultural currents in the world around them. They bought novels and paintings produced by middle-class artists; they listened to music produced by men and women from still more humble backgrounds. As important, however, nobles also contributed directly to the cultural worlds they moved in. Very few painted or wrote music, but many produced poetry, novels, and works of moral and political reflection. They also felt entitled to oversee the work of the professionals they supported. For better or worse, aristocratic patrons played a lively role in shaping the art that professionals produced for them, setting out for artists and writers themes to depict and styles to use.

Nobles' cultural involvements (this chapter argues) had two sources, in some ways contradictory but ultimately mutually reinforcing. A first was eminently practical. Starting in the sixteenth century, nobles were forced to educate themselves by the demands of political life, which increasingly required of them specific knowledge and broader attitudes. Nobles needed languages and rhetorical techniques if they were to compete effectively for administrative positions; some needed legal training; and, like their predecessors in Renaissance Italy, they needed to think about the difficult moral questions that political engagement posed. They turned readily to literature that reflected on the relations between religion and personal morality, on the one side, and the demands of state service on the other. Thus one aspect of the nobles' early modern cultural history was utilitarian adaptation; in this domain as in others, the nobles responded successfully to a changing world.

But the other side of the story was less utilitarian. Nobles involved themselves in early modern culture not just for its practical uses, but because it helped them understand their lives in broader terms. Their personal lives were changing along with their political situations, creating new relationships within families and between individuals. Responding to these changes encouraged thought about problems of human personality and about the bonds between people. It encouraged, in other words, personal uses of aesthetic experience, as a source of understanding, consolation, and distraction in a sometimes difficult world.

These two strands of cultural change – the one practical, oriented to university qualifications and state-service, the other an effort to make sense of private life – produced an apparent contradiction. Just as early modern nobles were acquiring a greater command of European high culture (and a larger array of university degrees), they increasingly voiced an alternative cultural ideal, that of the well-born amateur: a man or woman whose natural grace, wit, and taste gave cultural authority and creativity. These in-born qualities, it was increasingly argued in the seventeenth and eighteenth centuries, had more importance than mere learning, indeed might be damaged by learning. What counted was ability and experience of the world, not bookish citations or university degrees. In fact the contradiction was mainly apparent, for the grace that the period prized was often the result of extensive learning. Early modern aesthetic products required high levels of education for proper enjoyment, to appreciate the complicated patterns of allusion and argument that they often contained.

If the ideology of the graceful amateur cannot be taken entirely seriously, however, it nonetheless expressed an important fact. In the early sixteenth century, nobles in most parts of Europe had been at the margins of much cultural life – partly because of their military traditions, and partly because few of them had the education needed to participate in the Latinate culture of Renaissance humanism. But the ideal of the amateur was essentially aristocratic, in that it stressed nature over effort. This vision of culture suggested that nobles could play a leading role, and in many spheres they did just that.

A cultural revolution

Historians have been slow to view the nobles as full participants in early modern culture partly because of the group's own complaints. In many parts of sixteenth- and seventeenth-century Europe, nobles felt that they were living through a cultural revolution, and they disliked the experience. Standards of education and of cultural literacy seemed to be rising fast, in ways that annoyed conservatives. "In my time," grumbled an elderly French nobleman in 1656, "one made gentlemen study only to join the church. Those destined for the court or the army . . . learned to ride, to dance, arms, to play the lute, to leap, and that was all."[2] The new generation, he complained, expected much more. Nobles now had to display literary knowledge and polish, demands which seemed to challenge the essentially military basis of noble rank. Complaints like these echoed across early modern Europe, as nobles found themselves judged by rising cultural standards – standards that many opposed. "I'd rather my son should hang than study letters," an English gentleman was reported as saying in the early sixteenth century; ". . . the study of letters

[2] Quoted Jonathan Dewald, *Aristocratic Experience and the Origins of Modern Culture: France 1570–1715* (Berkeley, 1993), 81.

should be left to the sons of rustics."[3] New educational expectations seemed to raise questions about the dividing line between nobles and other social groups, implying that nobles could be judged by universal standards of achievement, rather than by birth.

In fact such complaints exaggerated the extent of change in nobles' educations. Even during the fourteenth and fifteenth centuries, many in the English gentry and peerage had in fact been highly educated. The first lay English peer known to have attended the University of Oxford did so in 1358, at a time when the university dispensed a rigorous Latinate education mainly to clerics and professional intellectuals, and many peers of his day held (and used) substantial libraries. There were highly educated nobles in fifteenth-century Spain as well. In 1475 the duke of Infantado made arrangements for preserving intact the family's library, "because I greatly desire that [my son] and his descendants should give themselves to study, as . . . I and our ancestors did, firmly believing our persons and house to be greatly improved and elevated by it." These men read because they were involved in government service. They needed to use written words, and they needed some familiarity with the law and with the broader terms of political debate.[4]

If they overstated the degree of change, however, observers after 1550 were correct in their belief that educational standards were rising. As late as the mid-sixteenth century, great nobles in both France and England might actually be illiterate, and few nobles made much use of books; among a group of fifty-eight German nobles who listed their losses in the 1525 peasant rebellion, only six seem to have owned any books at all.[5] But by this point such illiteracy had become a clear sign of backwardness, and nobles had begun crowding into universities across Europe. Between one-quarter and one-third of the Castilian nobility probably attended university, and comparable numbers have been suggested for the English gentry. Other regions showed lower, but still impressive levels of aristocratic education: at several German universities, well over 10 percent of the students were nobles, and nobles made up about one-quarter of the students at the early sixteenth-century University of Paris.[6]

---

[3] Quoted Lawrence Stone, *The Crisis of the Aristocracy, 1558–1641* (Oxford, 1965), 674.

[4] K. B. McFarlane, *The Nobility of Later Medieval England* (Oxford, 1973), 235, 228–47; Helen Nader, *The Mendoza Family in the Spanish Renaissance, 1350–1550* (New Brunswick, 1979), quotation 181.

[5] H. C. Erik Midelfort, "Adeliges Landesleben und die Legitimationskrise des deutschen Adels im 16. Jahrhundert," in Georg Schmidt, ed., *Stände und Gesellschaft im alten Reich* (Stuttgart, 1989), 246–47.

[6] Bernard Guenée, *Tribunaux et gens de justice dans le bailliage de Senlis à la fin du Moyen Age (vers 1380–vers 1550)* (Paris, 1963), 191; Richard Kagan, "Universities in Castile, 1500–1810," in Lawrence Stone, ed., *The University in Society*, 2 vols. (Princeton, 1974), II, 360–61; Charles McClelland, *State, Society, and University in Germany, 1700–1914* (Cambridge, 1980), 46–52.

University attendance tells only part of the story, for many parents found universities either excessively old-fashioned or insufficiently systematic in educational methods. In both Catholic and Protestant Europe a wave of college foundations marked the period, and nobles predominated among the students. In Protestant Sweden, the crown created eleven such schools between 1623 and 1643, and at the same time dramatically strengthened the university. Catholics responded after about 1560, most successfully with the foundation of hundreds of Jesuit colleges for boys. By the mid-seventeenth century, it was taken for granted that even members of the highest aristocracy, figures like the French prince de Condé, destined for a brilliant military career, would find themselves studying with the Jesuits. In the same years, it became normal for German nobles to spend a year or two visiting cultural centers throughout Europe.[7]

A later example suggests still more vividly the success of such campaigns for improving the aristocracy's educational standards. In the mid-eighteenth century, the notoriously uneducated Madame Du Barry became the mistress of the notoriously pleasure-loving French king Louis XV. Yet immediately after obtaining the king's favor Du Barry bought for herself a library of 1,068 volumes – so clear was it that bookishness now represented part of what contemporaries expected of the court nobility.[8]

Powerful forces underlay this expansion of aristocratic education during the sixteenth and seventeenth centuries. Religious competition between Protestants and Catholics encouraged each side to found schools. Education, it was believed, could inculcate both proper doctrine and moral self-control. As important, governments needed officials with the skills that schools and universities provided: familiarity with law, languages, and mathematics, command of rhetorical techniques. If members of the old nobility failed to educate themselves properly, so a variety of educational theorists warned, they risked losing their preeminence to lesser groups, who were only too eager to enter the new bureaucracies. Already in the mid-fifteenth century the situation was clear to at least one Burgundian aristocrat. "Those who have learned and

---

7 Michael Roberts, *Gustavus Adolphus*, 2nd edn (London, 1992), 85–86; François de Daimville, *L'Education des Jésuites (XVIe–XVIIIe siècles)* (Paris, 1978); Mark Motley, *Becoming a French Aristocrat: The Education of the Court Nobility, 1580–1715* (Princeton, 1990); Karen McHardy, "The Rise of Absolutism and Noble Rebellion in Early Modern Habsburg Austria, 1570–1620," *Comparative Studies in Society and History*, 34, (1992), 407–38. J. H. Hexter's classic article, "The Education of the Aristocracy in the Renaissance," repr. in Hexter, *Reappraisals in History* (New York, 1961), 45–70, set the terms for most current discussion of aristocratic education and still deserves close reading.
8 Maurice Rheims, *La Vie étrange des objets: histoire de la curiosité* (Paris, 1959), 313.

retained much, and who have the greatest desire to learn and know, attain great good, honor, and riches," Jean de Lannoy advised his son. "I was never put to school. I therefore know and can know nothing . . . No day passes that I do not regret this, and especially when I find myself in the councils of the king or of the Duke of Burgundy, and I know not nor dare not to speak my opinion." Around the end of the sixteenth century, a German nobleman made the same point. "Studies are a necessity for the nobility," he wrote in the course of a family chronicle; "neglecting them or quitting them prematurely means decline of the nobility."[9] Education, it was becoming clear even to distinguished families, was a means to power and honor.

Many nobles failed to respond, but enough did to flood sixteenth-century educational institutions. Even nobles who wanted to preserve more traditional modes of life, as warriors and estate owners, found themselves needing more education, for the development of gunpowder and firearms increasingly demanded a new kind of military man, one familiar with mathematics and with technologies of fortification. But military theorists also came to view familiarity with ancient military literature and history as directly relevant to their own craft. Partly because of the development of firearms, the early modern era (like the ancient world, but decidedly unlike the feudal Middle Ages) made heavy use of infantry warfare; and some of the most striking tactical innovations derived from ancient models. Nobles who hoped to succeed in the military, like their cousins destined for positions in the law and bureaucracy, had to go to school.

How much learning did these years at school and university actually instill? Answers, of course, varied according to individual circumstances and temperaments. Studies of the military nobles in several regions have shown how modestly such figures might be touched by literature. In mid-seventeenth-century England, a wealthy and educated peer might be satisfied with a library of only about 100 books. In Germany the situation was comparable: in the region of Franconia, most nobles had only a few dozen books, and few showed much interest in works of literature. In France, the lords of Pont-Saint-Pierre, wealthy Norman nobles with important relations in the high Parisian bureaucracy, owned just a handful of books before the 1760s. The situation was similar in seventeenth-century Paris, and even worse in the nearby territory of Luxembourg; there in the eighteenth century most nobles owned only a few books, and some owned none at all. For many nobles, it seems, rising

[9] Quoted Hexter, "The Education of the Aristocracy," 63; Eva Pleticha, *Adel und Buch: Studien zur Geisteswelt des fränkischen Adels am Beispiel seiner Bibliotheken vom 15. bis zum 18. Jahrhundert* (Neustadt a. d. Aisch, 1983), 21.

educational standards had little impact on later life.[10]

As a social norm, however, awareness of literature had more importance than such numbers imply. Nobles who expected to do well in high
society or at court were expected to display their culture; failure to do so
was taken as a sign of backwardness. And in fact examples of spectacular
learning could be found everywhere, even in apparently remote regions.
In early seventeenth-century Bohemia, there was the example of Peter
Vok Rozemberk, a great aristocrat whose library included more than
10,000 books and who regularly supported poets and scientists –
including the astronomer Johan Kepler. His friend Karel Zerotin,
another great aristocrat, court official, and landowner in neighboring
Moravia, spoke several languages, corresponded with scholars throughout Europe, and himself produced series of political tracts and reflections.
These men were typical of their time and place; early seventeenth-
century Prague produced an intensely intellectual court culture, and its
great nobles stayed in close touch with developments throughout Europe.
England witnessed a comparable flowering during these years, exemplified by the earl of Arundel; Arundel was not only the greatest art collector
of his age, but also someone deeply engaged by Renaissance literary
culture – to the point of buying two distinguished sixteenth-century
libraries.[11]

But nobles in much less favorable circumstances likewise sustained a
sincere cultural involvement. The Italian-born military commander
Ottavio Piccolomini led a roving and violent existence, and contributed to
some of the worst moments of the Thirty Years War – yet he was also a
well-informed and serious patron of Galileo, and assembled an impressive collection of art. Despite the repressive intellectual atmosphere that
the Catholic Reformation brought to Spain, the story there was similar:
several noble families assembled very large libraries, and used them
seriously. In the mid-sixteenth century the Osuna family, members of the
high nobility, endowed a university on their estate; in the early seventeenth century, they were the principal patrons of the poet Quevedo, and
of a series of lesser writers. More surprisingly, contemporaries described
reading as a normal occupation for the lesser Spanish nobles as well. "I
have about six dozen books," explains one such figure to the novel-

---

[10] Stone, *The Crisis of the Aristocracy*, 707; Pleticha, *Adel und Buch*, 101–03; Jonathan
Dewald, *Pont-St-Pierre, 1398–1789: Lordship, Community, and Capitalism in Early
Modern France* (Berkeley, 1987), 189–90; Roger Chartier, *Lectures et lecteurs dans la
France d'Ancien Régime* (Paris, 1987), 99–100; Calixte Hudemann-Simon, *La Noblesse
luxembourgeoise au XVIIIe siècle* (Paris-Luxembourg, 1985), 422–24.

[11] R. J. W. Evans, *Rudolph II and His World: A Study in Intellectual History, 1576–1612*
(Oxford, 1973), 140–45, 153; David Howarth, *Lord Arundel and His Circle* (New Haven,
1985), 154.

obsessed Don Quixote, "some novels, some in Latin, some history and some works of devotion. I enjoy the profane more than the devotional, provided that they are a source of honest entertainment." In Germany too there were strikingly cultivated nobles from unlikely backgrounds. Hans Pleickhard von Berlichingen, for instance, was the grandson of a famously uncultivated warrior – but he had studied at the universities of Jena and Bourges, owned books in Latin, French, and Italian, and displayed a serious interest in humanistic culture.[12]

For women, educational possibilities were far more limited during the early modern period, because schools and universities were largely closed to them. Yet they too participated in the cultural revolution of the sixteenth and seventeenth centuries. Religious reformers, both Catholic and Protestant, called for literacy on the part of women as well as men, since both religions attached new importance to reading religious texts. Though women had no possibilities of serving in government offices, they were expected to participate in the cultural exchanges of court life; and in many families they took on a large share of estate administration, since their husbands were so often absent at court or in the army.

As a result, female illiteracy largely disappeared from the nobility by about 1600, and a few women received strikingly advanced educations. In the early seventeenth century, Aletheia Talbot, the earl of Arundel's wife and the daughter of another earl, designed buildings, corresponded with artists and collected their works, and closely supervised her children's education; in 1620 she took them to Venice for this purpose.[13] By the late seventeenth century, England counted a number of women writers, some of them professionals, others writing only for their genteel families; at least one of them, the dramatist Aphra Behn, managed to earn a good living from her writings alone, an extraordinary accomplishment given England's still limited literary market. Across the Channel, the educated aristocratic woman had become common enough to stimulate satire from the comic dramatist Molière. His ridicule made clear the difficulties that educated women still faced, but it also suggested the cultural power that they had begun to acquire and the anxieties that they stimulated among many men. Power was especially clear in the literary salons that several aristocratic ladies had begun holding in mid-seventeenth-century Paris. These gatherings brought together intellectuals and socialites, and

[12] Ignacio Atienza Hernández, *Aristocracía, poder, y riqueza en la España moderna: la Casa de Osuna Siglos XV–XIX* (Madrid, 1987), 100–03; Antonio Domingez Ortiz, *Las clases privilegiadas en la España del Antiguo Régimen* (Madrid, 1973), 164, quotation 162; J. H. Elliott, *The Count-Duke of Olivares: The Statesman in an Age of Decline* (New Haven, 1986), 7; Pleticha, *Adel und Buch*, 41–42. (Goethe devoted a play to Berlichingen's grandfather, presenting him as an example of the German knights before their corruption by Renaissance learning and courtly manners.)
[13] Howarth, *Lord Arundel*, 14.

women were expected to contribute to discussions, rather than merely listening to men's ideas. As in England, a handful of aristocratic women novelists had established themselves by Molière's time. Madame de Lafayette, who was rich, published anonymously, though Parisian high society knew of her authorship; Mademoiselle de Scudéry, from the poor nobility, wrote to earn money. Her enormous novels (running to ten and more volumes each) were among the best-sellers of the mid-seventeenth century, though Scudéry could not live on her sales alone. Like most other seventeenth-century authors, she depended on gifts from wealthy patrons, and in return she had to produce works that celebrated their grandeur. By this point, European high society had a place for intellectual women, though it excluded them from many of its institutions of learning.[14]

Cultural patronage and cultural production

One result of this educational activity was to draw nobles into close involvement with contemporary art and writing, chiefly as patrons, less often as cultural producers themselves. Given their wealth and political power, nobles could scarcely have avoided playing a central role in determining the shape of the art and literature around them. They bought much of the art and subsidized many of the writers, and they heavily influenced institutional support for the arts, from church and state. Other forces pushed in the same direction. At court, nobles were expected to show knowledge of the arts and practical ability in some of them; until the late seventeenth century, for instance, young nobles at court were expected to dance in ballets, one of the many accomplishments expected of them. And still more basic conditions of aristocratic life demanded cultural involvement. For nobles who had the money, musicians, playwrights, and artists were a daily presence, because they supplied basic forms of indoor amusement. Wealthy nobles had string music playing as they dined, and they regularly had plays performed in their homes.

Nobles thus could not have avoided a prominent role in early modern culture. But the period brought something more, a readiness among nobles to appreciate artistic innovation, a surprising degree of support for what was new and even challenging in contemporary culture. Involvement of this kind intensified as the period advanced. By the late seventeenth century, nobles enjoyed the dominant voice in contemporary

---

[14] Boris Ford, ed., *The Cambridge Cultural History of Britain: Seventeenth-Century Britain* (Cambridge, 1989), 120, 128–29, 157–58; Carolyn Lougee, *Le Paradis des Femmes: Women, Salons, and Social Stratification in Seventeenth-Century France* (Princeton, 1976).

culture. This constituted a new situation. Nobles had been followers rather than leaders of late medieval culture, and in the sixteenth century cultural dominance remained with law school professors, theologians, and government officials. In the nineteenth century, nobles would return to this secondary role, as the bourgeois novel, journalism, and professional scholarship became primary modes of cultural practice. During the seventeenth and eighteenth centuries, however, nobles supported (and in some instances defined) the cutting edge of contemporary culture.

Their prominence could be seen in a variety of domains. During the seventeenth century, thus, enthusiasm for architecture touched the nobles of several countries. Nobles rebuilt their country houses, and many involved themselves in urban building projects as well. They did so for complex reasons. New building technologies such as glass-making made more comfortable buildings possible, and new military technologies such as gunpowder rendered medieval castles obsolete. New wealth enabled landowners to undertake the expenses of building, and competition with their neighbors made them eager to do so. But the striking fact about these rebuilding efforts was their aesthetic intent. From England to Bohemia, nobles who had the money sought to follow a new fashion for symmetrical and restrained design, based on the teachings of Roman architects and meant to convey classical values: of self-control and dignity on the one hand, of gracious and easy comfort on the other. The style had originated in sixteenth-century Italy, in urban palaces and in country villas designed for landowners who spent much of their time in the cities and who treated their country homes as pleasurable retreats rather than bases of power. In the early seventeenth century, both the style and the ideals behind it spread to England and France; by the eighteenth century, neo-classicism had become the norm for European architecture. It represented an especially influential effort by the nobles to employ aesthetic ideals of the ancient world. The effort sufficiently excited the British aristocracy that in the early eighteenth century a handful trained themselves as architects and designed their own country homes. The poet Alexander Pope celebrated the greatest of these aristocrat-architects, Lord Burlington, and noted the degree to which others were taking up the fashion: "Yet shall, my Lord, your just, your noble rules/ Fill half the land with Imitating-Fools." Wisely or foolishly, gentlemen were now expected to involve themselves in matters of architectural taste.[15]

Nobles involved themselves in contemporary painting almost as avidly. A small handful actually took up the brushes themselves.

[15] Quoted James S. Ackerman, *The Villa: Form and Ideology of Country Houses* (Princeton, 1990); see also 89–107, 140ff.

Wenceslaus Hollar, born into the Bohemian lesser nobility, left home in 1627 because his father refused to accept his choice to become an artist; in the 1650s prince Rupert, the descendant of German princes and an English king, collaborated in producing prints.[16] Much more often, of course, nobles became patrons and collectors. As with architecture, collecting paintings and encouraging contemporary artists became highly fashionable in the seventeenth century. Here too fashion began at the top of society. A mid-seventeenth-century Italian described the growing fashion for picture galleries in private houses, and emphasized that these "are suitable only for lords and great personages."[17] Fifty years later, an observer described the meteoric success of the Italian portraitist Rosalba Carriera, during her visit to Paris: "Ladies of the highest birth, and some of the most snobbish, came to her residence to pose from six in the morning." For many of these ladies and their husbands, no doubt, art meant little more than fashion, yet this was a fashion to which they readily sacrificed much of their customary haughtiness. The sacrifice became especially clear with regard to acknowledged contemporary masters. In the mid-seventeenth century, the French painter Nicolas Poussin refused to allow patrons to determine what subjects he would paint for them; hopeful buyers had to place their requests two years in advance. A Sienese nobleman did not even dare approach Poussin directly, but expressed to a mutual friend his desire to "have a work by one of the most distinguished modern painters," and his hope that the artist would be willing to paint a work religious in character.[18]

For works by leading contemporary artists, nobles were also ready to spend extraordinary sums of money. In 1655 the French finance minister, one of the richest men in Europe, was told that "it is difficult indeed to acquire a painting by Monsieur Poussin," because "the cost is astounding." The same could have been said of several seventeenth-century artists, for whose works collectors were willing to pay prices comparable to those of our own most successful contemporary artists.[19] Such expenditures suggest the seriousness of many nobles' involvement with the art world around them. At least some artists agreed. The Flemish painter Peter Paul Rubens described the English earl of Arundel as "one of the evangelists of our art" – reasonably enough, since Arundel had nearly bankrupted himself in his pursuit of paintings and other art objects. Like many of the nobles around him, Arundel was more than a

[16] Richard T. Godefrey, *Wenceslaus Hollar: A Bohemian Artist in England* (New Haven, 1994), 4, 107, 150.

[17] Quoted Jeffrey M. Muller, *Rubens: The Artist as Collector* (Princeton, 1989), 55.

[18] Quoted Rheims, *La Vie étrange des objets*, 81, 247.

[19] Quoted Rheims, *La Vie étrange des objets*, 247; see also 246–68 for striking examples.

mere buyer. He and his circle saw themselves as connoisseurs, seeking to develop autonomous tastes and expressing vigorous opinions.[20]

For even the least self-conscious art buyers among the nobility, portraiture came to matter a great deal. The genre had scarcely existed in the Middle Ages: the oldest extant French portrait bust dates from the mid-fourteenth century, and depicts a king. The taste for portraits began in the commercial republics of Italy and Flanders in the late Middle Ages, then was quickly taken up by kings and their courtiers. In the sixteenth century, however, nobles became increasingly fascinated with the genre, and portraits themselves became a normal backdrop to aristocratic life. By the seventeenth century, noble households of any standing had their collections of portraits, representing the family's own background and often including other notable figures. At his Burgundian castle, the French nobleman Bussy Rabutin covered the walls with dozens of portraits of the eminent captains and most beautiful ladies of his age – an extreme example of the preoccupation with individuality that Bussy shared with his contemporaries. The preoccupation was probably strongest at court (Bussy himself had spent much of his youth in close touch with the French court), and across Europe successful portrait painters grew rich in responding to this demand. From the sixteenth century on, each court had its favorite painters, who depicted both princes and courtiers.[21]

In some respects, this interest in portraits accorded well with traditional aristocratic values. Portraits allowed for the public display of familial pride, and they offered a means of conveying family feeling to unborn generations. These ideological functions help to account for the enthusiasm with which so many nobles commissioned images of themselves and their families. Yet alongside its conservative messages, much early modern portraiture included more radical implications. For early modern portrait painters became increasingly fascinated with their subjects' personalities. They continued to display their subjects' glamor, but they also showed personal complexity: aristocratic portraits from the seventeenth century convey their subjects' anxieties, melancholy, even disappointment and weakness. Seventeenth-century aristocratic portraiture offered nobles a mechanism for exploring and expressing individualism.

Painted portraits came first, but in the seventeenth century written

[20] Quoted Howarth, *Lord Arundel*, 2.
[21] César Rouben, *Bussy-Rabutin épistolier* (Paris, 1974); Jonathan Brown, *Velázquez: Painter and Courtier* (New Haven, 1986), 43–44 and *passim*; Lorne Campbell, *Renaissance Portraits: European Portrait Painting in the 14th, 15th and 16th centuries* (New Haven, 1990), 227ff.

portraits became almost as popular. Among the Parisian aristocracy, describing oneself and one's friends became a popular society pastime in 1640s and after; nobles sought to capture the main lines of their appearance, but also to bring out character, all in a page or two of witty prose. These passed back and forth in manuscript, and occasionally published versions appeared. So did more ambitious attempts at the same effect, lengthy memoirs tracing one's life and adventures and offering brief descriptions of the striking personalities one had encountered – in effect, miniature portraits within the larger portrait of one's life.

For the still more adventurous, the seventeenth century offered another avenue of self-depiction, the novel. Novels poured out of the seventeenth-century printing shops, few of them readable today but enormously popular with contemporaries. "The ease of printing and the passion for writing infinitely multiply these works," complained a French practitioner early in the seventeenth century. Their popularity seemed to derive from the double function they performed. On the one hand, they offered a glamorous, escapist version of aristocratic life, a dreamy series of adventures and love stories, often set in exotic locales. Yet everyone knew that the same novels presented contemporary stories and personalities in thin disguises, portraying leading contemporary nobles and tracing the events of their lives. These too were read as a form of portraiture, and the temptation to see them in this light became especially strong as novels became more psychological in orientation in the later seventeenth century. The seventeenth century's most revolutionary novel – revolutionary both for its avoidance of fantastic adventures and for its nuanced exploration of complicated emotions – was Mme de Lafayette's *The Princess of Clèves*, written by a noblewoman and dealing with an aristocratic milieu.[22]

This was only one instance of a larger process in seventeenth-century European culture. Over the sixteenth and seventeenth centuries, initiative in cultural matters tended to shift away from the highly educated circles attached to universities or to the middle classes, and came to lodge instead with courtiers and nobles, like Mme de Lafayette herself. Sixteenth-century culture had been largely dominated by men fluent in Latin and heavily influenced by Roman literature. A different figure dominated seventeenth-century culture: the elegant amateur, capable of writing and speaking well in vernacular languages, knowledgeable but unburdened by the heavy bookishness of the universities. Such an ideal of cultivation emphasized the value of native wit and personal style, and therefore offered a prominent place to women: if women had little access

---

[22] Quoted Dewald, *Aristocratic Experience*, 200; general discussion 199–201.

to Latin knowledge, they were seen as fully capable of speaking and writing cleverly. Above all, this ideal accorded well with nobles' images of themselves, for it emphasized the value of the courtier's natural grace and sensitivity to beauty. Though there were many exceptions, sixteenth-century culture had been dominated by men trained in the law, that is, by men who had passed through a demanding university training. Seventeenth-century culture, in contrast, was dominated by courtiers and gentlemen – and by gentle ladies.[23]

English drama illustrates the change with particular clarity. Before 1600, most English dramatists had been professional writers, many of them classically educated. After 1660, many leading London playwrights were gentlemen amateurs – and the plays they wrote described their own lives. In France few nobles actually wrote plays, but they were expected to participate in the process of composition and to be capable of offering intelligent comments to the professionals they patronized. Just as in England, moreover, late seventeenth-century comedy was expected to concern itself with the lives of the elegant upper classes, in contrast to the plebeian orientation of sixteenth-century comedy. At the same time, French nobles were expected to be able to write poetry – to the increasing annoyance of professional writers, who found themselves having to praise the half-baked productions of their social superiors.[24]

Finally, the development of early modern science too appealed to nobles and depended on their financial assistance. The courts of Florence and Prague saw some of the crucial work in early modern astronomy, sustained and followed in highly aristocratic settings. In the next generation, high nobles in Paris and London joined newly founded academies, watching experiments and accepting dedications of new works. As in so many other domains of early modern culture, support for science brought together a handful of genuine enthusiasts with a much larger number of the merely fashionable, who sought mainly the social status that being up-to-date conferred. But this was precisely the point: science – like other forms of cultural pursuit – had become so fashionable that even those with no actual interest felt obliged to attend scientific demonstrations and even to listen to scientific papers. By the late seventeenth century, it too was part of the cultivation expected of the fashionable man – and of the fashionable woman.[25]

---

[23] On women's place in the English literary marketplace, Janet Todd, *The Sign of Angelica: Women, Writing and Fiction, 1660–1800* (New York, 1989), 36ff.

[24] Ford, *The Cambridge Cultural History*, 120–21.

[25] Mario Biagioli, *Galileo Courtier: The Practice of Science in the Culture of Absolutism* (Chicago, 1993); Erica Harth, *Cartesian Women: Versions and Subversions of Rational Discourse in the Old Regime* (Ithaca, 1992).

The psychology of privacy

Examples such as these make it clear that nobles participated fully in the cultural movements of the early modern period. Indeed, given the extent to which they dominated Europe's economic and political resources, the situation could hardly have been otherwise. Writers, artists, and scientists turned to the nobles because they had the money to support cultural enterprises; and the professionals had little choice but to attend carefully to their patrons' cultural tastes. As important, however, these tastes proved surprisingly sophisticated. Nobles showed themselves willing to endorse, in many cases even to create, cultural forms that were distinctively new – and that have preserved considerable cultural force even in our own day. That force has resided partly in the fascination with individuality that seems to pervade many of the nobles' cultural enterprises. In diverse forms – glaringly in portraits, more subtly in psychological novels, poetry, and even in the design of elegant country retreats – nobles' culture reflected on the problems of selfhood.

This preoccupation suggests the need to look more deeply at the social contexts of the nobles' cultural involvements. Nobles (we have seen) had political reasons for educating themselves in the sixteenth and seventeenth centuries, as preparation for the competitive world of government offices and military commands. In addition, they confronted a widening range of economic changes. These too required them to be more alert to the world around them, and encouraged the use of reading and writing as means of coping with that world. Alongside these changes, however, came changes in the ways nobles lived, and these shaped their cultural choices in more specific, less utilitarian ways. In their daily lives, early modern nobles were becoming more interested in separating themselves from others, in creating private spaces. A popular mode of self-presentation made clear the links between cultural development and concern with privacy: starting in the sixteenth century, nobles and especially noble women began having their portraits painted holding books and reading. Bookishness had at least come to seem compatible with gentility, one of the accomplishments that a gentleman might properly seek to display and to have commemorated.[26]

Such images depicted more than just nobles' growing involvement in written culture. As an image of solitary activity, showing individuals engrossed in imaginative pursuits that had little reference to other people, these portraits also displayed early modern nobles' growing interest in privacy. Into the seventeenth century, nobles everywhere in Europe lived

[26] Chartier, *Lectures et lecteurs*, 199–203.

much of their lives surrounded by others, taking for granted a lack of privacy that most moderns would find intolerable. Even private doings would likely be witnessed by servants, followers, or friends – and this publicity extended to the intimate life of the body. Men very often found themselves sleeping together in one bed. Married couples had servants sleeping in the same room, and enjoyed only the limited privacy offered by bed curtains. Even in high society, bodily eliminations took place with others watching; in his early sixteenth-century manual of good manners, the Dutch humanist Erasmus advised that it was impolite to start a conversation with someone who was urinating or defecating, so little privacy did he assume in such matters.[27]

In fact no one wanted privacy. A great man or woman was expected to live surrounded by others, by dozens of servants and followers, often drawn themselves from the lesser nobility. Such crowds of followers demonstrated the great man's importance, the loyalty and service that he could command; privacy implied neglect and weakness. Great houses magnified the crowded quality of aristocratic life, by allotting almost no space to small, private rooms. Instead, aristocratic houses in the early sixteenth century consisted of a few great rooms, used interchangeably as bedrooms, living rooms, and dining rooms. Furniture was moved in and out as needs changed. Space within the house was in some sense impersonal, lacking designation as the bedroom or study of a specific person. The sixteenth century brought more divisions of space within the house, but no one felt the need for intimate rooms or for hallways, and thus other people continually trooped through the bedrooms and other private spaces of aristocratic houses. In the early eighteenth century, hallways were so new to the English aristocracy that an architect had to explain to the duchess of Marlborough that "the word corridor, madam, is foreign, and signifies in plain English no more than a passage."[28]

Placed constantly before an audience, early modern nobles knew that their lives had in some ways to be theatrical. They had to perform for those who watched their doings, some of whom, sooner or later, would report to the outside world what they had seen. Such lives required extraordinary degrees of self-control. They required, in fact, a relationship between inner life and outer action that was profoundly different from ours. In so theatrical a world, what was the place of sincere feeling or impulsive behavior? What places were there for solitude or intimate retreat? Until late into the sixteenth century, there were very few. Only hesitantly in the following two centuries did Europeans construct the

---

[27] Norbert Elias, *The History of Manners*, trans. Edmund Jephcott (New York, 1978), 130.
[28] Quoted Lawrence Stone and Jeanne Fawtier Stone, *An Open Elite? England 1540–1880* (New York, 1987), 345.

physical and psychological spaces that would allow for a different structuring of daily life.

By the end of the eighteenth century, however, this change – among the most powerful developments in European social history – had largely been completed. Those who could afford them had a range of private spaces available to them, and they had a culture that encouraged them to seek privacy often. Builders led the way, creating new dispositions of space within the home. Smaller rooms now became available, suitable for intimate conversations or solitary reading, and furniture makers supplied suitable furnishings: sofas for conversations, small and efficient stoves for heat, writing tables. Privacy had become an important ideal.[29]

So far-reaching a change had many sources. Religion contributed, for both Catholic and Protestant reformers wanted their followers to undertake private devotions, meditations, and readings. Political changes had similar effects, through both prohibitions and examples. Princes everywhere (we have seen) disliked seeing their aristocratic subjects surrounded by masses of followers. At the same time, they wanted to establish their courts as centers of elegance, with new standards of behavior, and in part this meant new demands to separate parts of one's life from others' gaze. At the German court of Brunswick, for instance, the prince sought to legislate privacy in bodily eliminations. "Let no one," proclaimed his court regulations of 1589, "whoever he may be, before, at, or during meals, early or late, foul the staircases, corridors, or closets with urine or other filth, but go to suitable, prescribed places for such relief." The prince's regulations echoed those of other courts. At the north German court of Wernigerode in 1570, the prince ruled "One should not, like rustics who have not been to court or lived among refined and honorable people, relieve oneself without shame or reserve in front of ladies."[30] Regulations like these betray the complexities of privacy in the late sixteenth century. Concern with privacy was partly a concern with social distinction, an effort to separate oneself from "rustics" and others who lived outside court society. Even to the refined, it was by no means an obvious value; courtiers had to be nagged into using toilets, and even in the mid-seventeenth century many failed to do so. By the early eighteenth century, though, these values could be taken for granted in the polite society that surrounded the courts.

There seems to have been a deeper psychological level to these changes.

[29] On sixteenth-century furnishings, Kristen Neuschel, "Noble Households in the Sixteenth Century: Material Settings and Human Communities," *French Historical Studies*, 15, 4 (Fall, 1988), 595–622; on the eighteenth century, Jean Nicolas, *La Savoie au XVIIIe siècle: noblesse et bourgeoisie*, 2 vols. (Paris, 1978), II, 966–72.

[30] Quoted Elias, *The History of Manners*, 131; *passim*, for pioneering discussion of these issues.

During the seventeenth and eighteenth centuries, European nobles experienced changing ideals about their bodies: they sought to establish boundaries between themselves and others. For this is what much early modern concern with cleanliness amounted to. The change was visible at the dining table. In the early sixteenth century, each diner had his or her knife and a spoon for soup, but most eating was done with fingers; forks existed, but only as serving implements. Hesitantly over the sixteenth and early seventeenth centuries, individual forks came into fashion – so hesitantly that a 1672 treatise of good manners advised "If everyone is eating from the same dish, you should take care not to put your hand into it before those of higher rank have done so." As hesitant was the development of ideas about the proper separation between diners: as the same treatise warned, "you should always wipe your spoon when, after using it, you want to take something from another dish, there being people so delicate that they would not wish to eat soup into which you had dipped it after putting it into your mouth." Ideas about cleanliness still remained uncertain, and an insistence on separate plates for each diner could seem excessive refinement even to such advice givers. Only with the eighteenth century can one see full acceptance even in court societies of the sharp separation of each diner from the others. An important psychological change had taken place. Practices that once had seemed normal – eating with one's hands, placing one's own spoon in the common plate – came to seem not merely impolite, but disgusting.[31]

Bodily cleanliness expressed similar concerns with separation, and developed at about the same pace as more elegant table manners. Sixteenth-century Europeans believed hot water to be harmful save in carefully controlled medical circumstances. Heat opened the body to the external threats of disease, and it stimulated inner lusts. Rather than clean bodies, sixteenth-century aristocrats attached fanatical importance to clean clothing, and especially to white linen. It became usual in the sixteenth century to change one's clothes several times a day. In the following century, bathing itself became important. The Moravian grandee and military commander Albrecht von Wallenstein illustrated the mid-seventeenth-century growing preoccupation with cleanliness by ordering for himself a bathtub made of silver.[32]

Concerned in these varied ways with establishing privacy around the self – with creating physical spaces for personal life, with separating off private functions from others' observation, with cleaning the self from

---

[31] Quoted Elias, *The History of Manners*, 92.
[32] Georges Vigarello, *Le Propre et le sale* (Paris, 1984); Golo Mann, *Wallenstein, His Life Narrated*, trans. Charles Kessler (London, 1976), 212.

others' touch – nobles naturally became preoccupied with another aspect of privacy, that is, with governing relations between masters and servants. Here was the most difficult aspect of privacy, for early modern technology seemed to demand servants to supply the comforts of elegance – yet their very presence limited privacy. In 1500 there had been unalloyed pleasure and honor in living surrounded by servants, for few wished to be alone. Thereafter the problem became increasingly acute. One answer was simply to treat servants as beneath notice, so inferior as to be invisible. Some nobles could carry this off – in eighteenth-century Paris, Madame du Châtelet bathed in front of her male servant, implying the irrelevance of his possible sexual interest and the absolute boundary between mistress and servant.[33]

Not all could act with such assurance, though, and one current of early modern thought stressed the sexual allure of the servant, even for very aristocratic ladies; and there were the more diffuse fears of theft and rebelliousness, the more strongly felt because most domestics were short-term employees, with little previous connection to their employers. Anxieties like these made the aristocratic household a very tense place. Servants could not be eliminated, but there began a movement to reduce their numbers and reduce their possible influence over the master's family. Architects helped, by planning aristocratic houses with sharply distinct servants' quarters. Moralists warned parents to keep chidren away from servants. "How can one imagine," asked a French observer in the 1780s, "that for twelve hundred francs a year some mercenary will bring up a real man?" Enlightenment philosophers agreed. Service, claimed Denis Diderot, "is the most abject of occupations." In some regions, observers claimed to see the effects of these ideas. "For some time now," wrote a resident of the French city of Montpellier, in 1768, "many have rejected the ridiculous luxury that consisted in filling one's household with servants bedizened in gaudy liveries. Nowadays people prefer to hire only those that are necessary, and to keep them as busy as possible." A numerous household of dependants had once seemed the essence of aristocratic life. In the eighteenth century, it increasingly seemed an unpleasant burden, which could only interfere with healthy family relations. Relations with intimate family members now came first.[34]

[33] Sarah Maza, *Servants and Masters in Eighteenth-Century France* (Princeton, 1983), 187.
[34] Quoted Maza, *Servants and Masters*, 290, 289, 278. Cissie Fairchilds, *Domestic Enemies: Servants and Their Masters in Old Regime France* (Baltimore, 1984) explicates the fears that surrounded servants and presents evidence of declining numbers. Cf. Hudemann-Simon, *La Noblesse luxembourgeoise*, 435–37, for the persistence of households with numerous servants in eighteenth-century Luxembourg.

The family and the self

Both nobles' amusements and their social ideologies (we have seen) helped to form individuals who were competitive, edgy, individuals who adapted readily to violence as a mode of life. The nobles' family arrangements contributed to the same result. Partly by design, partly by accident, aristocratic family patterns produced individuals who were well suited to the competitive, often violent world in which they moved.

In the nobles' own view of themselves, familial arrangements carried heavy burdens. For insofar as nobility rested on descent from distinguished ancestors and on purity of bloodlines, to a large degree nobility *was* family. The noble derived much of his/her identity from his lineage, and had an obligation to preserve this legacy for his descendants. Early modern nobles could become highly eloquent about what they owed their families. From the family came of course material advantages, but also honor and personal abilities. As a result (so ran contemporary theory) decisions about the family could not be left only to the individuals immediately concerned. Marriage, inheritance, education, and dozens of lesser matters affected the entire lineage. Its needs counted as heavily as those of any of the family's individual members.

Such tensions between the family's collective needs and the wants of its individual members emerged most visibly in the sphere of marriage, for here the individual's preferences conflicted most directly with the family's needs. Individuals may have wanted companionship, love, and sexual pleasures from marriage – but their families expected marriage to provide political power, status, and cash. As a result, through the sixteenth century personal choice played little role in most aristocratic marriage decisions. Families arranged marriages with little attention to the couple's wants, indeed often before the couple had reached puberty. At best sixteenth-century children might enjoy a veto over the partners their parents had selected for them.

Ideally marriage was intended to secure for a family distinguished connections, connecting the family with in-laws who could bring it new luster and powerful political connections. Far more important, marriage had to serve economic needs. More clearly than most domains of life, marriage illustrated the acquisitiveness and economic competitiveness that characterized even the most distinguished, most status-conscious aristocrats. Through most of the eighteenth century, all nobles married for money, in the sense that all girls in this milieu had to bring property to marriages: either cash, in the form of a dowry, or expectations of a substantial inheritance from parents and other relatives. No one could dispense with a dowry, and expectations as to its size rose over the period.

Marriage formed an important part of the process by which nobles sustained their economic dominance of early modern societies, however fecklessly they managed their own properties. Astute marriages brought infusions of capital to the husband's family, since contemporaries expected the bride to bring with her a substantial dowry. So important were the economics of marriage, in fact, that girls without the necessary resources had only the prospects of relegation to a convent or spinster-hood. After 1517 Protestantism removed even the former possibility across much of northern Europe, leaving a growing number of girls with no prospects but uncomfortable dependency on wealthier relatives.

The hard monetary calculations that dominated so many marriage choices made social inequality a common experience within marriage. A long succession of alliances joined aristocratic young men with wealthy women from lower ranks, the daughters of officials, bankers, and merchants; marriage of impoverished but noble women with wealthier men happened much less often, but certainly was not unheard of. Such marriages were not always comfortable. In his play *George Dandin*, the seventeenth-century French playwright Molière showed the humiliation of a commoner husband by his aristocratic wife – presumably expressing the anxieties his contemporaries felt about socially mixed marriages of all kinds. Yet most such alliances seem to have been more successful, not only for the couple but for their families. They strengthened bonds across the social barriers that might otherwise have divided upper-class society, giving nobles and officials alike connections that they regularly used.[35]

What then of marital love? Before the eighteenth century, few indeed accorded love between the couple importance equal to the financial and political stakes of marriage. This social consensus did not exclude the possibility of married love, or even of love matches, marriages entered into without arrangement by the families concerned. Historians have counted several such romances among the gentry of fifteenth-century England. More typical, though, were the mid-fifteenth-century efforts of Sir William Plumpton, who himself had married when he was twelve years old. Plumpton arranged for his teenage son to marry a wealthy girl who was then six years old; alas, his son died before the marriage could be consummated, but this proved no obstacle to the father's plans – not yet sixteen, the girl and her properties passed in marriage to Plumpton's younger son. Plumpton pursued exactly comparable arrangements for the next generation, marrying off his two granddaughters when they were about four years old.[36] Aristocratic families across Europe pursued

---

[35] I have described the workings of one such alliance in provincial France, in *Pont-St-Pierre*, 181–83.

[36] Keith Dockray, "Why Did Fifteenth-Century English Gentry Marry?: The Pastons,

comparable marriage strategies, with predictable consequences. Husbands and wives scarcely knew each other before the wedding, and few came to feel love afterward. Once they had consummated the marriage, in any event, their time together might well be limited. Men with careers of any significance spent much of their time living away from home, at court, in the armies, or in the lawcourts. Even the happily married found that such arrangements allowed them ample responsibilities and independence. Wives found themselves managing family properties, even, as we have seen with Margaret Paston, defending them against violent intrusions. They had to make decisions about lawsuits, harvesting, servants, provisions for the household. When husbands and wives lived together, they did so in ways that usually maintained their emotional distance. Sixteenth-century English mansions provided full suites of women's rooms, in which wives and other women of the household passed most of their time. French houses had similar arrangements.[37]

But efforts to strengthen the emotional connections between husbands and wives began in the sixteenth century and became more urgent in the seventeenth and eighteenth. One source of change was religious. As the nursery in which religious belief developed, the family seemed a crucial problem to Protestant reformers after 1517, and Catholics quickly came to a similar conclusion. Both sets of reformers demanded that the family better support children's religious lives, and to this end they called for more closeness between parents; a loveless household could not produce good Christians.[38] Secular moralists joined in the effort, demanding that children at least have a veto over their marriage arrangements and insisting that affection was the basis of real marriage. The French comic playwright Molière had little use for religious reform, but he filled his plays with examples that demonstrated the folly of arranged marriages – and the inadequacy of parents' concern for their children. "At least give us time to know each other," pleads one of Molière's heroines to her tyrannical father, "and to see develop in us that affection so necessary for a perfect union . . . Marriage is a bond that a heart should never be forced into."[39] A few seventeenth-century writers went further, arguing that marriage should begin with passionate love, not just with solid affection.

Plumptons and Stonors Reconsidered," in Michael Jones, ed., *Gentry and Lesser Nobility in Late Medieval Europe* (Gloucester-New York, 1986), 65.

[37] Alice Friedman, *House and Household in Elizabethan England: Wollaton Hall and the Willoughby Family* (Chicago, 1989), 47ff.; Jean-Pierre Gutton, *Domestiques et serviteurs dans la France de l'ancien régime* (Paris, 1981), 27.

[38] For the impact of Protestantism, Lawrence Stone, *The Family, Sex and Marriage in England, 1500–1800* (New York, 1977), 135–42.

[39] *Le Malade imaginaire*, Act II, scene vi.

"Young though I was, I could never understand how someone could decide to marry without love," recalled a French military nobleman late in the century.[40]

Talk of love and expectations that love might animate marriage were closely bound up with changing ideas about sexual relations themselves. European nobles through the sixteenth century held a complicated set of ideas about sexual relations, ideas that ultimately limited possibilities of real connection between men and women. On the positive side, women were assumed to have sexual needs and to enjoy sexual pleasure; in fact contemporary medical theory taught that women needed to reach orgasm in order to conceive. Such views implied a fundamental likeness between men and women, both driven by sexual urges and equal in their needs for sexual climax. Belief in women's sexuality encouraged a surprisingly bawdy atmosphere in much sixteenth-century high society, a readiness to talk and joke about sex that fitted easily with the era's indifference to personal privacy.[41] In the early sixteenth century the comic writer François Rabelais presented the ladies in his fictional land laughing at their young prince's penis; and early in the next century (we know) such interchanges actually took place in the court of Henry IV, with ladies-in-waiting fondling and laughing at *their* prince's penis.[42]

But the sixteenth century had its own forms of misogyny, to some extent bound up with its very attentiveness to female feeling. Precisely because women were so susceptible to physical arousal and sexual pleasure, sixteenth-century culture often described them as especially irrational and in need of close control. Michel de Montaigne in the later sixteenth century expressed a common view when he argued that women's innate irrationality made them incapable of real friendship, friendship of the kind that men could experience.[43] And the view of women's physical natures had a more sinister implication, for it implied a vision of how the woman might be reached and seduced. The seducer's main task, on this view, was to open the woman's physical feelings, for once these had been touched her passionate nature would make her incapable of further resistance – would reduce her in fact to loving dependence. Hence a series of essentially military images about how women should be approached – as fortresses to be captured, to be taken

[40] Quoted Dewald, *Aristocratic Experience*, 122.
[41] Stephen Greenblatt, "Fiction and Friction," repr. in Greenblatt's *Shakespearean Negotiations: The Circulation of Social Energy in Renaissance England* (Berkeley, 1988), 66–93; Thomas Laqueur, *Making Sex* (Cambridge, MA, 1990).
[42] François Rabelais, *Gargantua*, in *Œuvres complètes*, ed. Jacques Boulenger (Paris, 1955), 39 (Chapter 11); Philippe Ariès, *Centuries of Childhood: A Social History of Family Life*, trans. Robert Baldick (New York, 1962), 100ff.
[43] Discussed Dewald, *Aristocratic Experience*, 106, 120.

by force since compliance would follow force. Numerous sixteenth-century descriptions of sexual involvement begin with rape. One of the aristocratic interlocutors in Marguerite de Navarre's *Heptameron*, a series of bawdy tales from the mid-sixteenth century, typifies these views: "'Does it make sense,'" he asks, "'that we men should die for the sake of women, when women are made solely for our benefit? And does it make sense to hesitate to demand from them what God himself has commanded that they should let us have?'" A companion replies with enthusiastic agreement: "'Fortune favours the bold . . . you've only got to attack your fortress in the right way, and you can't fail to take it in the end.'"[44] To these men, rape seemed an unproblematic expression of male rights over women.

These ideas did not disappear from aristocratic culture after 1600, but they became less prevalent in elegant circles, for in the seventeenth century there developed a countervailing emphasis on women's delicacy, autonomy, and intellectual attainments. Expected to read and to have literary opinions, seventeenth-century noblewomen became more assertive in their dealings with men, and more critical of those who approached them without proper elegance. The newly developing literary salon gave women an opportunity to express their views, and to follow contemporary science. The intellectual distance between aristocratic men and women had narrowed significantly. As a result, companionship between men and women had become more of a possibility in the seventeenth century than in earlier times. These were ideals of family life that may have originated among the middle classes, but in the seventeenth century nobles adopted them with real enthusiasm.

Such ideas about the possibilities for emotional life between men and women developed alongside ideas about personality itself. The idea that marital choice was critical to individuals' happiness required strong belief that important differences set individuals apart – a belief that happiness rested with choosing the right spouse. Again, religious change contributed. Just as they agreed on the importance of the couple, early modern Catholics and Protestants agreed on the importance of self-exploration and analysis. Reformers of all stripes urged the faithful to undertake more careful soul-searching, to reflect on both sinful impulses and on signs of God's love. In some instances, notably in seventeenth-century England, this concern took the form of keeping a spiritual diary. But everywhere religious change produced greater self-awareness and an interest in exploring the complexities of character.

These changes brought greater warmth to many aristocratic homes

[44] Marguerite de Navarre, *The Heptameron*, trans. Paul A. Chilton (London, 1984), 119.

during the seventeenth and eighteenth centuries. But until then most nobles grew up without much parental affection – often, in fact, without much contact with their parents. Fathers had often to be entirely absent from home, serving as military men, courtiers, or officials. The risks of military service meant that many noble children grew up with no fathers at all. Few recorded what their experience of these intermittently present fathers was like, but probably the effect was jarring. Certainly this was true in the one case we do know well, that of the future French king Louis XIII and his boisterous father Henry IV. Henry visited his son rarely, but each time the event was traumatic, the child frightened, the father eventually angry that his son showed him more fear than love. Noble households across Europe must have witnessed similar interchanges, and there were other separations and absences. Noble families usually turned their children over to wetnurses for the first year or two of life – then removed them from the figure who had provided most of the mothering that the child had known. For all but the richest families, this meant a spatial as well as personal separation, for only very rich families could afford to maintain the nurse within the home. Boys underwent a further separation at about age ten, when they were sent off to one form or another of training. Those destined for administrative or church careers had then to begin serious schooling, often at some kind of residential college; future military men began at this age an apprenticeship in arms, serving as pages for older soldiers, from whom they picked up skills, lore, and habits. Few fathers sought to educate their own sons in these skills. To do so, most Europeans agreed, risked spoiling the child, leaving him too weak for the harsh world in which he would eventually have to move.

Such upbringings detached children from their childhood homes and from childhood itself, and this was the effect that parents sought. Children in these circumstances could scarcely have known their brothers and sisters, and their ties to parents had repeatedly been broken. For some these arrangements produced a bitter sense of personal loss. After the French Revolution, the aristocrat and one-time revolutionary Talleyrand wrote, "I say, . . . hoping never to think of it again, that I am perhaps the only man of distinguished birth . . . who has not for a single week of his life known the joy of staying under his parental roof."[45] By this time attitudes had sufficiently changed that Talleyrand could believe his childhood unusual. But even for the eighteenth century he was wrong, and in the sixteenth and seventeenth centuries childhoods like his were the norm. They left children with enduring grievances. Parents ignored such grief not because of indifference to children, but because of their

---

[45] Quoted Lewis Namier, *Personalities and Powers: Selected Essays* (New York, 1965), 2.

understanding of what children needed. The point was toughness, an ability to cope with a difficult, often hostile world. Children left too long at home (so it was generally agreed) would probably fail to acquire these qualities, surrounded as they would be there with indulgence and affection. Parenting and education had to accord with the violently competitive world that children would enter.

Such child-rearing practices had a further point: they prepared young men for early entry into the adult world. Aristocratic society in Europe for the most part was youthful, a society in which young men readily occupied important positions. In 1643 the great French noble the prince de Condé was twenty-two when he was placed in charge of the French armies at a crucial battle; his success there established him – barely out of adolescence – as the greatest general of his age. Roger de Bussy-Rabutin was a lesser figure than Condé, but he too began adult life early: at age sixteen he found himself leading a regiment in combat – after which his parents attempted to send him back to school! For officials the situation might be similar. The French government tried unsuccessfully for years to enforce regulations requiring that high court magistrates be at least twenty-five years old.

A double logic encouraged such careers. Nobles of course benefited from the privileges of birth and from parental connections, which placed them in high positions younger than their commoner competitors, who might have to advance through work and achievement. At the same time, the nobles' careers often demanded youth. Into the early nineteenth century warfare continued to require great physical vigor from even generals; no one could stay completely aloof from personal combat. Likewise, life at court demanded youthful grace; at court the old quickly became figures of fun, unable to keep up with fashions or amusements. Molière's comedies, performed before Louis XIV and his courtiers at Versailles, made the point clear to all: in them, to be old is to be foolish, selfish, and physically revolting. In one play after another, only the foolishness of the old – their inability to see that they are being duped – undermines their selfish tyranny and their indifference to others' happiness, including especially the happiness of their children. They have neither good sense nor affection for others. What Molière presented as comedy, other writers presented as mature political reflection: for the early eighteenth-century philosopher Montesquieu, for instance, the power of the young represented one of the essential markings of aristocratic societies.

At some point after 1700, this combination of assessments of age began to shift; youth and old age came to be looked at in somewhat different terms. Europeans of all classes became increasingly interested in childhood, indeed increasingly glorified the joys of both infancy and of caring for infants. In the second half of the eighteenth century, the philosophe and novelist Jean-Jacques Rousseau made parental care for children central to his program of moral and political regeneration, and his urgings found passionate response. Fathers and mothers began to hesitate about sending their children out of the house, and spoke instead of the joys of caring directly for them. Discipline became somewhat less central to educational theories, and in its place came stress on love as the source of psychic and social health. Such teachings touched middle-class as well as aristocratic families – but the evidence for aristocratic response is especially vivid. Indeed, long before Rousseau aristocratic parents had begun making a point of including children in their family portraits, in ways that accentuated the children's joyfulness and freedom. Some nobles even began speaking of the joys of playing with their children, even very young children.

In fact the eighteenth century brought into full flowering emotions that earlier generations had felt, but in profoundly ambivalent ways. In the late sixteenth century the essayist (and nobleman) Michel de Montaigne expressed uncertainties typical of his era, as he described the sorrow of one aristocratic father at his son's death in early adulthood. "Among his many regrets," reported Montaigne, was his grief "at never having opened his heart to the boy. He had always put on the stern face of paternal gravity, and had thus lost the opportunity of really knowing and appreciating his son, also of revealing the deep love he bore him, and the deservedly high opinion he had of his virtues. 'And that poor lad,' he said, 'never saw anything of me but a grim and scornful frown.'"[46] Montaigne's aristocrat expressed many of the ambiguities with which the sixteenth century regarded children. There was very powerful love and overwhelming grief at the child's death; yet contemporary theories of parenting demanded that love be concealed, so as not to spoil the child and diminish the force of paternal authority. As important, love here rested on the child's qualities, his "virtues" and the "deservedly high opinion" that they produced in the father. Love here rested on achievement. The child had to earn it.

In aristocratic circles, the eighteenth century thus brought not the invention of parental love for children, but its expansion and its detachment from the child's efforts. Children, so the new philosophy claimed, naturally drew their parents' love, as much for their failings as for their achievements. This appears to have been an important psychological change, a relaxation of that commitment to toughness and

---

[46] Michel de Montaigne, *Essays*, trans. J. M. Cohen (London, 1958), 149–50 ("On the Affection of Fathers for Their Children").

independence that characterized sixteenth-century families. Some historians have spoken of this change as the rise of "affective individualism," a new sense of love for individual persons and pleasure in their company. In fact we have plenty of evidence for love of this kind before the eighteenth century, love for children, spouses, and other intimates; and it is difficult to accept a view that discounts the psychological individualism of the sixteenth century, when we have such powerful examples of it in the portraits of the age. Yet something changed in the eighteenth century, something that should perhaps be described as a relaxation, an easing of the toughness that earlier generations had imposed on children and their parents alike. Many eighteenth-century parents determined not to undergo the sense of loss that Montaigne had described. They would love their children in the present.

Their elders as well. For as it treated children with more affection and sense of pleasure, so the eighteenth century treated elders with more respect and liking. There seem to have been fewer foolish oldsters in eighteenth-century humor, and there were a substantial number who were admired and even loved. Here the example was set by the American visitor Benjamin Franklin, treated as an elderly sage – but also as a sexual being, with widely noted love affairs among the English and French upper classes. Physical disgust in the face of old age had receded dramatically.[47]

The problem of religion

Nobles (so this chapter has argued) participated actively in the cultural changes brought by the sixteenth and seventeenth centuries. Their enthusiasm, however, presented them with a problem that many early modern Europeans faced, that of fitting intellectual interests with religious faith. For nobles, the problem took especially acute form because their relation to Christianity had always been complicated. Like virtually everyone else in Europe before 1500, nobles believed in the Christian God and in the teachings of the Christian church. These were simply basic realities of life, which no one questioned. For medieval nobles, Christianity had a further, ideological appeal. Christian doctrine accorded with aristocratic social theory in viewing the world as hierarchically ordered. To clerics and aristocratic warriors alike, society needed difference and deference to function properly; this was the age-old idea of dividing society between the three estates, one committed to prayer, one to defense, and one to work. Only if men and women knew their places

---

[47] David Troyansky, *Old Age in the Old Regime: Image and Experience in Eighteenth-Century France* (Ithaca, 1989).

within this system and respected their superiors could order survive. Such ideas had flourished throughout the Middle Ages, and they received new vitality in the thirteenth century, when the church made Aristotle its chief intellectual guide. For Aristotelian doctrines emphasized the role of the governor, and thus they gave new justification for the nobility's privileges. Christianity offered nobles a powerful ideological support, a way of viewing their privileges and powers as natural and necessary.

Nobles' involvement with religion, of course, had practical as well as intellectual dimensions. Especially in Catholic Europe, the church offered nobles careers and wealth. The church controlled huge landed estates and extensive judicial powers, and those who held church offices could count on using them for their families' benefit. Nobles received most of this bounty, and if anything, their control of high church offices tightened over the early modern period. In the Rhineland, site of some of the richest churches in Germany, old noble families acquired a complete monopoly on significant ecclesiastical office – to the point that access to these positions became the critical distinction between wealthy and poorer nobles.[48] Italy had still greater ecclesiastical wealth, offering huge fortunes for those who controlled high church office. Non-nobles enjoyed much of this bounty in the fifteenth century, but thereafter the nobilities tended to take over; indeed, holding church office became something of a sign of noble status.[49] In France, too, 85 percent of all bishops were noble in the early sixteenth century, 87 percent during the century after 1690. In the Habsburg territories of central Europe, a number of commoners received bishoprics in the sixteenth century, but after 1600 these positions fell almost entirely to the high nobility. Lower ranks within the church hierarchy also had incomes attached to them, and also attracted nobles' interest.[50]

Like marriage, then, nobles' religious practice was too important a matter for families to leave to individual consciences. Families' economic strategies required that some of their members take up clerical careers, however tepid their religious feelings. Growing up in the early seventeenth century, for instance, the future Cardinal Richelieu had planned on a military career. But an unexpected death in his family required that he change careers and take on a bishopric that the family controlled.

[48] Harm Klueting, "Reichsgrafen-Stiftsadel-Landadel. Adel und Adelsgruppen im niederrheinisch-westfälischen Raum in 17. und 18. Jahrhundert," in Rudolf Endres, ed., *Adel in der Frühneuzeit: ein regionaler Vergleich* (Cologne, 1991), 17–53.

[49] Richard Goldthwaite, *Wealth and the Demand for Art in Italy, 1300–1600* (Baltimore, 1993), 126–29.

[50] J. Michael Hayden, "The Social Origins of the French Episcopacy at the Beginning of the Seventeenth Century," *French Historical Studies*, 10 1 (Spring, 1977), 27–40; Evans, *The Making of the Habsburg Monarchy*, 137–39.

Richelieu's ready obedience to his family's needs paid off handsomely: his religious role provided him with a starting-point for a political career, and a succession of additional church offices provided a huge fortune.[51] Few noble families could boast such successes, but nearly every family included clerics and (in Catholic Europe) nuns among its members. Such intimate connections with religious life must have meant familiarity with its practical details and a broad commitment to the church interests.

But even in the Middle Ages the accord between aristocratic ideology and Christian religion had significant flaws. For the nobility, there was above all the problem of violence, the imperfect fit between a religion of peace and a warrior aristocracy, which found warfare glorious as well as necessary. The medieval church tried to erase this contradiction by creating a Christianized warrior, one whose violence was directed outward in crusading against religious enemies. But by the thirteenth century this effort had visibly failed, leaving the aristocratic warrior an uneasy participant in Christian communion. Kings' growing demands for absolute allegiance from their nobles added to the tension, for royal governments now demanded that nobles exercise their violence for purely political ends, without reference to personal moral standards or religious convictions. Sooner than most other subjects, in fact, nobles found themselves having to cope with the problem of secularization – the distinction between political and religious values. The issues were posed when the French king Louis XII in the first decade of the sixteenth century led his armies against the pope, and when his successor allied with Turks and Protestants against the Holy Roman Emperor.

As a man of violence and a devoted follower of the state, the nobleman had always occupied a difficult position within Christian belief. There were comparable problems with another of the nobleman's roles, that of man of honor, determined to assert his dignity and punish slights to it, if necessary with violence. At the core of aristocratic ideology was an assertion of self and family, and a sense of society as requiring constant struggle if self and family were to retain their rightful positions. Christ had taught submission to slights, humility to all others, and renunciation of outward glories; what place could honor have in such an ethic?

For many nobles, the Protestant Reformation of the sixteenth century offered temporary solutions to some of these tensions. Many found the doctrines of the Lutheran and Calvinist Reformations powerfully appealing, for these doctrines spoke to the contradictions between Christian practice and secular life, by affirming the importance of secular activity: to Luther and Calvin, the warrior performed a religious duty even if his

---

[51] Joseph Bergin, *The Rise of Richelieu* (New Haven, 1991), 38ff.

violence served only the secular aims of the state, for (as they taught) all
political power derived immediately from God's dispositions. There was
more. Sixteenth-century Protestantism glorified the role of the nobility
as an intermediary power in the state, responsible for governing churches, controlling the populace, and in extreme cases for checking the powers
of kings themselves, when they violated fundamental laws. Cynics might
note as well that Protestants promised to make church lands available to
lay buyers. But material calculation was less significant than the cultural
role that Protestantism seemed to offer. Luther and Calvin alike told
nobles that their military and governmental roles were an expression of
Christian piety, not a contradiction of it, and they offered an imposing
vision of the nobles' social role – far superior to that of the priest, at times
akin to that of the prince himself. It was for this reason that Martin
Luther addressed one of his most important early tracts directly to the
German nobility. According to Luther, this was the group that had the
authority to change their nation's official religion.

Thus across Europe sixteenth-century nobles responded enthusiastically to programs of religious reform, despite serious risks to themselves
and despite the force of religious traditions, which might have bound
them to Catholic doctrines. In most regions, in fact, they accepted
religious innovation more readily than most other social groups. Most of
the great nobles of central Europe turned Protestant, creating powerful
Protestant factions within the nobilities of Poland, Hungary, Bohemia,
and Moravia. By about 1560 as many as one-third of the French nobility
had turned to Calvinism, despite the unwavering hostility of the French
kings to religious innovation – and despite a series of well-publicized
executions of religious dissidents. In mid-sixteenth-century Holland
there was a Protestant majority among the nobles, and the great families
there supplied leadership and some early martyrs to the Protestant
rebellion there. England was a more complicated case, since there the
king himself led rebellion against Rome. Yet clearly Henry VIII found in
his nobility and gentry a willing and surprisingly sincere audience for his
complaints against Catholicism, one that quickly gave up its bonds to
traditional religious belief. Only in southern Europe did the reformers'
appeal to support from the nobilities fail: in Spain because of the strength
of crusading traditions and increasingly rigid ideas about race; in Italy
because all upper-class society was so tightly bound to the institutions of
Catholicism, which supplied positions, revenues, and grandeur to all
families of any significance. Elsewhere nobles supplied the reformers
with the core of their support, support far more important than mere
numbers would suggest. The nobles' presence gave reform movements
political respectability, a way of meeting Catholic claims that new

doctrines would lead to social upheaval; in many areas, the nobles offered the new doctrines military defense as well.

After about 1570, however, Protestantism ceased to expand among the nobles, and by about 1610 it was in rapid retreat. In part its failure reflected Catholic adaptations. By the late sixteenth century Catholic theologians better understood the needs of lay elites, and they developed messages akin to the Protestants'. Their writers too began to stress the importance of the nobleman's role in the secular world, and they began to develop forms of piety that could be adapted to such a life in the world. By 1610 Jesuit schools had been established across Catholic Europe. The excellence of the education they offered attracted large numbers of nobles, and so also did the Jesuits' concern to adapt Catholicism to the needs of social elites. Writers of the Catholic Reformation urged even material success itself as a Christian duty. Thus St. François de Sales, advising an aristocratic friend early in the seventeenth century: "Be much more concerned than worldly people to make your possessions useful and fruitful . . . God has given them to us to cultivate, . . . and thus we render him a great service in doing so . . . we necessarily have a greater and more solid care for our possessions than do the wordly, because they work only for self-love, whereas we work for the love of God . . . Let us, therefore, care in this loving manner for our temporal goods, even augmenting them if some legitimate opportunity arises and our situation demands it, because God wants us to do this for love of him."[52] Like Protestants, thus, Catholics could adjust Christian teaching for men and women who were heavily involved in worldly affairs.

More immediately important, however, was the role of the state. Where kings remained faithful to Catholicism, it proved difficult for nobles to sustain a position of religious dissidence. Most nobles found the resulting conflict of loyalties difficult to sustain. They simply could not place themselves in a position of permanent opposition to their kings' religious beliefs. Nor were most of them willing to endure the practical losses that religious dissent brought. Nobles who refused to conform to the monarch's religious convictions could expect exclusion from bureaucratic and military positions, and they might also lose the broader political influence that they might otherwise have enjoyed. The process was most dramatic in Austria and Bohemia, at the heart of the Habsburg empire. After 1600, the Habsburg rulers of central Europe became increasingly rigid in their religious stance, determined to eradicate Protestantism even among aristocratic families. Protestant nobles found

[52] Saint François de Sales, *Œuvres*, ed. André Ravier (Paris, 1969), 173; English translation available as St. Francis de Sales, *Introduction to the Devout Life: A Popular Abridgement* (Rockford, 1984), 174.

themselves under heavy pressure to convert to Catholicism; those who failed to respond faced significant financial penalties, and they had to watch as the emperor raised new, Catholic families to prominence, in effect creating a newly Catholic nobility. In France the pressures of Catholic restoration were less intense, but there too Protestant families found themselves pushed away from the centers of power – until finally Protestantism was altogether banned from the kingdom, in 1685. Long before that point, aristocratic Protestantism had virtually disappeared from the country.

How much anguish did such religious choices cause? How seriously did nobles in fact take their commitment to either Catholicism or Protestantism? For a significant minority of seventeenth-century nobles, religion had enormous importance. It led some of them to take grave personal risks, and it led many to work at remaking the world in accordance with Christian teachings. In the early 1580s, the wealthy English earl of Arundel found himself moved by the Catholic priests he encountered in Protestant London, and soon converted, at a time when the English government viewed such a choice as treason. Queen Elizabeth had him arrested almost immediately and kept him in jail for a decade, where he finally died of dysentery. He died without ever being allowed to see his only son, who was born just after his arrest.[53] Comparable heroism could be encountered across Europe, on both sides of the religious divide.

So also could more mundane efforts to bring society into conformity with Christian teachings. In Protestant England, the late sixteenth century brought what contemporaries already called puritanism. Numerous gentry and some high nobles sought legislation to restrict such immorality as theater, dancing, and popular festivities.[54] In Catholic France pious nobles had strikingly similar ideas about social improvement. New religious orders formed, allowing pious nobles to play a more socially engaged role in such areas as teaching and poor relief. For nobles who remained in the secular world, there developed a series of tightly organized, highly effective groups devoted to improving the quality of French religious life – and to subordinating political to religious decisions. They sought to end the government's support of non-Catholic allies, and they sought to restrict what they viewed as licentious behavior. Just as in England, in France "the devout" (as they were known) sought to close theaters and outlaw dancing; "one must not go to a ball if one is a

[53] Howarth, *Lord Arundel*, 5–8; John Martin Robinson, *The Dukes of Norfolk* (Oxford, 1982), 68–79.
[54] Jean-Christophe Agnew, *Worlds Apart: The Market in Anglo-American Thought* (Oxford, 1986).

Christian," as one of them wrote late in the seventeenth century.[55] Spain too witnessed a rise of aristocratic puritanism in the seventeenth century. There a Junta de Reformación in 1624 proposed a ban on publishing all "plays, novels and other works of this kind, because of their unfortunate effect on the manners of the young," and in fact all such works were banned in Castile for the next decade. These were striking plans, in view of the vitality of Spanish drama and literature in the previous decades; theatrical performances had been especially appreciated at the Spanish court.[56]

Heroic religious enthusiasm and puritan morality touched many seventeenth-century nobles, and at moments these groups managed to dominate public policy. Yet the larger movement of contemporary feeling was against them. The majority of early modern nobles seem to have had lukewarm religious feelings, and they rarely allowed theology to stand in the way of worldly interests. More typical than the earl of Arundel, who risked his life for his religious convictions, were figures like his son, who quietly converted back to Protestantism and (in the words of a contemporary) "was rather thought to be without religion than to incline to this or that party of any." In keeping with this coolness, he remained close after his conversion to his Catholic wife and in-laws. In the very year of his conversion, he arranged that a proper monument be built for his Catholic father; familial pride mattered far more than any religious differences.[57] Albrecht von Wallenstein, the Bohemian nobleman who would lead the Catholic military forces during the Thirty Years War, had been brought up Protestant but casually converted to Catholicism in about 1606, for political advantages. He remained very close to his Protestant brother-in-law, who vigorously advanced his political career, and when politics required saw no problem about allying with the Protestant Swedes.[58] Given the sprawling nature of most great aristocratic families, coexistence like this was commonplace. Even during the burning religious conflicts of the sixteenth century, many noble families had included both Protestants and Catholics. Tolerance was especially striking in central Europe. Before 1618, for instance, Czech nobles managed to sustain a peaceful community that included both Protestants and Catholics.[59]

Such relative tolerance of religious diversity should not surprise us. Most nobles had always attached too much importance to family pride and personal honor to be very consistent Christians, whether Protestant

---

[55] Quoted Dewald, *Aristocratic Experience*, 135.
[56] Quoted Elliott, *The Count-Duke of Olivares*, 187; Ruth Kleinman, *Anne of Austria, Queen of France* (Columbus, 1985), 36, 116.
[57] Quoted Howarth, *Lord Arundel*, 220; see also 57, 105.
[58] Mann, *Wallenstein*, 73–75.
[59] Evans, *Rudolph II and His World*, 84–115.

or Catholic. But specific events further encouraged the nobles' essentially secular, skeptical outlook. The very ferocity of religious conflict during the sixteenth century encouraged such views. Observers could see the destructiveness of strong religious belief, most strikingly in the massacres that each side committed during the French Wars of Religion. Some could draw skeptical conclusions from what they saw, asking whether any religious doctrine could be so clearly right as to justify such violence. This was the question posed by the French magistrate and country gentleman Michel de Montaigne, and his essays were among the widely read books of the late sixteenth century. Others had asked a further question: at different times during the French Wars of Religion, both Protestants and Catholics had rebelled against the king, forcing contemporaries to ask whether one could be both a good citizen and a devout Christian. Religious enthusiasm seemed to undercut civic obedience.

During the 1620s and 1630s, religious belief received further challenges. The French minister Cardinal Richelieu was both the greatest aristocratic statesman of his age, leading France toward eventual triumph in the Thirty Years War and to dominance of European politics, and an exponent of harshly amoral political reason. French national interests, he argued, required alliance with Protestant princes against Spain and Austria, the great Catholic powers of the age. His example posed problems for puritan moralists, for his successes seemed to demonstrate the superiority of a politics divorced from religious standards. And Richelieu did win, both in foreign wars and in struggles against the relgious party within France, high nobles and bureaucrats who argued for a religious basis to French policy. To thoughtful Europeans of all parties, Spain seemed to embody an antithetical vision of politics, a politics based on religious loyalties and Catholic unity. Spain's humiliating failures in the seventeenth century seemed to teach a clear lesson: as Richelieu argued, politics had its own logic and its own moralities. Machiavelli had taught this lesson a century earlier, but for many Europeans it was the seventeenth century that demonstrated its truth. Early modern nobles took the lesson to heart more than most other groups, for they defined themselves as essentially a political class, destined to govern.

The impact of Enlightenment

The vigor of such ideas during the seventeenth century helps to explain nobles' relatively easy acceptance of the Enlightenment of the eighteenth century. To be sure, the eighteenth century brought radical challenge to important European traditions. Enlightenment writers criticized ideas about the proper organization of society and pointed to the injustices of many current practices. They denounced clerics, raised questions about religious belief itself, and mocked aristocratic vanity. They found the lesser nobles especially tempting objects of satire; Voltaire, Goethe, and numerous others offered exaggerated depictions of the lesser nobles' poverty, ignorance, and pride. Such caricatures appeared in some of the eighteenth century's best-selling books, and they were eagerly imitated by less serious writers, in dozens of pamphlets and pornographic novels. Criticism of nobility formed an important element in the Enlightenment's program.[60]

Yet a variety of indicators suggest the eagerness with which eighteenth-century nobles adopted Enlightenment views. Some of the best-known Enlightenment writers were themselves nobles, and so were many of their lesser-known imitators. More important, nobles represented a significant portion of those who bought Enlightenment books, and many of them participated in the institutions where Enlightenment ideas were discussed. Across Europe, nobles joined salons, literary societies, and Masonic lodges. In late eighteenth-century Spain, fully 10 percent of the high nobility subscribed to one periodical devoted to Enlightenment ideas – and this was only one of several such periodicals published in the country. In one region of France, nobles made up nearly half of those who bought Denis Diderot's *Encyclopedia* – one of the Enlightenment's most important publications. Throughout France, fewer nobles became priests after the mid-eighteenth century, and noblemen tended to give less money to the church (though noblewomen apparently remained more traditional in their religious practices). The situation was similar in the neighboring duchy of Savoy. "Gentlemen are becoming more and more rare in the Clergy," a mid-eighteenth-century observer complained; and in this region women as well as men were distancing themselves from the church. Nobles' detachment from their religious traditions made itself felt in such personal choices as well as at the level of high ideas.[61]

In later years, after the French Revolution suggested to social elites the

---

[60] Characteristic examples from the high culture of the period include Voltaire's *Candide*, Goethe's *The Sorrows of Young Werther*, and Fielding's *Tom Jones*; even apparently positive depictions of nobles, as in Goethe's play *Götz von Berlichingen*, in fact made the same point, suggesting as they did that true nobles (like Götz himself) were profoundly unsuited to the modern world. For the intensity with which criticism of the nobility was pursued in the eighteenth century's pamphlet literature, see Robert Darnton, "The High Enlightenment and the Low Life of Literature," repr. Darnton, *The Literary Underground of the Old Regime* (Cambridge, MA, 1982), 1–40.

[61] Richard Herr, *The Eighteenth-Century Revolution in Spain* (Princeton, 1958), 198; Robert Darnton, "The *Encyclopédie* Wars of Prerevolutionary France," *American Historical Review*, 78, 5 (December, 1973), 1331–52; Gilles de Regnaucourt, *De Fénelon à la Révolution: le clergé de l'Archevêché de Cambrai* (Lille, 1991), 101–02; Michel Vovelle, *Piété baroque et déchristianisation en Provence au XVIIIe siècle* (Paris, 1973), 133–35; Nicolas, *La Savoie*, II, 983–88; quotation 988, n. 22.

dangers of such radical ideas, some nobles expressed bewilderment at their ancestors' enthusiasm for the Enlightenment. Commentators suggested that nobles had been carried away by frivolous fashion, and that their interest had reflected a characteristic political immaturity. French nobles accepted Enlightenment criticism of their societies, so Alexis de Tocqueville suggested in the mid-nineteenth century, because they lacked experience with the real political world around them.[62]

But such views are fundamentally misleading. To be sure, for many nobles the Enlightenment was simply one fashion among many. They attended salons or literary assemblies because this was expected of educated people, and they bought advanced books in the same way. Yet for the nobility as a whole the Enlightenment meant more than fashion, because so many of its concerns accorded with their own. Enlightenment writers raised issues that confronted nobles in their daily lives, and used concepts that resonated with the nobles' own longstanding cultural orientations. Such accord might apply to specific issues. When Enlightenment writers praised constitutional government and urged that French politics become more like English, for instance, most nobles found themselves in vigorous agreement – for such views flattered their hopes for a larger voice in political life. Criticism of religion, likewise, fitted with many nobles' already tense relations with Christianity. Courtiers who had laughed at Molière's comedies in the later seventeenth century (despite the playwright's excommunication by the Catholic church) would not have been shocked by eighteenth-century criticism of religion; and they would have found much that was familiar in eighteenth-century writers' defense of human impulses to pleasure against the fears of ascetic Christianity. More broadly, the Enlightenment's preoccupation with useful knowledge appealed to nobles – for the nobles had succeeded over the previous century in converting themselves into a well-educated ruling class.

In fact, nobles could read with pleasure even Enlightenment critiques of their own order, such as those contained in Voltaire's *Candide* or Goethe's *Sorrows of Young Werther*. Novels like these made fun of the vanity and narrowmindedness of provincial nobles, whose claims to social superiority rested only on birth. Such figures certainly existed in the later eighteenth century, and occasionally they made their influence felt. Yet increasingly the more prosperous nobles saw themselves in different terms, as a propertied elite sharing values and interests with other social elites. Across Europe nobles' public language praised entrepreneurship and work, and their actions increasingly meshed with

[62] Alexis de Tocqueville, *The Old Regime and the French Revolution*, trans. Stuart Gilbert (New York, 1955), 138 ff.

this rhetoric. Relatively few nobles actually turned to trade, but (as we have seen) many treated their lands as objects of entrepreneurial calculation. They concerned themselves with producing food for distant markets and with making their lands more productive. Those who occupied political offices worried about such problems at national levels. They sought to improve agricultural and industrial production within the regions they administered, and they sought ways of dealing with contemporary social problems. During the mid-eighteenth century, the Prussian and the Austrian governments, both heavily dominated by nobles, undertook large programs of educational reform, designed to diffuse literacy within their borders. The effort had self-consciously economic dimensions: literacy was to improve national economic performance.[63]

Nobles who participated in such ameliorative efforts, whether public or private, found much to enjoy in Enlightenment criticism of traditionalist backwardness – including criticism of backwardness among their poorer and more provincial fellow nobles. Enlightenment criticism of nobility in fact often represented a call for a new kind of nobility, one based on public service and economic activity rather than on arbitrary privilege.

Across Europe, nobles adapted with striking success to psychological and cultural change during the seventeenth and eighteenth centuries. Their success was clearest in the realm of high culture. Nobles educated themselves, and they subsidized much of the culture produced around them. They supported much that was advanced in the cultural life around them, and indeed many participated actively in cultural life. Their enthusiasm grew over the sixteenth and seventeenth centuries, so that European culture acquired a more aristocratic texture by 1700 than it had had in 1550. Other adaptations were slower, but ultimately successful as well. Nobles gave up habits of personal violence, and acquired new forms of self-control. They became closer to their families, more affectionate to spouses and children. Many became somewhat less emphatic about their superiority to other social groups. Increasingly, they came to see social privileges as resting on ability and property, rather than on genealogy. They mingled more often with commoners, and they did so on closer terms.

In important ways, such adaptations reflected changes imposed on the nobles by the world around them. Nobles educated themselves because they were increasingly required to do so. States needed better training

[63] James Van Horn Melton, *Absolutism and the Origins of Compulsory Schooling in Prussia and Austria* (Cambridge, 1988).

from their officials, and even warfare called for bookish education; both Protestant and Catholic reformers held up education as an important element of Christian practice; an increasingly market-oriented economy made reading, record-keeping, and numerical calculation more valuable to landowners. The development of courts made the display of culture valuable. New forms of personal relationship, such as the increasing warmth felt toward family and friends, seem to have originated in the middle ranks of society. Nobles acquired these habits by imitating those whom they regarded as social inferiors.

Yet adaptation to outside forces does not fully explain nobles' cultural role during the early modern period. From about 1550 until the French Revolution, nobles dominated European cultural life far more completely than they ever had during the Middle Ages. They involved themselves passionately (and at great expense) in a variety of arts, and they accorded immense respect to artists, most of them humbly born. By the mid-seventeenth century, painters such as the Spaniard Velázquez and the Fleming Rubens enjoyed both the formal trappings of nobility and the informal social acceptance of other nobles. Nobles rarely became painters, but they often participated directly in other arts, some in architecture, a great number in literature. In the course of the seventeenth century, indeed, the ideal of the gentleman amateur came to dominate some forms of literature, and the direct style of the courtier became the model of good writing. In the two centuries before the French Revolution, the nobles defined the main lines of European high culture – and the art and literature that they patronized retained a central place in Europe's canon into the twentieth century.

Cultural involvement of this order is an important fact in itself, and it tells us something about the nobles' psychology in these years. Clearly that psychology extended beyond impulses to grandeur and the preservation of the past – impulses that often have been seen as defining the aristocratic mind. Early modern nobles certainly had such impulses, but they had others as well. Above all, they seem to have been fascinated by the varieties of emotional life. They found the literary and artistic exploration of the feelings endlessly interesting. Nobles' investment in such artifacts of high culture, in other words, served important social needs. Early modern high culture interested the nobles because they were in fact trying to live in new ways.

Conclusion
Toward a new society: the French Revolution and beyond

In 1789, the largest and grandest of the European states experienced unexpected shocks. Burdened with heavy debts from a century of warfare, the French king confronted a fiscal crisis that risked incapacitating his government. Meeting the crisis, it was clear, would require the king to restructure his government and impose new burdens on his subjects, but he could not make such decisions on his own. Doing so would undercut his most urgent need, for a restoration of public confidence – and of bankers' readiness to lend his government more money. Thus at the king's orders, on May 4, 1789, 1,248 representatives of the French population began meeting in Versailles. Significant constitutional changes, nearly everyone agreed, would be needed to end the government's troubles, but few observers expected the Estates General to transform French government or society.

In the event, of course, the calling of the Estates General led rapidly to fundamental changes in both government and society. For a full generation after 1789, French men and women experienced revolution. The monarchy and the Catholic church were first restructured, then abolished; in 1793–4 the king and queen were placed on trial and executed. Nobility suffered a similar fate. Specific privileges attaching to noble status were abolished almost immediately, and the status itself disappeared soon after; significant numbers of nobles went into voluntary exile, and the French government arrested others whose loyalty to the Revolution seemed suspect; some forms of property from which the French nobles had benefited were abolished, and the government confiscated lands belonging to suspects and exiles.

Nor was the Revolution's impact limited to France. From 1792 on, revolutionary France found itself at war with the rest of Europe. French military successes brought the Revolution's institutions and social values to large parts of the continent. By 1799 France controlled the Low Countries, the Rhineland, and much of Italy; in 1808 a puppet state was established in Spain. Before the French arrival, the Spanish government had already begun an effort at land reform, with the intention of breaking up great estates held by the aristocracy and the church – demonstrating that even nations that resisted France found themselves affected by the French example. Faced by the need to organize effectively against the French and in some cases under direct French pressure, the German states too had to organize themselves in new ways. In the decade after 1805 German princes established a series of written constitutions, for the first time codifying citizens' rights and diminishing inequalities between them. Most of these constitutions significantly lightened burdens on the peasantry, improving their chances of mobility and lightening seigneurial dues. Prussia and Bavaria, two of the larger and more influential German states, ended serfdom in the same years.[1] The Chancellor of Prussia described the atmosphere in which his government made these concessions: many landowners, he explained, "say that it is better to give up voluntarily than be forced to sacrifice everything . . . frightful consequences will be unavoidable if the common man . . . takes matters into his own hands."[2]

The French Revolution thus opened a new phase in the nobility's history – not just in France, but throughout Europe. The nobles' history (and their successes) continued after 1789, but on fundamentally different terms. Nobles now had fewer advantages in their dealings with other social groups, and the society around them was rapidly changing. For this study, the Revolution raises important questions. The simplest concern the Revolution's direct impact on the nobility. How serious were the economic and personal losses that the nobles sustained? What remained to them in 1815, when monarchy returned to France and to other European countries? More complicated questions center on the extent and the sources of revolutionary anger at the nobility. Why did the order elicit such dislike from contemporaries? Did revolutionary anger reflect deep feelings within eighteenth-century society, or did it result from the accidental events of the Revolution itself? Interpretation of the Revolution has important implications for understanding eighteenth-century nobles' relations to the society around them.

The nobility's problematic place within French society became obvious with the calling of the Estates General itself. Well before the start of serious conflict over France's political future, widely followed writers called for the nobility's destruction. Probably the strongest such call came

---

[1] James Sheehan, *German History, 1770–1866* (Oxford, 1989), 265–67.
[2] Jerome Blum, *The End of the Old Order in Rural Europe* (Princeton, 1978), 356, quotation 361.

from one of the privileged themselves. This was the abbé Sieyès, a priest and thus a member of the first estate, but also a brilliant political writer in defense of the third estate. His famous pamphlet *What Is the Third Estate?* is in fact a small book, suggesting the high level of political debate in the months leading up to the Revolution and the seriousness of the issues involved. But despite its form, Sieyès's message was violent. French nobles were parasites, he argued, who contributed nothing to society but absorbed a large share of its wealth and honor. Their destruction would invigorate France rather than weakening it. The real nation was the third estate; only this nation produced goods and used its abilities. *What Is the Third Estate?* ended with a violent proposal. The nobles must choose, either to allow themselves to be absorbed into the third estate itself or to face violent destruction; they were a disease to be eradicated. "The nobility is not part of our society at all; it may be a *burden* for the nation, but it cannot be part of it," Sieyès argued. His argument inverted one of the nobility's own favorite claims, that of belonging to a race separate from other Frenchmen, as descendants of Germanic conquerors. "The nobility," he wrote, ". . . is a foreigner in our midst."[3]

What Is the Third Estate? must have shocked contemporaries by its rejection of current social arrangements. For the book proclaimed the propriety under certain circumstances of social war, and it urged the expulsion of a large social group from the nation; in fact it proclaimed that the nobles had never belonged to the nation and had no rights within it. The violence was all the more striking because it came in so scholarly a format and from a man who was not an extreme revolutionary. A decade later Sieyès would play an active role in promoting Napoleon Bonaparte's restoration of authoritarian government and aristocratic style in France; and even during the first years of the Revolution he appeared a moderate figure. If men like Sieyès could express violent anger against the nobility, hostility in 1789 must have run deep indeed. That it did so is suggested by the successes of the book and its author: the book sold out several editions during 1789, and Sieyès became one of only three clerics elected to represent the third estate at the Estates General. Clearly his ideas had a wide appeal in early 1789.[4]

The Estates General in fact applied Sieyès's vision almost immediately after convening, with the enthusiastic assent of educated public opinion. In calling together the Estates, the crown had followed the division of French society into three orders, as these had been understood for nearly eight centuries. There was to be a first estate of clergy, a second of nobles, and a third of commoners. As a concession to middle-class opinion, the

[3] Keith Michael Baker, *The Old Regime and the French Revolution* (Chicago, 1989), 156–57.
[4] R. R. Palmer, *The Age of the Democratic Revolution*, 2 vols. (Princeton, 1959–64), I, 491.

king allowed the third estate twice as many representatives as each of the other orders, but he insisted that each order deliberate independently of the others and that voting be by order: clergy, nobles, and third estate each had one vote, ensuring that no measures could be passed without the assent of at least one of the privileged orders. But even the announcement of these arrangements aroused middle-class indignation, and the members of the third estate simply refused to follow the king's constitutional directives. In place of an Estates General divided by social ranks, they insisted on a single assembly of equal representatives. They were to be something entirely new, a National Constituent Assembly, embodying by their very organization an egalitarian conception of political rights and social organization. Following a tense stand-off with the crown, they prevailed. Willingly or not, members of the privileged orders were forced to join the Assembly on these terms. In effect, the representatives had carried out Sieyès's program, submerging the privileged in an egalitarian nation. Nobility had disappeared as a fundamental element of the French constitution; a vision of equal citizenship had replaced it.

Within three months the erasure of privilege had gone still farther. In a dramatic session on the night of August 4, 1789, the National Assembly did away with most external marks of nobility itself and with a host of privileges and positions that had long been associated with it. Seigneurial authority disappeared, ending the nobles' most vivid expression of leadership in the countryside; so too did venal offices, their principal form of political power, and the venal military offices. If the integration of the three distinct estates into a single national assembly marked the end of nobility as a constitutional idea, the Night of August 4 marked its end in daily affairs. The delegates had eradicated privilege, the thousands of small actions and expectations that made nobility a lived reality in the eighteenth century. After August 4 nobility ceased as a visible reality – at least so official legislation would have it. In June 1790 the Assembly took the final step and abolished nobility itself as a social status.

To this revolution in ideas about citizenship and society, the summer of 1789 soon added practical revolution – expressing in action the dislike of distinctions that representatives to the estates had established in law and theory. In a few rural areas, crowds rioted and attacked aristocratic properties, burning papers and a few houses. But the most important events came in Paris, where a large crowd besieged and finally captured the Bastille, the great royal fortress on the eastern edge of the city. Following their triumph, they killed two notable aristocrats, the military man in charge of the fortress and the royal governor of the city, and then mutilated their bodies; the crowd paraded through the streets with the two men's heads stuck to the ends of pikes. Here was an event to shock contemporaries across Europe, for they had come to think of their age as one of civilization, progress, and order. Violent crime had diminished, and violent rebellion had become far less frequent than in previous centuries. No one expected the savage mutilation of respected personages in one of the continent's most civilized cities. Powerful and unexpected political forces had suddenly emerged.

In both theory and action, then, the summer of 1789 marked an explosion of hostility against nobility itself. The king had wanted political reforms, which would allow his government to tax social elites and function more effectively. The representatives of the French middle classes had arrived at Versailles with a fundamentally different vision of their task. From the outset, they sought to erase the nobility's privileged standing within the French constitution. Popular violence during the summer of 1789 confirmed this vision of radically different social arrangements. This was to be a revolution about the place of privilege and distinction within society, about the existence of nobility itself. Middle-class representatives asked such questions even before arriving at the Estates General.

Where had this radicalism come from? Probably not from below, from the mass of peasants and artisans who constituted the large majority of French society. Some peasant rebellions marked the early phases of the Revolution, and a few nobles' houses were burned. But these incidents were much less frequent than historians once believed. In fact most peasant activism during the Revolution was directed against revolutionaries rather than nobles, as villagers sought to restore the Catholic church and resist revolutionary taxation.[5] The social experiences of middle-class reformers probably counted for more in 1789. Snubs and exclusions were a commonplace experience in Old Regime society, in both private and public life. Late eighteenth-century regulations kept non-nobles out of certain occupations, and made their access to others difficult. Ambitious outsiders might have little difficulty in taking advantage of the openings that eighteenth-century society offered, but many failed to do so. The German novelist Goethe clearly spoke for many in his generation when he described his hero Werther at a gathering of provincial nobles. The commoner Werther had a strong sense of self-worth, but nonetheless felt unbearably humiliated when the nobles refused to accept him as an equal.[6]

---

[5] For critical review of instances of peasant violence during the Revolution, Hilton Root, "The Case Against Georges Lefebvre's Peasant Revolution," *The History Workshop*, 28 (Autumn, 1989), 88–102; for the peasants' involvement in counter-revolution, Donald Sutherland, *France 1789–1815: Revolution and Counterrevolution* (London, 1985).

[6] Discussed above, Chapter 1.

But stress on middle-class anger shields from our view the reasoning that underlay this assault on nobility – as well as the fact that many nobles shared the political philosophy offered by the third estate. Sieyès himself (we have seen) belonged to the first estate; and many of those who led the destruction of nobles' privileges during the Night of August 4 were from the high nobility. These figures were seeking to reconfigure the nobility's place in French society, in the manner of enlightened reformers across Europe. In Germany, Spain, Austria, and northern Italy, groups of nobles participated in efforts to improve their societies by reducing the force of social distinctions. In the decade before the Revolution, the Habsburg emperor Joseph II (Marie Antoinette's brother) brought dramatic reforms to Italy and central Europe. He eliminated serfdom from much of his territory, reduced the nobles' political voice, and ended their fiscal privileges. Just as important, he sought to promote the social mixing of nobles and commoners, opening the imperial gardens to all social classes and inviting commoners to his ballroom. "For industry, for commerce," he proclaimed, "nothing is more necessary than liberty, nothing more harmful than privileges and monopolies." In the 1780s, it seemed that thoughtful members of all social classes could agree on the need to end nobles' privileges and make them full members of the larger society.[7]

Anger, it seems, mattered less than philosophy in 1789 – though there was certainly plenty of anger as well. As both enlightened nobles and commoners expressed it, privilege stood in the way of social development. They believed that French nobles should become the core of a broader social elite, whose dominance would rest on superior wealth, taste, and ability, rather than on irrational privileges accorded to birth. We have seen that, across Europe, the nobilities were in fact moving closer to this social ideal. Writers like Sieyès told the nobles that they could preserve their leadership only on such terms – and many nobles agreed, playing a constructive role in the unfolding of a new, liberal regime.

But the course of revolutionary events during the following years brought much sharper doubts about the possibility of integrating the nobles

---

[7] Nicholas Till, *Mozart and the Enlightenment: Truth, Virtue and Beauty in Mozart's Operas* (London, 1992), 85–96; quotation 88; Calixte Hudemann-Simon, *La Noblesse luxembourgeoise au XVIIIe siècle* (Paris-Luxembourg, 1985), 239ff. For the view that nobles themselves wanted some such integration within a liberal political order, Guy Chaussinand Nogaret, *La Noblesse au XVIIIe siècle: de la féodalité aux Lumières* (Paris, 1976); for critical review of this line of thought, Michel Vovelle, "L'Elite ou le mensonge des mots," *Annales ESC*, 29, 1 (1974), 49–72.

within society. From the outset, those nobles who attended the Estates General acted in ways that deepened their alienation from other social groups. Their language, their dress, even their habits of sociability – all proclaimed distance from the third estate. Even after joining the National Assembly, the nobles' voting patterns remained distinctive, and they soon formed a political club devoted to defending their own interests.[8] During 1789 itself, some highly visible nobles left France, established themselves in Belgium and the Rhineland, and publicly denounced the Revolution. Thousands of others followed in the next three years. They lobbied the great powers to undertake war against France; when war came, in 1792, many joined the foreign armies. Faced with a nobility apparently willing to betray its own nation, the revolutionaries' own rhetoric became correspondingly more violent. By 1793, numerous revolutionary politicians argued that the taint of nobility was so grave that no virtuous actions could compensate for it: "it's a delusion . . . to believe that equality can penetrate the soul of someone who has learned, from the cradle on, to treat his fellows as beasts of burden." Others attached nobles' guilt to birth itself: "their hearts are hardened from birth," concluded another leading Jacobin. Even intensive political reeducation, such statements implied, could not make the nobles acceptable members of a democratic society. There could be no accommodation with such enemies.[9]

Hence the war opened a period of brutal assaults on even those nobles who had remained peaceably at home and had supported the Revolution. All titles ended; "aristocrat" became a political denunciation, signifying opposition to the Revolution and the threat of subversion; symbols of the old society were uprooted, and those who clung to them, however harmless they might seem, were subjected to arrest and trial. In one village in northern France, an impoverished seigneurial gamekeeper who persisted in wearing his silver-buttoned coat was arrested in 1794 – and executed as an aristocratic enemy of the Revolution.[10] Throughout France comparable events unfolded. Harmless widows, distinguished magistrates, loyal country gentlemen – all found themselves under suspicion for their symbolic or real attachments to the old social order. At Toulouse, in southern France, nearly half of the members of the Parlement, the great lawcourt of the Old Regime, were arrested and

[8] Timothy Tackett, "Nobles and Third Estate in the Revolutionary Dynamic of the National Assembly, 1789–1790," *American Historical Review*, 94, 2 (April, 1989), 271–301.

[9] Patrice Higonnet, *Class, Ideology, and the Rights of Nobles During the French Revolution* (Oxford, 1981), 59, quotations 150.

[10] Liana Vardi, *The Land and the Loom: Peasants and Profit in Northern France, 1680–1800* (Durham, 1993), 35.

executed as aristocrats, despite the fact that many of them had advocated liberal opinions before 1789.[11]

Paralleling this effort against symbolic enemies were efforts against the declared enemies of the Revolution, the émigrés. Into 1792 nobles had been able to move freely back and forth across French borders – and they could transfer the funds needed for life in exile. War brought this liberty to an end and made the exiles seem clear national enemies. In keeping with this new suspicion, the government seized their properties and began auctioning them off. Their relatives fell under suspicion, and their arrests began. Closer controls were established on travel outside France, so as to make emigration itself more difficult. A new system of passports and identity controls made even movement within France problematic – and made it easy for local enemies to place even the most right-thinking nobles in jeopardy. The Revolution's attacks on the nobility were frightening partly because of their injustice. Even by the terms that the revolutionary authorities set out, their efforts hurt many essentially innocent people.

Yet the limits of revolutionary violence also need to be emphasized. Only about 7 percent of the nobles emigrated and exposed their properties to seizure – though their number included much higher percentages of the greatest families. Still fewer nobles faced the revolutionary tribunals; in the country as a whole, about 1,200 were executed in the course of the Revolution, roughly 1 percent of the order. This meant that large regions had little experience of revolutionary trials and executions. In the large and wealthy province of the Franche Comté, twenty-six nobles were executed, frightening instances of revolutionary injustice, but only a small blow to the order as a whole. To be sure, nobles suffered in disproportionate numbers from the effects of revolutionary justice – but the typical victims of the system in fact were peasants, and the large majority of nobles managed to escape the Revolution's direct violence. Even families that did suffer confiscations proved amazingly adept at protecting their properties. Properties could be handed over to relatives or to discreet front-men, and some nobles made astute use of inheritance laws to detach property from politically threatened émigrés. Some families lost, but most probably did not – and in any case significant compensation came in 1825, when a newly royalist government, headed by Louis XVI's brother, set aside money to reimburse their losses.[12]

In other ways too, most of provincial France had a far milder experience of Revolution than Paris. Many village nobles continued

---

[11] Philippe Wolff, ed., *Histoire de Toulouse* (Toulouse, 1974), 417.

[12] Higonnet, *Class, Ideology, and the Rights of Nobles*, 58; Claude Brelot, *La Noblesse en Franche Comté de 1789 à 1815* (Paris, 1972), 119; Sutherland, *France 1789–1815*, 386–87.

tranquilly to levy seigneurial dues (theoretically abolished on August 4, 1789) into 1791. Even more frequently, nobles continued to enjoy the deference and respect that they had long claimed. Many marks of their claimed superiority had been abolished, but they retained their status as local leaders and moved easily into the offices that the revolutionary legislature had created. Partly because of their suspicions of monarchical tyranny and partly because of their belief in property owners' rights, the early revolutionaries exalted the role of the local notable. As important landowners, enjoying local eminence, many nobles found themselves in a new position of local political leadership, new if only because local positions had been so much less numerous in the previous regime; and this prominence of the local notables remained a permanent legacy of the Revolution, despite all the constitutional variations that followed 1789. There were other compensations. In 1790 the revolutionary government began selling lands that had belonged to the Catholic church, as part of its effort to settle the state's financial problems. Like other prosperous Frenchmen, nobles recognized these church lands for the bargains they were, and many bought. The Revolution had brought benefits as well as costs.

And after the summer of 1794 the threat of revolutionary violence diminished quickly. By this point the French of all classes had come to find revolutionary justice oppressive, and in July the most radical revolutionary leaders were themselves arrested, tried, and executed (all in the space of twenty-four hours). Revulsion at the extraordinary violence of the previous two years played its part, and so also did a growing confidence about the future of the new society itself. French armies and administration had disproved the expectations of aristocratic Europe, had in fact shown that the new form of government might be *more* powerful, *more* effective than the old. The revolutionaries' successes had made the nobility seem less impressive, less necessary – and also less dangerous to society. Compromise now seemed possible, because the new society seemed so strongly established. Thus émigrés slowly began returning to France, in small numbers after about 1795, in much greater numbers after Napoleon's seizure of power in 1799 "reopened the gates of France to the nobility" – in the words of one noble lady who gratefully benefited from the new order.[13]

We should not understate the losses that both émigrés and other nobles had suffered. Nobles found that some forms of property simply had vanished. Many families had owned official positions during the Old Regime, and these the Revolution abolished without compensation. Most

[13] Quoted Robert Forster, *The House of Saulx-Tavanes: Versailles and Burgundy, 1700–1830* (Baltimore, 1971), 179.

noble families owned some feudal dues (also abolished), and for some these constituted an important percentage of family revenues. Property disappeared under revolutionary legislation, and other economic advantages also disappeared. No longer could pensions and other forms of assistance be expected from the government, as the Old Regime's high nobles had experienced; and no longer could the estate owner profit from the advantages that feudal law had offered Old Regime lords. Other properties survived but were especially vulnerable to the economic shocks that Revolution inevitably brought. Intermittent periods of hyperinflation destroyed the value of bonds and other obligations that the nobles held. Of course the process worked both ways: the nobles found that their own debts had vanished as money lost its value. But the balance was negative, especially since by the end of the eighteenth century many nobles relied so heavily on money-lending as a source of income. The Revolution brought higher taxes on all large landowners than nobles had ever confronted during the Old Regime. And properties that were seized even for short periods underwent significant depredations. Furniture was damaged or lost, buildings fell into dilapidation, lands were neglected. A near-decade of neglect could do enormous damage to both rural and urban holdings.

These losses were real and had long-term effects on aristocratic finances. Many noble families never regained the economic momentum that they had enjoyed in the eighteenth century – momentum which had derived partly from the advantages they enjoyed over non-noble competitors in such matters as taxation, inheritance, and connections with government officials. But survival remains the most important fact about the nobility's experience of Revolution. Most nobles avoided both exile and arrest. The minority who suffered these misfortunes often managed to hold onto their properties through adroit legal maneuvers, and enjoyed eventual compensation for what losses they did sustain. Nobles could no longer view themselves as the unchallenged leaders of French or European society after 1815. But they remained rich and powerful, sufficiently so to play a large role in the culture, politics, and economics of the nineteenth century.

The French Revolution, then, largely completed the long-term processes of change that this book has attempted to sketch. It did not destroy the nobility, but it did undermine the last substantial differences that separated nobles from other wealthy and powerful members of their societies. It turned the nobles into one among several elements within a larger ruling class in European society. As such, the nobles had to follow the rules of a new social order, without many longstanding economic and

psychological props. These were genuinely new circumstances, especially because they included an element of fear that the nobles had never
experienced before 1789. Their encounter with revolution left all propertied men and women with the conviction that popular movements might
again threaten their well-being. Such fears touched all of Europe, and
they proved enduring even in countries that had been immune to
revolution. From the 1880s on, thus, a series of leading English nobles
sold off their London properties, for fear that rising political pressures
would destroy their value.[14]

This book has argued, however, that such anxieties were not quite so
new as they seemed to contemporaries, for nobility had never been so
solid and stable as conservatives later imagined. Nobility had in some
ways always been an artificial element within European society, its claims
to ancient origins and public service visibly false. Contemporaries could
see around them new families rising and old ones disappearing; they knew
that most families did not descend from medieval conquerors. To this
vague awareness of instability, the early modern period brought further
challenges. Intellectuals like Erasmus challenged the nobles' claims that
they served society through warfare. The rise of administrative nobilities
established an alternative model of nobility, one that rested on learning
and the peaceful exercise of administrative responsibilities – to some
extent, on personal achievement rather than familial inheritance. Relations between rich and poor nobles became more strained, and as mutual
support within the order weakened poorer nobles tended to drop out of
the order altogether. Eighteenth-century nobilities were very small
groups indeed, probably about half as large as their medieval predecessors.

In this sense, the nobles' absorption into a larger ruling class was
already largely complete before 1789. It had become steadily more
difficult over the early modern period to hold the status of nobility
without holding substantial wealth. There had always been poor nobles
in European society, indeed the poor had formed the large majority of the
order. Through the sixteenth century, honorable social roles had been
available to such figures, as dependents of the great. What had once been a
normal aspect of society's functioning, however, by 1700 had come to
seem a contradiction within the social order. Poor nobles survived, but
they suffered increasing mockery from the world around them. Most
painfully, rich nobles themselves joined in the laughter and made it clear
that they preferred the company of talented or wealthy commoners to that
of ignorant country gentlemen.

In part this disaggregation of the nobility reflected the cultural

[14] David Cannadine, *The Decline and Fall of the British Aristocracy* (New Haven, 1990),
122.

transformations of the early modern period. Educational standards rose rapidly, under the influence of both religious reformers and new political needs. Nobles had to educate themselves if they were to appear at court or receive administrative positions, and even if they were to be successful military commanders. To a surprising degree they succeeded in this effort. During the seventeenth century, European culture took on an aristocratic and courtly tone that it had not previously had. In the fifteenth and early sixteenth centuries, the leading roles in European culture had been played by highly educated specialists, university-trained theologians and Latin-speaking humanists like Erasmus. In contrast, the seventeenth and eighteenth centuries glorified the aristocratic amateur, the man or woman of taste and ability, who had avoided the stultifying effects of specialized training. Such men and women had an increasing role to play as European high culture shifted from Latin to vernacular languages. It came to be expected that nobles would write poetry, novels, and essays, and that they would offer informed judgments on others' efforts. They followed other arts closely, and an influential handful even tried their hand at architecture.

So central a role in contemporary culture testifies to the nobles' capacity for adaptation to change over the early modern period. But cultural adaptation also brought with it new divisions within the nobility. Access to culture was expensive, requiring both education and familiarity with the fashions of the court and the city. It excluded poor nobles and village squires, and it made exclusion public. And just as cultural engagement increased the distance between rich and poor nobles, it established close contacts between rich nobles and able commoners. Though social boundaries remained important in eighteenth-century salons and learned academies, these institutions nonetheless offered a formal ideal of positions open to talent. These were settings in which high nobles mingled with professional writers, artists, and scientists. Backward nobles had no place there.

Other changes that this book has traced worked in the same directions. Specifically aristocratic forms of property tended to decay in early modern Europe. Lordship, the form of landed property that combined economic value with public authority, disintegrated most quickly. Despite institutional variations across Europe, noble landlords everywhere became more purely economic actors, whose incomes depended on selling what their land produced. After 1600, land itself lost some of its centrality as well. Alternative sources of income became numerous, and non-specialists had much easier access to them. As a result, after 1700 it was by no means certain that the nobleman would be a landowner; and in most regions the odds were against his residing in the countryside even if he did own property there. Economically (as in their social relations), nobles became less different from other social groups. Indeed, eighteenth-century nobles' rhetoric celebrated the similarity, praising mercantile entrepreneurship and indicating approval of young nobles who took up business careers.

By the eighteenth century, changing manners and modes of life too had created new resemblances among the rich of all backgrounds, and new differences within the nobility itself. Sixteenth- and seventeenth-century moralists increasingly made gentility a matter of behavior and psychology, rather than of pure birth. They schooled Europeans in habits of self-control and cleanliness, and urged greater respect for individuals' privacy and emotional autonomy. By implication, such counsels challenged the primacy of birth as a marker of worth. They suggested the importance of inner qualities, which might have little to do with status. They explicitly raised questions about the legitimacy of patriarchal authority, the metaphorical basis of nobles' powers over others in their society.

Finally, early modern nobles confronted changes in the functioning of political power. Probably the expansion of state power was the greatest social change that Europe experienced in these years; and the state's expansion touched every aspect of nobles' lives. Much of the change was negative. Nobles found themselves excluded from the easy familiarity they once had enjoyed with their kings, and in western Europe they lost powers that they had once exercised in the countryside. They had to submit to new taxes and regulations. Old noble families had to watch as a wave of new administrators and judges established themselves in the sixteenth century, and these new figures quickly won for themselves both wealth and social status. They challenged the old nobles' sense of social superiority, and they challenged ideas about the nature of nobility itself. These were nobles who did not fight, yet they enjoyed more authority than most of those who did.

Nobles had complicated responses to the expansion of governments during the early modern period. Many, including some of the richest and most distinguished, responded with hostility and intermittent violence. Aristocratic rebellions dominated the political history of sixteenth-century England and France, seventeenth-century France and Spain. In their indignation at the state's expanding powers, some nobles even proved willing to encourage peasants in rebellion. Irritation with central authority, it seems, mattered more than the nobles' perennial anxiety about lower-class rebelliousness.

Sooner or later, however, nobles who could do so joined the state rather than continue in opposing it, for the state had much to offer. There were governmental positions, both as civil servants and, in keeping with the nobles' ancient traditions, as soldiers. There were business possibilities, as states sold land, borrowed money, and contracted with private entrepreneurs to collect taxes. There was the excitement of life at court, which during the sixteenth and seventeenth centuries became the focal point of society, and for the greatest nobles there was direct financial support, in the form of pensions and gifts from the crown. Perhaps most important, there were the indirect results of stronger government. Across Europe – in the later sixteenth century in England, after 1650 in most continental countries – stronger government brought pacification to the countryside. Brigandage and private warfare disappeared; international warfare continued, but became much less destructive for ordinary people. For landowners, this achievement of public order meant enlarged economic opportunities. It supplied the necessary background to improvements in cultivation and marketing. Nobles relinquished the autarky of the fifteenth and sixteenth centuries because they could rely confidently on large market networks, and these functioned because governments had succeeded in pacifying European societies.

Alexis de Tocqueville, we saw, believed that the European nobilities had declined steadily since the time of the Crusades. Clearly he was wrong in important ways. Despite numerous fluctuations and variations, nobles became richer and more powerful over the early modern period, and their impact on European culture deepened. But there are truths that may be drawn from Tocqueville's beliefs. The nobles survived and prospered only by relentless adaptation to a modernizing society, and not all could adapt. Poor nobles had little room for maneuver, and tended simply to drop from the order. Others failed to understand the economic or political currents around them. It was easy for nobles to bankrupt themselves in the early modern period, especially as steadily more consumer goods became available after 1650; and excessive political ambition might lead to arrests and executions – though families of such political victims proved extraordinarily successful in maintaining wealth and status. Even for successful nobles, however, adaptation required becoming something new. The European nobilities survived by fitting themselves to their societies, by giving up elements of their separate identity. Hence a final paradox in the nobles' history: the group became stronger through this process of renunciation, as it increasingly blended into a modernizing society.

Suggestions for further reading

The following suggestions are meant to orient readers to the large and uneven literature on the European nobles. I include here only works in English, and works that will be of broad use to students attempting to make sense of the field. Notes in the text offer guidance on more specific topics and indicate important works in other languages.

1 GENERAL STUDIES

Recent surveys offer excellent introductions to the period discussed here: see M. L. Bush, *Noble Privilege* (New York, 1983), and *Rich Noble, Poor Noble* (Manchester, 1988); H. M. Scott, *The European Nobilities in the Seventeenth and Eighteenth Centuries*, 2 vols. (London, 1995); and the important forthcoming work by Samuel Clark.

2 PRIMARY SOURCES

A number of readily-available primary sources provide insight into the nobles' lives, outlooks, and concerns. These include Jean Froissart, *Chronicles*, ed. Geoffrey Brereton (London, 1968); Norman Davis, ed., *The Paston Letters: A Selection in Modern Spelling* (London, 1963); Baldesar Castiglione, *The Book of the Courtier*, ed. Charles Singleton (Garden City, NY, 1959); Madame de Sévigné, *Selected Letters*, ed. Leonard Tancock (London, 1982); Elborg Forster, ed., *A Woman's Life in the Court of the Sun King: Letters of Liselotte von der Pfalz, 1652–1722* (Baltimore, 1984); Frederick Pottle, ed., *Boswell's London Journal, 1762–1763* (New York, 1950).

3 THE MEDIEVAL BACKGROUND

Thomas Bisson, "The 'Feudal Revolution,'" *Past and Present*, 142 (February, 1994), 6–42, offers a superb introduction to medievalists' current thinking about how the nobility developed. A more radical approach is taken by Susan Reynolds, *Fiefs and Vassals: The Medieval Evidence Reinterpreted* (Oxford, 1994), who questions most of what historians once believed about how medieval nobilities functioned. Guy Bois, *The Crisis of Feudalism: Economy and Society in Eastern Normandy, c. 1300–1550* (Cambridge, 1984; first published 1976) offers an unusual attempt to see late feudal society whole, integrating the history of aristocratic politics with that of estate organization and economic life. Finally, Johan Huizinga, *The Waning of the Middle Ages* (Garden City, NY; first published 1919) remains astonishingly relevant to current thinking.

4 NATIONAL EXAMPLES

Though uneven in coverage, there are important English-language studies of most European nobilities:

ENGLAND

Lawrence Stone's *The Crisis of the Aristocracy, 1558–1642* (Oxford, 1965; an abridged paperback edition is available) set the agenda for recent studies of the nobilities everywhere; it presents an especially rich version of the thesis that landed elites underwent a significant crisis in the early modern period. Stone has since broadened some of his conclusions and revised others (notably regarding the idea of crisis itself) in a series of other important works: notably *The Family, Sex and Marriage in England 1500–1800* (New York, 1977), and with Jeanne Fawtier Stone, *An Open Elite? England 1540–1880* (New York, 1987) (abridged paperback editions of both are available). G. E. Mingay, *The Gentry: The Rise and Fall of a Ruling Class* (London, 1976), remains a good introduction to English issues. The work of Robert Brenner represents an important effort to contrast English developments with those occurring elsewhere in Europe: see Trevor Aston, ed., *The Brenner Debate: Agrarian Class Structure and Economic Development in Pre-Industrial Europe* (Cambridge, 1985).

FRANCE

Robert Forster played a pioneering role in drawing historians' attention to the French nobility: see especially his books *The Nobility of Toulouse in the Eighteenth Century* (Baltimore, 1960) and *The House of Saulx-Tavanes: Versailles and Burgundy, 1700–1830* (Baltimore, 1971). More recent works include Emmanuel Le Roy Ladurie, "In Normandy's Woods and Fields," repr. in *The Territory of the Historian*, trans. Ben and Siân Reynolds (Chicago, 1979), a brilliant exploration of a unique primary source; Jonathan Dewald, *Pont-St-Pierre, 1398–1789: Lordship, Community, and Capitalism in Early Modern France* (Berkeley, 1987), and *Aristocratic Experience and the Origins of Modern Culture: France 1570–1715* (Berkeley, 1993); Ellery Schalk, *From Valor to Pedigree: Ideas of Nobility in the Sixteenth and Seventeenth Centuries* (Princeton, 1986); Kristen Neuschel, *Word of Honor: Interpreting Noble Culture in Sixteenth-Century France* (Ithaca, 1989); J. Russell Major, *From Renaissance Monarchy to Absolute Monarchy: French Kings, Nobles, and Estates* (Baltmore, 1994). Guy Chaussinand Nogaret, *The French Nobility in the Eighteenth Century*, trans. William Doyle (Cambridge, 1980), though flawed, remains well worth reading; as does Marc Bloch's classic study, *French Rural History: An Essay on Its Basic Characteristics*, trans. Janet Sondeimer (Berkeley, 1966).

ITALY

Italy presents special problems for students of the nobility, since its feudal nobility shaded easily into the commercially oriented urban patriciate. For insights into this situation, Richard Goldthwaite, *Wealth and the Demand for Art in Italy, 1300–1600* (Baltimore, 1993); Werner Gundersheimer, *Ferrara: The Style of a Renaissance Despotism* (Princeton, 1973). Tommaso Astarita, *The Continuity of Feudal Power: The Caracciolo di Brienza in Spanish Naples* (Cambridge, 1992), is a model study of the older nobility of southern Italy.

SPAIN

The important works on the Spanish nobility by Antonio Dominguiz Ortiz have not been translated into English. In their place, readers may turn to a series of fine but narrowly focussed studies and to general studies of early modern Spain, which usually give considerable attention to the nobles. Notable among the former are J. H. Elliott, *Spain and Its World: Selected Essays* (New Haven, 1989); Charles Jago, "The 'Crisis of the Aristocracy' in Seventeenth-Century Castile," *Past and Present*, 84 (1979); and Helen Nader, *The Mendoza Family in the Spanish Renaissance* (New Brunswick, 1979). Among more general studies, J. H. Elliott, *The Revolt of the Catalans: A Study in the Decline of Spain, 1598–1640* (Cambridge, 1963) and *Imperial Spain, 1469–1716* (New York, 1963); John Lynch, *The Hispanic World in Crisis and Change* (Oxford, 1992).

HOLLAND

H. F. K. Van Nierop, *The Nobility of Holland: From Knights to Regents, 1500–1650*, trans. Maarten Ultee (Cambridge, 1993) is a carefully researched and wide-ranging study.

GERMANY

R. J. W. Evans, *The Making of the Habsburg Monarchy, 1550–1700* (Oxford, 1979), makes the nobles' evolution a guiding thread of central European history; see also the studies of Karen McHardy, most recently "The Rise of Absolutism and Noble Rebellion in Early Modern Habsburg Austria, 1570–1620," *Comparative Studies in Society and History*, 34 (1992), 407–38. William Hagen's recent studies promise to revolutionize views of the eastern German nobilities: see "How Mighty the Junkers? Peasant Rents and Seigneurial Profits in Sixteenth-Century Brandenburg," *Past and Present*, 108 (1985), 80–116 and "Seventeenth-Century Crisis in Brandenburg: The Thirty Years War, the Destabilization of Serfdom, and the Rise of Absolutism," *American Historical Review*, 94, 2 (April, 1989), 302–35; Gregory Pedlow, *The Survival of the Hessian Nobility, 1770–1870* (Princeton, 1989), offers both an excellent case study and a clear overview of developments elsewhere in Germany.

5 THE NEW NOBILITIES

A number of works deal with the rise of administrative nobilities in the sixteenth and seventeenth centuries. These include R. Burr Litchfield, *Emergence of a Bureaucracy: The Florentine Patricians, 1530–1790 (Princeton, 1987)*; Jonathan Dewald, *The Formation of a Provincial Nobility: The Magistrates of the Parlement of Rouen, 1499–1610* (Princeton, 1980); George Huppert, *Les Bourgeois Gentilshommes: An Essay on the Definition of Elites in Renaissance France* (Chicago, 1977); Hans Rosenberg, *Bureaucracy, Aristocracy, and Autocracy: The Prussian Experience, 1660–1815* (Cambridge, MA, 1958). William Beik, *Absolutism and Society in Seventeenth-Century France: State Power and Provincial Aristocracy in Seventeenth-Century Languedoc* (Cambridge, 1985) is a pioneering investigation of relations between a seemingly modernizing state and provincial elites.

6 COURTS AND ARMIES

Many works on the nobles touch on life in the European courts and armies. Among those that deal more specifically with these institutions are A. G. Dickens, ed., *The Courts of Europe: Politics, Patronage and Royalty, 1400–1800* (New York, 1977); Ronald G. Asch and Adolf M. Birke, eds., *Princes, Patronage, and the Nobility: The Court at the Beginning of the Modern Age, c. 1450–1650* (Oxford, 1991); Robert Hanning and David Rosand, eds., *Castiglione: The Ideal and the Real in Renaissance Culture* (New Haven, 1983). Two important works chart Europeans' organization of violence and the ways this changed – subjects crucial to understanding the nobles: J. R. Hale, *War and Society in Renaissance Europe, 1450–1620* (Baltimore, 1985); and Geoffrey Parker, *The Military Revolution: Military Innovation and the Rise of the West* (Cambridge, 1988). François Billacois, *The Duel: Its Rise and Fall in Early Modern France*, ed. and trans. Trista Selous (New Haven, 1990), is a remarkable explication of another characteristic form of aristocratic violence.

7 CULTURE AND DAILY LIFE

Biographies offer especially clear insights into how nobles lived and thought. Among many excellent studies, readers might begin with Golo Mann, *Wallenstein, His Life Narrated*, trans. Charles Kessler (London, 1976); J. H. Elliott, *Richelieu and Olivares* (Cambridge, 1984); Nancy Nichols Barker, *Brother to the Sun King: Philippe, Duke of Orléans* (Baltmore, 1989). David Howarth, *Lord Arundel an His Circle* (New Haven, 1985), provides an extraordinary view of one nobleman's cultural interests. Norbert Elias's important studies have shaped much current thinking about nobles' changing behavior in the early modern period: see *The Civilizing Process*, trans. Edmund Jephcott, 2 vols. (New York, 1978). Roger Chartier, *A History of Private Life*, vol. III, trans. Arthur Goldhammer (Cambridge, MA, 1989) both exemplifies Elias's influence and offers a wealth of detail on nobles' lives.

8 THE FRENCH REVOLUTION AND THE NINETEENTH CENTURY

Several excellent studies trace the nobles' nineteenth- and early twentieth-century history. Though in different ways, these all respond to a classic work of the mid-nineteenth century: Alexis de Tocqueville's *The Old Regime and the French Revolution*, trans. Stuart Gilbert (Garden City, NY, 1955), which argued that the French Revolution only completed processes of aristocratic decline that had begun in the seventeenth century. In contrast, more recent works have argued for the complexity of the nobles' fate after 1789 – and have drawn particular attention to the group's nineteenth-century vitality. See for instance Patrice Higonnet, *Class, Ideology, and the Rights of Nobles during the French Revolution* (Oxford, 1981); Jerome Blum, *The End of the Old Order in Rural Europe* (Princeton, 1978); David Cannadine, *The Decline and Fall of the British Aristocracy* (New Haven, 1991); Dominic Lieven, *The Aristocracy in Europe, 1815–1914* (New York, 1992); Arno Mayer, *The Persistence of the Old Regime: Europe to the Great War* (New York, 1981); David Higgs, *Nobles in Nineteenth-Century France: The Practice of Inegalitarianism* (Baltimore, 1987).

Index

poor nob =
sacrific[e]

European-wide trends
> gap rich/poor nob over e mod period
Nobs as part of larger history, ec⁻/pol⁰/
    not confined to Court or castles   social

Cap^{sm}/consumerism

distinction

career: army/state service